Python for Psychology, Social Sciences, and Education

Programming Made Easy for Psychologists, Educators, and Social Scientists

Josep M. Roig-Fusté

Apress®

Python for Psychology, Social Sciences, and Education: Programming Made Easy for Psychologists, Educators, and Social Scientists

Josep M. Roig-Fusté
BARCELONA, Barcelona, Spain

ISBN-13 (pbk): 979-8-8688-2354-1 ISBN-13 (electronic): 979-8-8688-2355-8
https://doi.org/10.1007/979-8-8688-2355-8

Managing Director, Apress Media LLC: Welmoed Spahr
Acquisitions Editor: Celestin Suresh John
Development Editor: Laura Berendson
Editorial Assistant: Gryffin Winkler

Cover designed by eStudioCalamar

Cover image designed by pixabay.com

Distributed to the book trade worldwide by Springer Science+Business Media New York, 1 New York Plaza, New York, NY 10004. Phone 1-800-SPRINGER, fax (201) 348-4505, e-mail orders-ny@springer-sbm.com, or visit www.springeronline.com. Apress Media, LLC is a Delaware LLC and the sole member (owner) is Springer Science + Business Media Finance Inc (SSBM Finance Inc). SSBM Finance Inc is a **Delaware** corporation.

For information on translations, please e-mail booktranslations@springernature.com; for reprint, paperback, or audio rights, please e-mail bookpermissions@springernature.com.

Apress titles may be purchased in bulk for academic, corporate, or promotional use. eBook versions and licenses are also available for most titles. For more information, reference our Print and eBook Bulk Sales web page at http://www.apress.com/bulk-sales.

Any source code or other supplementary material referenced by the author in this book is available to readers on GitHub. For more detailed information, please visit https://www.apress.com/gp/services/source-code.

If disposing of this product, please recycle the paper

This book is dedicated to the memory of my parents and to my entire family, who for many years supported my interest in computing, which took up their time and limited my availability to be with them, and also to the countless fellow psychologists who for years have used diagnostic and rehabilitation programs developed in our professional office, and especially to my high school colleagues Jordi Gomà and Heribert Mestres, computer experts who selflessly helped me in my endeavor when I began programming.

Table of Contents

About the Author

Dr. Josep M. Roig-Fusté is a licensed clinical psychologist with more than 40 years of experience across hospital, corporate, and private practice settings. He earned a bachelor's degree in psychology from the Universitat de Barcelona, and a PhD in medicine from the Universitat Autònoma de Barcelona. He earned a degree in clinical psychology from the Ministry of Science and Innovation and a master's degree in psychiatry from the Universitat Autònoma de Barcelona. In addition to his clinical work, Dr. Roig-Fusté has spent the last three decades developing software for psychological applications—ranging from administration, correction of psychological tests, automatic generation of reports from psychological test data, and development of computerized cognitive rehabilitation tools. His programming journey began with QBasic and Visual Basic, and today he works primarily in Python 3.

About the Technical Reviewer

Siddhant Agarwal is a seasoned developer relations professional with more than a decade of experience building and scaling developer ecosystems globally. Currently leading developer relations across APAC at Neo4j and recognized as a Google developer expert in GenAI, he is passionate about empowering developers to reimagine data and AI through graph technology. Known for his unique ability to tell powerful stories through technology, Sid translates complex ideas into narratives that inspire action and innovation. With his signature "Local to Global" approach, he turns grassroots creativity into global impact. Previously at Google managing flagship developer programs, he continues to shape communities, share insights on GenAI and graph databases, and drive meaningful connections across the tech world. Learn more at meetsid.dev.

Introduction

I imagine that when starting a project of this kind, it is necessary to ask two questions and to answer them as clearly as possible. The questions are: Why should a psychologist or a social scientist know about computer programming or learn to program? And why choose Python programming in particular? I will therefore try to answer both questions in a way that can be satisfactory to everyone reading this book.

It is an unquestionable fact that in the last 40 years computers have invaded our lives and our work, since they are applied to all fields of knowledge and human activity, also naturally to psychology, social sciences, and education (Roig-Fusté, 2018), so no professional in these areas can be left out if they want to be efficient in their work. Any scientist who must collect information and process a large amount of data will need a computer, and the computer can be applied to many other tasks and in quite diverse ways. But the computer has no initiative and does nothing if it is not told, in a convenient way, what it must do. This means it will be necessary to decide which applications are made and who makes them, telling the computer what it must do in a way that it understands, in other words, who programs the computer. I can think of basically three possibilities, each of them with its advantages and disadvantages. These possibilities are that it be done by a psychologist, that it be done by a computer scientist or a programming specialist, or that it be done by a multidisciplinary team made up of social scientists and computer scientists. This third option would be by far the most appropriate, but that does not mean it does not have drawbacks or limitations, mainly that it will be the most expensive option and that it will not work if the social scientists do not have any knowledge of computer science or interest in it and the computer scientists do not have, in turn, knowledge of social sciences or interest in them. In addition, it will be a more viable and effective option in the case of institutions or large projects, and it is difficult to apply to individual projects, which may only be of particular interest to a few specific people.

It is possible to commission a project to a computer scientist, but it will also be expensive, and many concepts of the subject matter will have to be explained, which may be important for carrying out the work correctly. Even when commissioning a project, it would be advisable for the person commissioning it to have knowledge of computer science, since this will allow them to prepare the information for the project more conveniently and be aware of the true complexity of the project.

We are left with the psychologist carrying out the entire project, since they know what is needed and how it should be done. This option would be ideal if computing were easy and accessible to everyone. Computing is not easy and is becoming more complex every day. Fortunately, young people are more accustomed to using computers and have a greater interest in using them; in addition, universities usually offer programming courses in all branches of education. Whatever the drawbacks and difficulties, professionals must have enough ambition to incorporate all those tools that can facilitate, improve, and advance our knowledge.

Psychologists, like everyone else, have been forced to work with computers, but we often lack knowledge and ambition in marginal tasks, and we settle for the first thing we have learned or what is simply closest to hand, thereby limiting our possibilities for progress, especially taking into account the rapid evolution of information technology and its undoubted increase in complexity as the years go by.

So, learning to program seems to be something essential for any scientist or technician; from here there are various possibilities in terms of programming languages: Basic, SmallBasic, Java, JavaScript, Pascal, Python…, some older ones like Fortran, and others more complex like assembler, C, C++ or C#, to name just a few possibilities. I recommend Python, but whatever you choose from these options, I hope this book can be useful to see new possibilities and find the way to facilitate your daily professional work.

Computer science has many possibilities, and although it is true that it requires a significant effort at the beginning, it is also true that it usually gives spectacular results when it can be used to its full potential once the initial learning stage has been overcome. It should also be noted that learning a programming language helps with greater intellectual development, offers more possibilities and flexibility in the use of computers, and completes a professional curriculum.

Given the interest in computing and its application options, you must consider the paths you are going to choose for your objective. If this is programming, even if they are simple applications, you will have to choose a programming language among the hundreds that exist. So why do it in Python? In fact, for many applications in the field of psychology there are some alternatives, such as Matlab (Borgo, Soranzo and Grassi, 2012; Rosenbaum, Vaughan, and Wyble, 2015), which is expensive, and learning it is not easy either. Another alternative is the R language (Adler, 2010; López, 2012, Mair, 2018), designed mainly for data processing and statistical calculations, which can be complicated if not used with a menu such as R-commander (Elosua, 2011; Navarro, 2013) or with the help of RStudio (Kronthaler and Zöller, 2021). This is free and powerful, replacing the SPSS program that psychologists and social scientists have used so much since the 1980s to do our statistical calculations. But if you want a more general, flexible option with more possibilities and broader horizons, this could be Python.

Python is undoubtedly in fashion, which means there are many people working with it and many resources available: books, in Spanish and English, in-person and online courses, tutorials, specialized websites, support groups to solve difficulties, and so on. Python defenders say that it is an easy language to learn; personally I do not believe that this is true because there are no easy languages to learn, especially for someone who is not a computer scientist and is starting out in programming, as can often happen in the case of professionals in our areas of knowledge.

Learning to program from scratch is not an easy task; but, although it has its complexities, in the case of choosing Python we will surely have the advantage of working with a language that will not be the most technical or most difficult to handle. The choice of Python may also be for other reasons: it is a free, powerful, multiplatform, and well-documented language (van Rossum, 2012, 2020). For all these reasons, it has been used on many occasions to introduce people to the world of programming, replacing the old BASIC[1] or the Pascal language in more technical environments, both very popular just a few years ago, but which have become obsolete or have disappeared from the market. Furthermore, Python has already been widely used in psychology and social science applications (Dalmaijer, 2017; Peirce, 2007, 2009, 2019; Peirce, Gray, Simpson, S., MacAskill, Höchenberger, Sogo, Kastman, & Lindeløv, 2019; Peirce & MacAskill, 2018; Bexter & Kampa, 2020) and is very powerful for statistical applications (Nawaz, 2020).

Some of the concepts and terms that we will use in this work may be unknown to a beginner, but if you want to program, you will have to become familiar with them and many more. If you have many years of computer use behind you, you will probably know many of the terms that we are forced to use and the task will become easier; if not,

[1] The BASIC language, which became popular with the arrival of personal computers, was introduced in 1964 by John George Kemeny (1926–1992) and Thomas Eugene Kurtz (1928–2024) at Dartmouth College, with the idea of offering an easy procedure so that everyone could program.

I recommend you first take an introductory book on computing (for example Norton, 2006; Farrell, 2013), familiarize yourself with the subject in general, and do not miss any opportunity to read about computing topics that particularly interest you. This will expand your computer culture and the information you have on the subject and will facilitate your understanding, while making you see how interesting it can be to spend a little more time on computing and improve the use of it in your daily work, taking advantage of all its potential.

To begin, I will explain a little about what the mentioned advantages of using Python refer to and to expose some of its characteristics: Python is free, meaning you don't have to pay anything to use it; you can get it on the Internet and start using it right away.

It is multiplatform, meaning that it works on computers with the most common operating systems, i.e., Windows, Apple, or Unix, and others that are not so common such as Android. This has the advantage that an application does not have to be programmed, i.e., written, three times, or more, if we want to use it on some of these operating systems.

Python is an interpreted language, which means it runs on the fly and allows you to see the results of your programming efforts, as well as to correct errors, when they occur, by applying the desired modifications. The fact that it is interpreted does not mean it cannot be compiled to obtain a directly executable file. There are also simple options for this, which can be used when the program has already been finished and has been tested in the interpreter, to rule out errors or any type of malfunction. You will learn about these options later.

Python is a powerful and well-documented general-purpose language (Van Rossum, 2012, 2020). Languages allow you to do simple things, such as adding two numbers, and some of them allow you to do complex things, such as managing and directly collecting values from a measuring device, such as those found in experimental psychology, or consulting a database on the Internet. A general-purpose language is more flexible and better suited to a wide variety of tasks.

If you choose a language that has technical limitations, for example the already mentioned BASIC, which has nevertheless been used in psychology (Deni, 1986), and you progress in its use, there will possibly come a time when the language is not useful for what you want to do, and you will also have the difficulty that some modes of the simple and easy-to-learn language can compete with those of a more powerful language and even make it difficult to learn a second language that is better, when learning this one is necessary. The lack of documentation can also make it difficult to learn and to obtain optimal use once learned. Python has extensive documentation by its authors, and hundreds of books have also been published on the subject, some of them very specialized and in some part of the field of our interest (Dalmaijer, 2017, 2024). However, both the documentation and most of the books are in English, which is sometimes a drawback for some people, because they are less accessible documents: more difficult to acquire or understand.

You will surely ask yourself other questions: Why read a programming book written by a psychologist? Simply because this book talks about both programming and its possible applications to psychology, social sciences, or education, and of these two topics perhaps the first is not the most important for a scientist in our area; therefore, it does not intend to usurp the teaching of programming and create experts in programming computers, but rather to introduce a topic and help professionals in a specific area to use programming effectively for their daily work, giving some basic concepts and looking in greater depth at some fields, in which it can be applied with advantage, such as psychology, social sciences or education. In my experience, one of the things that most facilitates learning a complex subject like this, is having a clear idea of what you want to do with what you are learning. If you know how you want to apply what you learn about programming, you will be more consistent and will advance more easily.

You should also consult other books that allow you to delve deeper into the field of strict programming and expand your experience with your own practice. Therefore, this book does not propose to teach programming in Python, a goal that may be too difficult for someone who is not a computer professional, but we will refer to how to program in Python, since we are going to deal with the application of this programming language. This book aims to study how to make some computer applications that may be useful for psychologists and social scientists, stimulating the interest of professionals in these sciences in computer science and programming, starting from the basis that we have already chosen the programming language of Python and providing a guide to get started effectively.

If you want to delve deeper into the topic of the importance of learning to program for any human being and how computers and programming are changing and will continue to change not only our lives but also our way of thinking, you can find some philosophical reflections in Rushkoff's book (2010).

To read this book, I assume that no prior knowledge of computer science or programming is required, although it may be advantageous to have used a computer and to understand the most basic aspects, such as what an operating system is and how to use it, what applications are and how to interact with a computer, etc. If you have no experience in these fields, supplementing the information in this book with a general Python programming book (Matthes, 2022) or searching the Internet for specific information about these concepts or fundamental knowledge may be necessary and extremely helpful.

I have already said that learning to program is not easy, and learning to program in Python is not either, no matter what its defenders say; you have to learn new concepts and new ways of doing things or handling abstract concepts, all without seeing the utility until you have mastered the language and can create an application from start to finish, hoping that it is useful and efficient and works correctly; this makes it easy to get bored or discouraged, when in reality it is only possible to learn by persisting. There is a point in learning where things get complicated and getting past this point; becoming a real programmer requires time and dedication, as well as a lot of perseverance and effort.

On the other hand, some of the advantages of Python that we have mentioned, such as working on various platforms or operating systems or the large number of libraries available or the multitude of development environments, can confuse the beginner; for all this we will limit ourselves to the most fundamental: exposing the essentials of the language, using a single version of Python, version 3, to a single development environment, Python's own, which is called IDLE (Integrated Development and Learning Environment). IDLE is an environment consisting of an editor in which programs are written and that accompanies the original language by default. We will also focus on a single operating system: Windows. At the end of the book we will mention, in passing, other possibilities that can facilitate the work so that you can continue to delve deeper into the subject and chart your own path of progress toward where you want to go.

Computer science evolves very quickly, and professionals cannot be satisfied with the first thing they have learned; they need to learn new things and incorporate everything that can facilitate their understanding or their daily work, even if this requires more effort. This book has been written in this spirit, to point out possibilities and start new paths. It is up to the professional to integrate them into their daily practice. To achieve this, the best thing is to have an objective. Learning to program, in this case, is not an objective for a social scientist; it is only a means to achieve the objective that you have. By having an objective when starting this adventure, you will have a truly clear idea of what you want to do with the knowledge you acquire in computer science, that is, what this knowledge will be applied to. Knowing, for example, that you want to plan experiments with the help of a computer and which ones, or that you want to write teaching programs or automate tasks such as collecting survey data or correcting tests, preparing reports based on test results, doing statistical research, etc., will greatly help progress, will force you to look for solutions, will consolidate what you have learned sooner and, above all, will make the journey more enjoyable.

It will certainly not be possible to develop in detail all the possibilities of applying programming to psychology, partly because some of them are very new and have not yet reached a wide diffusion, but we will be able, or will try, to expose their bases and their infinite possibilities for the future. Finally, I would like to point out that writing a programming book can be complicated because, in programming, there are many ways of doing the same thing, reiterating that the objective of this book is not so much to teach how to program as to show the advantages of having a tool such as programming for research and for daily practice, while stimulating the interest of social science professionals in the application of computer science in their work.

Since computer science is of great interest to all fields of psychology and psychological software is an area of great potential and future, the current panorama is rather bleak; an Internet search using the terms *psychological software* or, more advisable, *psychological software,* to try to obtain a greater number of results, can convince us of this. Although in recent years some researchers have addressed the issue and a multitude of companies with applications in this field have emerged, few of them have evolved, and many have already disappeared, which indicates that the subject has not yet taken root strongly or has found a safe path to evolve, being at the moment situated between two extremes: that of the programs that are too expensive or that of those that are not very useful. Nevertheless, some collaborative or public domain applications have been developed; we can refer as an example to the PEBL Test Battery (Mueller and Piper, 2014), an open-source program that has the disadvantage of being written in C^{++}, a very powerful language as well as very specialized and more complex, less known by professionals in the human sciences, or to PsyToolkit (Stoet, 2010, 2011), an application for Unix, a valuable operating system, but not very widespread among less professional users or personal computers in our country. In both cases, they can be used immediately and are useful for professionals, provided they are skilled in the use of computers and are particularly familiar with these applications. In comparison, Python is a longer path, because you have to learn to program, but it is also more flexible and promising, since it is not necessary to limit ourselves to what is already done. As you will see, you can take advantage of much of what is already done to expand your work and make it more useful.

Any suggestion or comment that may contribute to improving this book or correcting errors in subsequent editions can be sent to info@mtrpsicologia.com, putting the title of this book in the subject of the message.

CHAPTER 1

Installation and First Steps in Python

Welcome! In this first chapter, you will be introduced to the Python language. You will learn the commands it uses and its structure, and you will be exposed to different data types and how to handle them. Topics such as libraries or compilation, which are fundamental to developing software, also are covered.

Get the Tools You Need

Before starting work, it is necessary to obtain the required tools for the task. You must visit the Internet and download the necessary files. By entering **Python** into a search engine, multiple sources will appear where you can obtain the files and documentation. Alternatively, you can visit Python's official website at `https://www.python.org/` to acquire the required materials.

Upon reaching the Python website, your first dilemma arises: you must choose between different versions of the language and various usage platforms. This book is based on Python 3.8.0 and a 64-bit Windows operating system. Other common options include 32-bit Windows, macOS, or Unix. There are also options for large computer platforms or Android devices, all available on the website.

In principle, the programs written in this book should work for any Python 3 version and any platform but not for its predecessor, Python 2. On Python's official website, you can find version 2.7, which stopped receiving updates in January 2020 and is no longer supported, despite still being widely used. This version may be of interest if you need to run legacy programs written in Python 2. Many Python programs available on the Internet may not function in Python 3, as they were likely written for version 2. It is

J. M. Roig-Fusté, *Python for Psychology, Social Sciences, and Education*,
https://doi.org/10.1007/979-8-8688-2355-8_1

possible to automatically translate these programs to version 3, but such translations do not always guarantee full functionality due to compatibility issues—particularly with certain Python 2 libraries that do not work in Python 3.

Version 2 has been maintained mainly because early adopters of Python have numerous applications written in this version that are not easy to migrate to version 3, whether manually or automatically, often due to library dependencies that are not available for Python 3. However, these programs remain useful for their creators. One proposed solution to this issue, as suggested by Dalmaijer (2017), is to install the WinPython package, which provides a portable version of Python 2.7 to run legacy programs while using the latest version of Python 3 for new development. Naturally, for those starting programming now, it is undoubtedly best to use the latest version of Python 3.x, currently 3.14.0, although this version is not compatible with Windows 7 or earlier but offers better long-term prospects.

I will not elaborate on why the language we have chosen is called Python, nor on who its creator was, when it was created, or why; these are anecdotes that can be found on the Internet and are at the beginning of all the Python programming books. You will repeatedly encounter answers to these questions. If interested in the topic, you can consult other documents.

Python is an open-source and collaborative language, which has multiple advantages and perhaps, I say, some disadvantages. The main advantage is that many people are working with it and have contributed resources that you may utilize at some point. The primary disadvantage is that the possible ways to handle the language are numerous, which can again mislead and confuse beginners. We will see this throughout the book.

You will find details about the installation on the official page or in any programming book about the Python language. The installation on Windows is straightforward. Install the basic options by executing the installer program (python-3.12.0.exe or Python-3.x.x, depending on the newest version you have downloaded from the official page) and follow the instructions provided by the installer program. You may choose some options or allow the program to install with the default options, which are the most common and recommended for beginners. If you have doubts or are installing a version that is not for Windows, consult the original page or conduct an Internet search engine to find the specific information you need.

On Windows, the installer will provide you with a console, which is a text-only screen for issuing commands directly to the operating system, and a comfortable working environment called IDLE (Python's Integrated Development and Learning

Environment), as previously mentioned. In addition to all the necessary documentation for working with this language, there are thousands of documentation pages in various languages that you can download from the official website, which are useful to have on hand, even if you do not intend to read them all, to consult specific topics and questions when necessary.

The Python Development Environment

The standard development environment (IDLE) appears in Figure 1-1. Upon calling it, it informs us of the version of the language installed and some options that may provide additional information to the user.

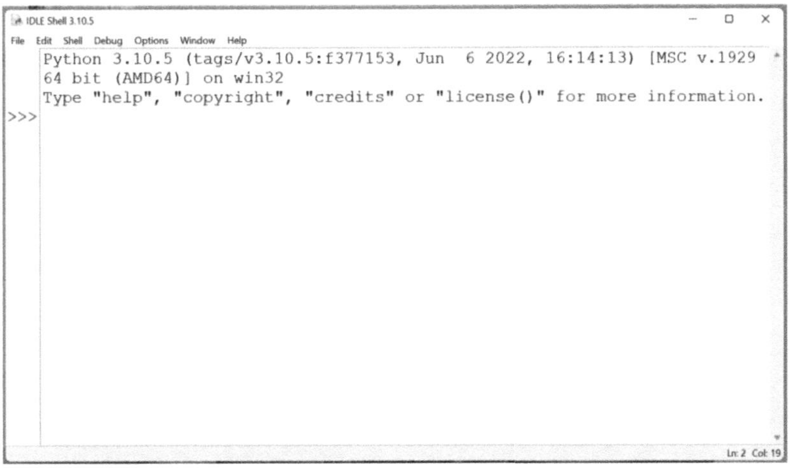

Figure 1-1. *The standard development environment (IDLE)*

The symbol >>> followed by a blinking cursor, visible on the screen after the startup message, is the operational indicator. In this line, where the blinking cursor is located, you should type the commands of the language you want to execute. If you type the word `help` followed by two parentheses, one opening and one closing, as in `help()`, and then press the Return or Enter key, you will obtain help information.

To exit the help, you must type the word `quit` and press the Return or Enter key. To close IDLE, you can go to the File menu and select the Exit option, or you can type `exit()` at the language prompt you see on the screen (>>>) and press the Return key.

IDLE can be used immediately or to open a text editor. Selecting File ➤ New File allows you to write a program that will be saved in a disk file with the extension `.py`.

You can later select this file with File ➤ Open to execute it or continue working on it to improve or make any changes you find necessary. Conversely, any command written at the command line will be executed immediately, but it will not be saved, and to execute it again, you will have to write it anew.

If you type the following in the IDLE shell and press the Return key, you will see the result in the same window, following the line you wrote:

```
>>> 3 + 3
```

However, if you go to the upper menu File and select the New File option, a text window will open where you can write, as mentioned, a more extensive program consisting of several lines, even hundreds or thousands of them. When you finish writing your program, you can execute it by selecting Run ➤ Run Module or by pressing F5. Before executing any program you have written or modified, Python will prompt you to save it to avoid losses due to a potential computer crash. You will not be able to execute any program from the editor, whether short or long, that has not been previously saved; this is equally valid for any modification of a program that had already been saved.

As mentioned, you can open the IDLE editor by selecting File ➤ New File; when you click this menu, a text editor window opens, allowing you to write extensive programs, which you can then execute in the same IDLE environment or compile if you want (see Figure 1-2).

Figure 1-2. *Text editor window*

In the lower-right corner of the text processing window, you can observe the line and column number, as shown in Figure 1-3, where the cursor or writing indicator is located. This is important information since the interpreter, when an error occurs, will indicate which line of the program the error occurred in, and this information will help us locate the line within the program and correct the error. By moving the cursor and observing how this number changes, you can locate the exact line to which the interpreter refers. It is also possible to request that IDLE display all line numbers on the left side by selecting Options ➤ Show Line Numbers.

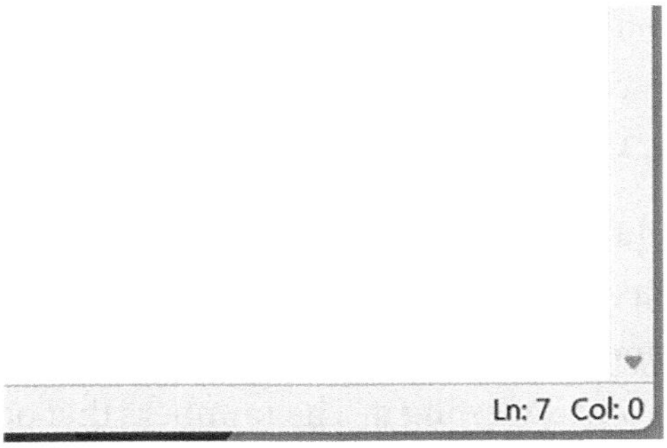

Figure 1-3. *Line and column numbers are shown*

Once the program is written, it can be saved through the menu File ➤ Save and executed with the menu Run ➤ Run Module, or F5. As previously mentioned, if the program is not saved beforehand, the interpreter will always prompt you to save it before executing.

Once the program is written, it can be saved through the menu File ➤ Save and executed with the menu Run ➤ Run Module, or F5. As previously mentioned, if the program is not saved beforehand, the interpreter will always prompt you to save it before executing it.

Programs are fundamentally composed of variables, constants, and commands. Variables and constants store information, while commands refer to the actions that the computer must execute. Variables and constants can be strings or numbers and can be assigned within the program itself or introduced from the outside by a user or read from an auxiliary file when the program itself is executed.

Variables have a name, and their value is assigned with the equal sign. If they are character strings, they must be written in single or double quotes; if they are numbers, integers, or floating-point numbers, they should not be quoted. The name of a variable can be any combination of characters, must start with a letter or an underscore, and may contain numbers; there are a few words that are reserved for the language and cannot be used as variable names.

Examples of Variables

These are some examples of variables:

```
edat = 33  # the variable contains an integer
media = 28.50  # the variable contains a decimal number
nombre = "Antonio"  # this is a string variable
prueba = True  # this is a Boolean value
```

What is written after the # sign is a comment that does not affect the programming and is included as guidance or clarification for the programmer. This is useful for future maintenance or improvement of the program, especially if the program was written by a person different from the one reviewing it. The numbers that occupy the variables can be integers, floating-point, or complex.

There is another type of variable called a Boolean, whose value can be only True or False. Constants are values that do not change throughout the program. Although Python does not differentiate between variables and constants, programmers usually do. Constants are written at the beginning of the program or in a separate file to be imported at the beginning of the program, and their names are usually written in uppercase. Here is an example:

```
PI_NUMBER = 3.1416
```

Keep in mind that Python differentiates between uppercase and lowercase; therefore, variable names such as `Edat`, `EDAT`, `edat`, and `EdAt` are distinct. This peculiarity is a frequent source of errors. There are also certain words that are reserved by Python; see Table 1-1 for a list of words that cannot be used as variable names.

Table 1-1. *Reserved Words That Cannot Be Used As Names*

and	as	not	assert	Finally
or	break	for	pass	class
from	nonlocal	continue	global	raise
def	if	return	del	import
try	elif	in	while	Else
is	with	except	lambda	yield
False	True	None		

Keep in mind that variables have a local scope in Python, which means that a variable used in a function cannot be accessed from the program, and the program variables are not available in functions. If you need any value or values from a function, you must return them using the `Return` statement.

The reason for local variable scope is to prevent interference between them; for example, if you have a variable that performs a count within a function, you can have another variable with the same name in the main program without any interference between them, thus avoiding the need to check the names assigned to variables to prevent repetitions that could cause problems.

The local scope of variables can be altered by declaring those variables you want to have a global scope at the beginning of the main program with the global statement, for example:

```
global edat
```

This means the variable `edat` will be recognized in all parts of the program, including within functions, where you will also need to write global edat at the beginning of the function, taking indentation into account. It is considered that using global variables is not a good practice and that there must be very compelling reasons to do so.

Operators

Variables are used in conjunction with operators. Table 1-2 shows the operators accepted in Python.

Table 1-2. *Python Operators.*

Operator	Description	Example
+	Addition	2 + 2 = 4
-	Subtraction	9 – 3 = 6
*	Multiplication	3 * 4 = 12
/	Division	9 / 2 = 4.5
%	Modulus	9 % 2 = 1
**	Exponentiation	3 ** 4 = 81
//	Floor Division	9 // 2 = 4

Mathematical operators have an order of precedence in their execution, which can be overridden using parentheses. In programs, both numbers and variable names can be used to perform operations, for example:

```
>>> a = 9
>>> b = 2
>>> a / b
4.5
```

There are language functions for handling numbers:

```
type(numero)
```

This returns the type of number, which can be integer, floating-point, or complex.

```
abs(-20)
returns 20.
```

The `abs()` function returns the absolute value of a number. The same result can also be obtained with `fabs()`, by first importing the math library:

```
import math
math.fabs(numero)
```

The installation, importation, and use of libraries, some of the most important aspects of this language, will be discussed later. The math library allows for many other mathematical operations to be performed easily and quickly, such as obtaining the factorial of a given number:

```
math.factorial(numero)
```

This command easily and quickly calculates the factorial of a positive integer. For example:

```
import math
math.factorial(49)
362880
```

```
math.floor(numero)
```

This returns the integer part of a number.

Table 1-3 describes the assignment operators.

Table 1-3. *Assignment Operators*

Operator	Description	Examples
=	Assigns a value to a variable	a = 30
+=	Assigns to the left expression the value it already had plus that of the right expression	a += 10
-=	Assigns to the left expression the value it already had minus the value of the right expression	a -= 10
*=	Assigns to the left expression the value it already had multiplied by the value of the right expression	a *= 2
/=	Assigns the value to the left expression to the value it already had divided by the value of the right expression	a /= 2
**=	Assigns to the left expression the value of the specified power	a **= 3
//=	Assigns to the left expression the value of the exact division by the value of the right expression	a //= 2
%=	Assigns to the left expression the value of the modulus of the division by the value of the right expression	a %= 2

a += 10 can also be written as a = a + 10; the same applies to the other assignment operators.

Comparison operators (Table 1-4) are used differently from assignment operators.

Table 1-4. *Comparison Operators*

Operator	Description	Examples
==	Equal	`if a == b:`
!=	Not equal	`if a!= b:`
>	Greater than	`if a > b:`
<	Less than	`if a < b:`
>=	Greater than or equal to	`if a >= b:`
<=	Less than or equal to	`if a <= b:`

Note in the first case of the table: if a is equal to b, two equal signs are placed here; failing to do so will result in an error message and will break the execution of the program.

Data Types in Python

Let's talk about data types in Python.

Strings (Character Strings)

Character strings, or strings, are written in the program between quotes, which can be single or double, and they support some operators, but only those that make sense, such as addition and multiplication, for example:

```
>>> 'Juan' + ' García'
'Juan García'
>>> 'Juan' * 3
'JuanJuanJuan'
```

String manipulation allows for many more possibilities through the so-called built-in functions of the language. For example, if we have a string that we will call cadena:

```
cadena = "abcdefghijklmnñopqrstuveyz"
```

We can find out the number of characters it contains:

```
>>> len(cadena)
26
```

Or identify a character from it, selected by its position within the string:

```
>>> cadena[1]
'b'
```

Note that the numbering string indices start at 0; the 0th element in this string is a, and the 1st element is b, while the 18th element is r. If a negative index is indicated, the count starts from the last element of the string, for example:

```
>>> cadena[-10]
'p'
```

Substrings can be extracted in various ways:

```
subcadena = cadena[ start  end]
subcadena = cadena[: end]  # from zero to the indicated final index
subcadena = cadena[ start:]  # from the indicated starting index to the end
subcadena = cadena[:]  # copies the entire string
```

Here's an example:

```
>>> subcadena = cadena[10:18]
>>> print(subcadena)
klmnñopq
```

If the indices are out of range of the string, the substring will be empty.

The most common operations with strings are:

`cadena.count('subcadena')` returns the number of times the substring is found within the string.

`cadena.find('subcadena')` returns the index of the first occurrence of the substring. The result is -1 if the specified substring is not found.

`cadena.index('subcadena')` returns the index of the first occurrence of the substring.

`cadena.lower()` returns a version of the string in lowercase letters.

`cadena.upper()` returns a version of the string in uppercase letters.

`cadena.swapcase()` returns a string changing each letter from uppercase to lowercase or from lowercase to uppercase.

`cadena.lstrip()` removes whitespace from the left side of the string.

`cadena.rstrip()` removes whitespace from the right side of the string.

`cadena.strip()` removes whitespace from both the beginning and the end of the string.

`cadena.startswith('text')` returns True if the string starts with the specified text; otherwise, it returns False.

`cadena.title()` returns a version of the string in which the first letter of each word is capitalized, and the rest of the word is in lowercase.

`cadena.replace(text to replace, new text)` returns a version of the string in which a part has been replaced by another new one.

Strings can be sliced to obtain parts of them.

Other data types in Python that we will discuss next include lists, tuples, and dictionaries.

Lists

Lists are a data type that allows for the storage of information of any type: strings, integers, floats, other lists, and so on. The data in the list is written between brackets and is mutable. Lists are equivalent to arrays or matrices in other languages.

```
unaLista = ['Juan', 'Antonio', 'Pedro']
myLista = [] # An empty list
```

This serves to initialize a list.

Values can be added or removed from lists:

```
unaLista.pop()
```

This removes the last value from the list. A value can also be removed by its index:

```
unaLista.pop(8)
```

This removes the value at index 8. Values can also be removed by their value:

```
unaLista.remove("value")
```

This removes the specified value from the list.

Values are added to the end of the list using the `append()` command.

```
myLista.append(180)
```

If we want to change an existing value in a list, it is done using the index of the value to be changed:

```
unaLista[2] = 35
```

This replaces the value at index 2 with 35.

Lists can be sorted:

```
unaLista.sort()
```

They can be reversed:

```
unaLista.reverse()
```

They can count the number of occurrences of a specific element:

```
unaLista.count('Juan')
```

In lists containing numeric content, the maximum and minimum values can be determined:

```
lista = [12, 2, 21, 31, 4, 3, 1, 144, 122, 55, 62]
max(lista)
returns 144
min(lista)
returns 1
```

In lists with character or string values, `max` and `min` will follow alphabetical order.

To find out the number of elements in a list, the `len()` command is used. The following program yields a result of 3:

```
myLista = ['1', '2', '3']
print(len(myLista))
```

This program will print value 3.

Tuples

Tuples contain values separated by commas; they are like lists, but the information is enclosed in parentheses and cannot be modified, thus allowing the program to manage tuples more quickly than lists.

```
miTupla = ('Juan', 'Antonio', 'Margarita')
num = (12, 14, 16, 18, 20, 22)
```

An element of a tuple can be selected by its index; with `len()`, as in the case of lists, we can determine the number of elements in a tuple:

```
len(num)
returns 6.
```

Dictionaries

A dictionary is a set of data grouped in key-value pairs, where each value can be accessed via its key. They are indicated using braces: {}. Here's an example:

```
Capitales = {
    Francia: París
    Alemania: Berlin
    Italia: Roma
    England: Londres
}
```

Dictionaries can contain all types of data such as integers, strings, lists, tuples, and even other dictionaries, but the keys must be unique and formed by a string or a number. The value can be obtained using the key:

```
capital = capitales["Francia"]
```

In this case, the variable capital will take the value `Paris` for use in the program.

```
a = 'Hola' # is a string.
a = [Juan, Antonio, Pedro] # is a list.
a = (Juan, Antonio, Pedro) # is a tuple.
a = {'Juan':' carpenter', 'Anna':'cook'} # is a dictionary.
```

Methods

Methods are used to alter the state of an object. An object is anything in Python, such as a variable, identified because it is written following the object, separated by a dot:

```
x = 'hello'
print(x.upper())
HELLO
```

Note that, in this case, `.upper()` does not change the variable `x`, which remains `'hello'`; to change the variable, we would have to write this:

```
x = x.upper()
print(x)
HELLO
```

In this case, the variable `x` takes the value `'HELLO'` instead of `'hello'` and will remain `'HELLO'` until it is changed.

Built-in Functions of the Language

print()

The `print()` function is the one that, in the case of Python 3, allows for the presentation of information on the screen, known as standard output; printing to a printer is much more complicated and must be done through some library, as we will see later. This function allows for printing strings, numbers, or any variable that is placed within the parentheses. In earlier versions of Python, parentheses were not used, and the command `print` was not a function. This fact is one of the causes of incompatibility between different versions of Python: Python 2 and Python 3. Whenever you see a Python program where `print` is not accompanied by parentheses, you will know it is a Python 2 program.

`print()` can be used in various ways, combining strings with variables. Here's an example:

```
print('Name: ', nom)
```

This will print `"Nombre"` followed by the name contained in the variable `nom`.

```
print(a, b, c, sep = '+')
```

This will print the contents of variables a, b, and c, interspersing the separator + between them.

```
print(a, b, c, end = '')
```

This will print the contents of the variables joined and, on the same line, the content of the next print. If nothing is indicated, the print assumes by default that at the end of the command there is a character `\n` (new line) that forces the next output to be written on the following line.

Input()

The input function allows for reading information from the keyboard. It always reads it in the form of a string and stores it in a variable; if you want to use the input as a number, you will have to convert it using the `int()` or `float()` function. Care must be taken not to convert with the float function if it is an integer and vice versa, as this would result in an error and cause the `program to break`:

```
variable = input()
```

Inside the parentheses, a message can be written to inform the user what is being requested, for example, `'Please enter your name:'`.

```
nombre = input('Please enter your name:')
```

When the program encounters this instruction, it will pause until the user types something and presses the Return key. The input provided by the user will be stored in the variable `nombre`.

chr()

The `chr()` function converts an integer between 0 and 255 into its corresponding ASCII character.

ord()

This converts a character into the corresponding integer value of its ASCII character. Here's an example:

ord('a') will print the value 97 on the screen.

strip()

This removes whitespace from the beginning and end of a string.

There are other built-in functions in Python that we will mention later.

Using input() and print()

Variables can be written or calculated within the program or introduced via the `input()` function through the keyboard:

```
nombre = input('Please enter your name:')
edad = input('Please enter your age:')
```

These commands will accept input for name and age in a console environment. Note that all variables introduced via `input()` are strings; therefore, if a number is requested, it cannot be operated directly; it must first be transformed into a number using other functions such as `int()` or `float()`. Transforming a string entered as a decimal number into an integer using the `int()` function will yield an error message and break the program. Transforming a string that does not represent a number with any of the mentioned functions will also yield an error message. Sometimes it will be necessary to transform a number into a string, which is done with the `str()` command.

sum(), min(), and max()

These built-in functions in the Python language sum all the elements of a list, identifying their minimum and maximum values, respectively. Type the following in the Python prompt:

```
>>> data = [5, 3, 2, 8, 9, 1]
```

Press the Return key; nothing will happen. Next, type this:

```
>>> sum(data)
and press 'return'
28
```

Then type this:

```
>>> min(data)
and press 'return'
1
```

Then type this:

```
>>> max(data)
and press 'return'
9
```

Commands

Commands are used to manage variables and events, being essential for communicating to the computer about what it needs to do. They have a specific syntax that, if not respected, the computer will not understand what it is supposed to do and will cause the interpreter to issue an error message and stop executing the program. In the following sections, we will examine conditional statements and loops.

If Statements

These allow for changing the flow of execution of a program based on whether a condition is met; `if` statements may be accompanied or not by one or more `elif` statements and a final `else` statement, which indicate the path to follow when the initial condition is not met but another specified condition is met, or none of the mentioned conditions are met. Here's an example:

```
numero = input("Please enter an integer: ")
calculo = (int(numero) % 2)

if calculo == 0:
    print(numero, " is an even number")
else:
    print(numero, " is an odd number")
```

In line 1, an integer is requested. This must be transformed from a character to a number in line 3, where the modulus or remainder of the division by two is calculated and assigned to the variable calculo. In line 5, it is checked whether this variable is equal to zero; in this case, a message is printed indicating that the number is even; otherwise, it prints that it is odd in line 8.

It is also possible to make several successive checks with `if... elif`:

```
python
numero = input("Please enter an integer: ")

if numero < 0:
    print("The number is negative")
elif numero > 0 and numero < 10:
    print("The number has a single digit")
```

```
elif numero > 9 and numero < 100:
    print("The number has two digits")
else:
    print("The number is very large")
```

You can write as many elif statements as you want; the last statement is not mandatory.

Loops

In programming, it is common for an action to need to be performed repeatedly; for this, there are different types of loops: the for loop and the while loop. When we know the number of times a loop will be used, we use the for statement; when we do not know, we use the while statement; however, both forms can be interchanged at the programmer's discretion, as they have a break mechanism for interruption.

While Loop:

The while loop will repeat until a specified condition is met. Now that we know part of the language, let us create a small program that involves the while loop; the program will calculate the factorial of a number entered by the user:

```
# Calculation of the factorial number.

numero = input('Enter the number for which you wish to calculate the
factorial: ')
numero = int(numero)

factorial = 1  # initialize the factorial variable

i = 1  # initialize a counter
while i <= numero:
    factorial = factorial * i
    i = i + 1

print('The factorial of ' + str(numero) + ' is ' + str(factorial))
```

As we have seen, the # sign allows for writing comments, and what is written after this sign is ignored by the Python interpreter. In the first line, the program is identified; other details such as the program name, author name, version, and date can be added.

In line 3, the user is asked to enter the number for which they want to calculate the factorial using the input() instruction; note how a message is written inside the parentheses of this instruction, which will be displayed on the screen when the program is executed, and how this instruction is assigned to the variable numero to capture the number typed by the user, which will then be used to calculate the factorial. The number entered with the input() function is considered a string; therefore, it must be transformed into a number using the int() function. If the user enters anything that is not an integer, the program will break, giving an error message; thus, it will be necessary to ensure that the user has entered a number. As we will see later, try/except statements can be used to prevent the program from breaking.

Line 5 initializes the factorial variable to 1. Line 7 initializes a counter, and line 8 begins the while loop, which has a condition that the counter must not exceed the number entered by the user. Lines 9 and 10 are part of the loop, and line 11 increments the counter by 1 with each iteration of the loop. Observe the indentation; these lines are four spaces to the right of the initial line, which allows the interpreter to recognize that they are part of the while block. When the value of i exceeds the entered value by 1, the loop will stop. Line 12, now outside the loop, will print the result.

Of course, the factorial of a number can be calculated in other ways in Python, for example, in a simpler manner using the math library:

```
# Calculation of the factorial of a number using the math library.

import math
num = input('Enter the number for which you wish to calculate the
factorial: ')
num = int(numero)

factorial = math.factorial(num)

print('The factorial of ' + str(num) + ' is ' + str(factorial))
```

This second method, without a loop, makes the program much simpler; however, the first program allowed us to introduce the while loop. As we will see in the for statements next, just like in the while statements, it is possible to intervene in the loop with the keywords break and continue. The first breaks a loop before its completion, and the second skips the current iteration to proceed to the next.

The For Loop:

The `for` loop functions, if not interrupted, a predetermined number of times as follows:

```
for i in range(0, 100, 3):
    print(i, end=", ")
```

The `range()` function, specific to Python, generates a sequence of numbers, which is especially useful when we need to execute a loop a specific number of times. The numbers in the range function refer to the start, end, and interval of the loop. In this case, counting starts at 0; the iterations are from 0 to 100, in intervals of 3. The `end = ""` command ensures that the numbers are printed one after the other, on the same line; if this code is omitted, the numbers will be printed in a single column, one below the other, meaning that after printing each number, there will be a carriage return. What is placed within quotes after end is what will separate the numbers; if nothing is placed, they will not be separated at all.

As explained, loops can be influenced by the commands `break` and `continue`. Consider the following example and think about what will happen:

```
for i in range(10):
    if i == 3: continue
    if i == 5: break
    print(i, end=", ")
```

Indeed, the computer will skip the number 3 and stop before printing 5 on the screen; it will not print this number because it interrupts before the `print` command, resulting in this:

```
0, 1, 2, 4,
```

Since in this case the start of the loop has been omitted, it is assumed to be zero, and the step, also omitted, is assumed to be 1.

Loops can be interrupted with the `break` command or skip certain cycles with the `continue` command. Here is an example:

```
number = 0

for number in range (100):
    print(str(number))
    if number == 15:
```

```
        break     # ends the loop
        print('The loop ended at: ' + str(number))
```

This loop, which was supposed to provide 100 iterations, is interrupted at iteration 15. The continue statement allows skipping the part of a loop where it is activated, but the loop can continue until the end. For example:

```
number = 0

for number in range(10):
    if number == 6:
        continue    # will skip the number 6

    print('Number: ' + str(number))
```

You can also place a pass command that will leave the condition ineffective; this is useful when you know that consequences need to be introduced but have not yet been programmed. If you remove the line containing pass, the program will give an error message and stop, as the language does not accept the existence of an empty block. For example:

```
number = 0

for number in range(10):
    if number == 6:
        pass # will skip this part of the program

    print('Number: ' + str(number))
```

Loops can be nested to generate tables and matrices or to solve complex problems:

```
for i in range(2):
    for j in range(2):
        for k in range(2):
            print(f"Now i = {i}, j = {j} and k = {k}")
```

This will yield the following result:

```
Now i = 0, j = 0 and k = 0
Now i = 0, j = 0 and k = 1
Now i = 0, j = 1 and k = 0
Now i = 0, j = 1 and k = 1
```

```
Now i = 1, j = 0 and k = 0
Now i = 1, j = 0 and k = 1
Now i = 1, j = 1 and k = 0
Now i = 1, j = 1 and k = 1
```

Random Numbers and Time Control

Two tasks that we will frequently need in psychology and social sciences are generating random numbers and controlling time.

Let's see different possibilities for generating random numbers:

randint(a, b)

This returns a random integer between a and b, inclusive.

```
import random

numA = random.randint(0, 1)
print(numA)
```

randrange(a, b, step)

This generates random integers between a and b, separated by a fixed interval:

```
import random

for i in range(10):
    print(random.randrange(5, 27, 4))
```

random()

The random() function returns a float between (0.0 and 1.0):

```
import random

for i in range(5):
    print(random.random())
```

uniform(a, b)

This returns a floating-point number between a and b, inclusive.

```
import random

for i in range(5):
    print(random.uniform(100, 200))
```

choice()

This returns a random element from a list.

```
import random

fruits = ['pears', 'apples', 'bananas', 'plums']
for i in range(3):
    print(random.choice(fruits))
```

shuffle()

This shuffles the elements of the list. In a card game, this would be like shuffling the cards:

```
import random

cards = [1, 2, 3, 4, 5, 6, 7, 10, 11, 12]
random.shuffle(cards)
print(cards)
```

sample()

This returns random elements from a list; in a card game, this would be like dealing cards (see Program 1-1).

Program 1-1.

```
import random

cartas = [1, 2, 3, 4, 5, 6, 7, 10, 11, 12]
random.sample(cartas, 5)
```

All these programs start by importing the random library; then the program is asked to execute a command according to the programmer's needs.

Time control, which is necessary in psychological experiments, is done through the time library, as shown in Program 1-2.

Program 1-2.

```
import time

tInitial = time.time() # The start time is noted.
```

```
4   tAsignado = 10 # How long the test will last
5
6   tPrueba = tInitial + tAsignado
7
8   while tPrueba > time.time():
9       pass
```

This program starts with the import of the time library in line 1. The time at the start of the test is noted in the variable `tInitial` in line 3; the time that the test will last in seconds is assigned in line 4, in this case 10 seconds. In line 6, the value of the test time is calculated in Python notation, and in line 8 the 10-second loop that the test will last is started. The `pass` command does nothing, in its place would be the lines of code that make up the test to be performed. The `pass` command has been placed provisionally while the program has not been finished writing. If this program were executed without the `pass` command, it would throw an error, since Python does not allow any control structure to be an empty block. If it is executed with the `pass` command, the program will do nothing for 10 seconds, after which it will end, but it will not break either, which guarantees that the structure written so far is correct in Python code. Later, we will have to write the missing code that will be contained in the loop.

Sometimes you will need your program (see Program 1-3) to delay its execution for any reason. This is done with the `time.sleep()` or `time.delay()` function, from the time library, placing inside the parentheses the number of seconds you want to delay it.

Program 1-3.

```
import time

time.sleep(2)
```

It works by suspending the execution of the calling process for the specified number of seconds. The parameter passed to the function can be a floating-point value, if you want to pause the program for a fraction of a second.

An alternative is to use the `Event.wait` function from the threading library, as shown in Program 1-4.

Program 1-4.

```
from threading import Event

retraso = 1 # value in seconds

print('Now stop...')
Event().wait(retraso)
print('Go back to work... and finish the program')
```

Functions

Functions are a block of instructions within a program. There are predefined functions in the Python language and others from libraries that must be installed and imported at the beginning of the program, which make the programmer's work easier. We have already mentioned and used some of them, such as `print()` or `input()`, and there are many more. Other functions can be written by the programmer, as subprograms, having specific purposes with the advantage of being able to be reused as many times as necessary, without having to write them again each time or making the program longer unnecessarily by repeating code.

Functions can have parameters or not and return results or not. Let's look at an example:

```
def sumar(a, b):
    resultado = a + b
    return resultado
```

In this case, the add function accepts two values or parameters, `a` and `b`, and returns their sum.

Functions are placed at the beginning of the program, because they cannot be executed without the interpreter having read them and placed them in the computer's memory, but they do nothing if the program does not call them. Functions are called by assigning them to a variable and passing them the required values; the variable will contain the value returned by the function, as we see in the following lines:

```
suma = sumar(12, 15)
print(suma)
```

This code will print the result of the sum on the screen: 27.

The advantage of this procedure is that if the task that the function performs is very complex, it can be called from different points in the program, obtaining results with a single line of code. The parameters that are sent to the function can be program variables. Let's suppose we want to correct one or more scales of a questionnaire; we would have to create a function that receives the answers to the questionnaire and the correction key and that returns the score of the corrected scale, so that for each scale that we want to correct we would call the function, passing the answers and the key and then collecting the result. These saves writing a lot of code and makes the program smaller, more readable, and easier to correct or modify.

Functions are distinguished by the parentheses that are seen after their name.

In the predefined functions that the language contains, it is not necessary to know how things happen, only what each function does. As we have seen, you can also define your own functions, which allow you to perform specific tasks within the program. These have the advantage that they can be reused and save space or programming time.

The Python language includes functions, some of which we have already used. See the functions shown in Table 1-5 and also at `https://docs.python.org/es/3/library/functions.html?highlight=built`.

Table 1-5. *Python Functions*

`abs()`	`dir()`	`isinstance()`	`range()`
`aiter()`	`divmod()`	`issubclass()`	`repr()`
`all()`	`enumerate()`	`iter()`	`reversed()`
`anext()`	`eval()`	`len()`	`round()`
`any()`	`exec()`	`list()`	`set()`
`ascii()`	`filter()`	`locals()`	`setattr()`
`bin()`	`float()`	`map()`	`slice()`
`bool()`	`format()`	`max()`	`sorted()`
`breakpoint()`	`frozenset()`	`memoryview()`	`staticmethod()`
`bytearray()`	`getattr()`	`min()`	`str()`

(*continued*)

Table 1-5. *(continued)*

bytes()	globals()	next()	sum()
callable()	hasattr()	object()	super()
chr()	hash()	oct()	tuple()
classmethod()	help()	open()	type()
compile()	hex()	ord()	vars()
complex()	id()	pow()	zip()
delattr()	input()	print()	__import__()
dict()	int()	property()	

Classes

Classes and objects are structures that allow you to create your own data types, i.e., user-defined data types, and provide a way to package data and functionality together. Classes are created with the class command, as follows:

```
class ClassName:
    statement 1
    statement 2
    ...
    statement n
```

The class starts with the word `class` followed by the name and a colon. The class name follows the same rules as Python variable names, and it is recommended that the name of a class starts with a capital letter. Like functions, classes must be defined at the beginning of the program before being called; otherwise, an error will occur.

Classes have attributes, which are properties that we have added to the class type, and methods, which are Python functions that are defined within the class, with the word `def` and must necessarily have a self-argument.

Modules and Libraries

An important part of the Python language is the modules and libraries that allow the power of the language to be extended with minimal effort, since it is not necessary to program everything that is already programmed. A module is a portion of a program that performs a specific task. A library is a set of preprogrammed modules that the programmer can use to do certain tasks without having to program them.

Libraries are an essential complement to any language, since they contain modules written, sometimes in other languages, that provide access to system functionalities such as reading and writing files, performing complex calculations or voice recognition and synthesis tasks that would be inaccessible, or very difficult to perform, for Python programmers without them, as well as modules written in Python that provide standard solutions for the various problems that a programmer has to face every day. Some of these modules are explicitly designed to allow the portability of Python programs, abstracting platform specificities to achieve platform-neutral APIs.

Libraries such as NumPy, Python's contraction of number (Idris, 2015), are very useful for performing all kinds of numerical calculations. This is an open-source library for scientific computing. It allows, for example, to work with arrays or matrices in an efficient, easy, and fast way. This library also contains a long list of useful mathematical functions, including functions for linear algebra, Fourier transformation, or random number generation routines.

Other important libraries are Matplotlib and Pandas. The former is used to draw graphs, while the latter is a Python package that provides data structures; it is fast, flexible, and expressive, and is designed to make working with relational or labeled data easier and more intuitive. It aims to be a high-level building block for performing practical, real-world data analysis in Python. We are working with version 1.4.2.

The libraries are installed with the pip program, as we will see later. Once installed, to find out if these libraries are working correctly, you can run the program in Program 1-5.

Program 1-5.

```
import pandas as pd
import numpy as np
import matplotlib.pyplot as plt

np.random.seed(0)
valores = np.random.randn(100) # Create an array of random numbers with normal distribution
s = pd.Series(valores) # generate a pandas series
```

```
s.plot(kind='hist', title='Randomly distributed normal values')
plt.show()
```

The result of this program is an image like the one you can see in Figure 1-4.

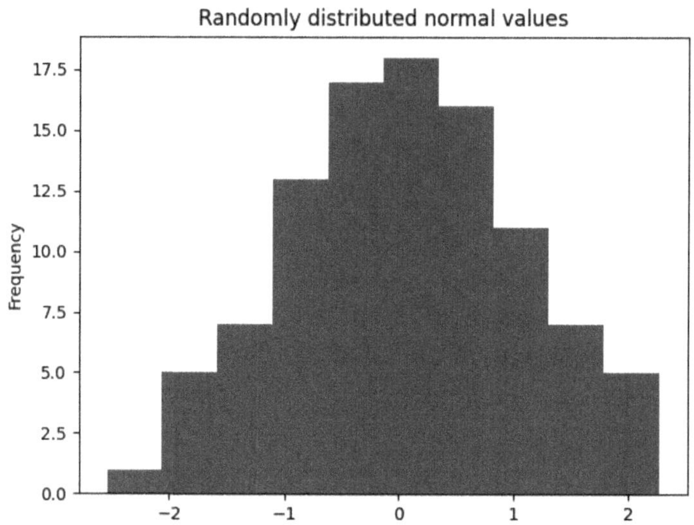

***Figure 1-4.** Randomly distributed normal values*

There are many libraries, and throughout the book we will mention those that we consider most useful for the tasks we have to face.

When importing libraries, keep in mind that all import statements should be at the beginning of the program, thus avoiding placing them where you need them or in random order. The recommended order is 1) system libraries, such as `os` or `random`; 2) third-party libraries, such as `psicopy`; and 3) your own modules. Within each section, it is advisable to put the libraries in alphabetical order to locate them more easily, like this:

```
import os
import random
```

This may not seem particularly useful for a short program, but as your projects grow, you will need to include more and more libraries. Keeping them in that order makes it easier to understand which libraries you use and which are nonstandard. Alphabetical order means you can quickly check whether a library is included in the program or not, since you can quickly find the location where its `import` statement appears.

Installing Python Libraries and Using the pip Program

As we have already mentioned, Python works with libraries to extend its functionality. Libraries are basically reusable program fragments that allow you to avoid having to repeat things that have already been programmed before. Libraries are in a central repository called PyPI (Python Package Index) and must be installed on the computer you are working on before you can use them. Installation is done with a specific program called pip. In the latest versions of Python, the pip program (Pip Installs Packages) is installed by default. If you want to check that it is really installed on your computer, type in the Windows console prompt:

```
> pip --version
```

The computer will respond with a message like this:

```
pip 24.2 from c:\python38\lib\site-pakages\pip (python 3.12)
```

This message extends to the bottom of the screen and may vary slightly depending on the version of pip and Python you have installed. You can also use the command `pip -h` or `pip -help`. This command will print a few lines of text informing you how to use the pip program.

pip is updated with the following command:

```
> python -m pip install --upgrade pip
```

Or this:

```
> pip install -upgrade pip setuptools
```

The `pip freeze` command lists all the libraries you have installed on your computer and their versions. And the following command will create a file called `requirements.txt`:

```
pip freeze >requirements.txt
```

This is useful if you need to provide a `.py` program to be executed on another computer without compatibility problems. This file contains the name and versions of all the Python libraries you have on your computer and allows you to install them on the target computer with the following command:

```
pip install -r requirements.txt
```

You can also list your libraries with the `list` command.

```
> pip list
```

This will also list, on screen, all the packages installed in Python and their versions.

All pip commands can be viewed by typing `pip -h` or `pip help` at the operating system prompt, which will produce a response like the one shown in Figure 1-5.

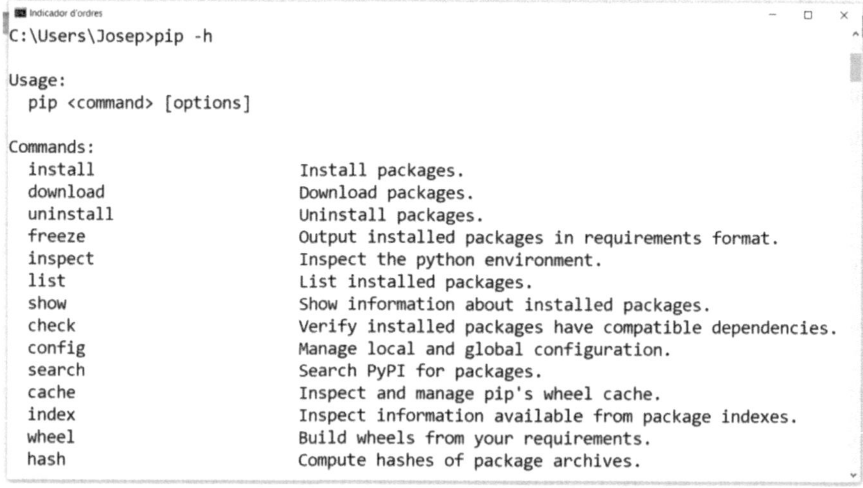

Figure 1-5. *pip commands*

To install a new library, you can first check if it exists with the command `pip search <library name>`. However, please note that the search command is an old command, destined to disappear. Another way is to search the website `https://pypi.org/` where you can find an index of available packages.

Libraries can be installed directly with the following command:

```
> pip install <library name>
```

Or with this:

```
> pip install --upgrade <library name>
```

This last command installs the latest version of the specified library, overwriting the previous version if it was already installed.

It is also possible to install older or specific versions of a library:

```
> pip install <library name> == <version>
> pip install <library name> -= <version>
```

For example:

```
> pip install pandas == 0.25.0
```

You can also get a list of installed libraries that have registered new versions:

```
> pip list --outdated
```

Note that some libraries are updated quite frequently and quickly become outdated. On the other hand, `pip show <library name>` provides information about the installed package. Here's an example:

```
> pip show psychopy
```

This command will produce the screen output shown in Figure 1-6.

```
Name: PsychoPy
Version: 2022.1.4
Summary: Psychology experiment software in Python
Home-page: https://www.psychopy.org/
Author: Open Science Tools Ltd
Author-email: support@opensciencetools.org
License: GNU GPLv3 (or more recent equivalent)
Location: c:\users\drroi\appdata\local\programs\python\python310\lib\
site-packages
Requires: arabic_reshaper, astunparse, cryptography, esprima, freetype-
py, gevent, gitpython, glfw, google-api-core, google-auth, google-cloud,
google-cloud-speech, googleapis-common-protos, imageio, imageio-ffmpeg,
javascripthon, jedi, json_tricks, markdown-it-py, matplotlib, moviepy,
msgpack, msgpack-numpy, numpy, opencv-python, openpyxl, pandas, pillow,
pocketsphinx, psutil, psychtoolbox, pygame, pyglet, pyo, pypiwin32, pyqmix,
pyqt5, pyserial, python-bidi, python-gitlab, python-vlc, pyWinhook,
pyyaml, pyzmq, questplus, requests, scipy, sounddevice, soundfile,
SpeechRecognition, tables, ujson, websocket_client, wxPython, xlrd
Required-by:
```

```
Name: PsychoPy
Version: 2022.1.4
Summary: Psychology experiment software in Python
Home-page: https://www.psychopy.org/
Author: Open Science Tools Ltd
Author-email: support@opensciencetools.org
License: GNU GPLv3 (or more recent equivalent)
Location: c:\users\drroi\appdata\local\programs\python\python310\lib\site-packages
Requires: arabic_reshaper, astunparse, cryptography, esprima, freetype-py, gevent, gitpython, glfw, google-api-core, google-auth, google-cloud, google-cloud-speech, googleapis-common-protos, imageio, imageio-ffmpeg, javascripthon, jedi, json_tricks, markdown-it-py, matplotlib, moviepy, msgpack, msgpack-numpy, numpy, opencv-python, openpyxl, pandas, pillow, pocketsphinx, psutil, psychtoolbox, pygame, pyglet, pyo, pypiwin32, pyqmix, pyqt5, pyserial, python-bidi, python-gitlab, python-vlc, pyWinhook, pyyaml, pyzmq, questplus, requests, scipy, sounddevice, soundfile, SpeechRecognition, tables, ujson, websocket_client, wxPython, xlrd
Required-by:
```

Figure 1-6. *Screen output*

The name of the library, its features, and its dependencies are displayed. Dependencies are other libraries necessary for its operation; if they are not installed, the library in question will not work.

At the end of the installation, pip will issue a message indicating that it has successfully installed the library. If the requested package cannot be installed, due to a lack of compatibility with the version of Python you have on your computer or for any other reason, pip will issue an error message.

Libraries can also be uninstalled:

```
> pip uninstall <library name>
```

Here's an example:

```
>pip uninstall PyQt5
```

The system will respond with a message:

```
>Succesfully uninstalled PyQt5
```

This assumes the library was previously installed; otherwise, it will print a warning message informing that this library was not installed, like so:

WARNING: Skipping PyQt5 as it is not installed

To update a library, type this:

```
>pip install --U <library name>
```

If you want to update the library but not its dependencies, use this:

```
>pip install --U -no-deps <library name>
```

In this case, the library will not work, and you will have to install its dependencies one by one for it to work correctly.

Some Python programs come with a file called `requirements.txt`, which contains the libraries needed for the program to work correctly. This file can be used to install these libraries:

```
> pip install -r requirements.txt
```

This command must be run from the directory containing the `requirements.txt` file.

This command will upgrade the pip program itself:

```
>python.exe -m pip install -upgrade pip
```

Library management in Python is a complex and fundamental issue, because they are necessary, there are many of them, they may have incompatibilities between them and with the version of Python you are using, or they may not be updated and available for the version of Python installed on your computer; this means it is possible that a program that works well in one version of Python and in a certain environment, in which all the necessary libraries are installed, does not work with another version of Python and in another environment. This may force you to have several versions of Python installed if you want to run third-party programs that are not compiled. To avoid problems in this case, it is common to install several versions of Python or the same version with different library packages, in so-called virtual environments. I will not go into this topic in detail, but I will mention that it is possible to create virtual environments from the language itself with `venv`. Another solution is to use Python on a web page or in the cloud. For example, with Google Colab, you will find information at `https://colab.google/`.

Libraries extend the capabilities of the language and are a great help in carrying out different tasks that otherwise could not be carried out or would be more difficult and time-consuming to program or much slower in their operation. It is common that even if an application works correctly, any change in its libraries or in the versions of those libraries can damage it and make it stop working or that with a version of Python and various libraries installed, you cannot install a library that you need to run a new program. If you have a problem with this type, the only way to solve it is, as we have said, to work in virtual environments.

From the Windows console, you can find out the version of Python you have installed with the command:

```
> python --version
```

Or find out how many installations you have installed:

```
> where python
```

Compiling a py and pyw Program

Once the program has been written and its correct operation has been checked and any errors have been corrected in the Python interpreter, it can be compiled to create a stand-alone executable file. Executables have some advantages over interpreted programs. For example, they are faster in their operation, they are protected against accidental modifications, and they can be run by themselves without having to have Python installed or to be opened through the interpreter. Also, in some cases it seems that the program can work differently in the interpreter than once it is compiled as an executable. Compiling a program makes it much easier to distribute it and improves user experience.

Compiling a program also has its disadvantages. The compilation process itself is a task that takes time; if an error is found in the compilation process, the executable program will not be created, and the source file will have to be corrected and compiled again. In addition, a compiled program cannot be changed, so it cannot be improved or modified. You must go back to the source program, make the necessary modifications or improvements, and recompile it.

There are several ways to create an executable from a `.py` file. One of them is to use the PyInstaller program. To do this, you must have this program already installed on your computer. If you do not have it installed, you must install it with this command:

```
>pip install pyinstaller
```

You can find the PyInstaller manual here:

`https://pyinstaller.readthedocs.io/en/stable/`

Once the program is installed, from the console environment, you must go to the directory where the file with the extension .py that you want to compile is and write the following command:

```
>pyinstaller --windowed --onefile <filename.py>
```

Or this one:

```
>pyinstaller --noconsole <filename.py>
```

It is also possible to add an icon to the program with this command:

```
--icon=file.ico
```

The windowed command is only in the case of a Windows graphical application; if it is a console application, this command should not be used, since the program would compile incorrectly and would not work when trying to run it. The onefile command is used when you want to distribute the executable without attachments; if this command is not indicated, the executable will be smaller, but it must be accompanied by a lot of auxiliary files for it to work correctly on another computer, or these auxiliary files must already be on the target computer. Otherwise, the executable will not work either.

The final file size can also be reduced by compressing the executable with UPX, using the --upx-dir option, which must specify the folder where the compressor is installed. Here's an example:

```
pyinstaller --onefile --upx-dir=C:\upx main.py
```

Finally, PyInstaller can encrypt Python source code files provided a 16-digit key is provided via --key=16_digit_key:

```
pyinstaller --key=1234567891234567 main.py
```

This option requires the tinyaes package, installable with pip:

```
pip install tinyaes
```

On Windows, the PyInstaller compilation process will create three subdirectories in the directory we are working with: __pycache__, build, and dist. The executable file to be distributed will be found at the end of these subdirectories, with the same name as the source file that has been compiled but with the extension .exe.

Other compilation options are the use of the py2exe program and cx_Freeze.

Using py2exe is suitable only for Windows.

To use py2exe, you first need to install the utility with pip:

```
pip install py2exe
```

To generate an executable file, with py2exe, you must first create a file called `setup.py`, indicating the name of the main file.

```
from distutils.core import setup
import py2exe
setup(console = [<"program name.py"])
```

This file is then invoked by passing it the `py2exe` option:

```
python setup.py py2exe
```

Like PyInstaller, the executable file will be found in the `dist` folder along with its dependencies, while the build folder can be discarded.

For desktop applications, the `windows` argument is used instead of `console` to avoid displaying the console.

To specify an image as an icon, the `icon_resources` option must be used.

```
from distutils.core import setup
import py2exe
setup(
    console=[{
        "script": " program_name.py",
        "icon_resources": [(1, "archivo.ico")]
    }]
)
```

All dependencies can be included in a single file, like PyInstaller's `--onefile` option, using this:

```
from distutils.core import setup
import py2exe
setup(
    options={"py2exe": {"bundle_files": 1}},
    console=[{
```

```
        "script": "<program_name.py>"
    }]
)
```

Compiling with cx_Freeze requires the prior installation of this utility with pip:

```
>pip install cx_Freeze
```

Next, we compile with the following command:

```
>cxfreeze -c <program name.py> --target-dir dist
```

The -c option indicates the name of the file to be converted and --target-dir the folder where cx_Freeze will store the executable file.

To set an image as an icon, the --icon option must be used.

```
cxfreeze -c main.py --icon=file.ico --target-dir dist
```

In this case, to hide the console, which is an unsightly element in programs with graphical presentation, the following command is used:

```
cxfreeze -c ain.py --base-name=Win32GUI --target-dir dist
```

Summary

In this chapter, you learned about the Python language and how to interact with the computer. In the next chapter, you will see some simple examples of programming for psychology, and you will have your first contact with graphic presentations.

CHAPTER 2

Put into Practice What You Have Learned and More

Now that you have learned about the Python language and how to interact with the computer using this language, we will move on in this chapter to simple examples of programming for psychology, and you will have your first contact with graphic presentations.

Subject-Computer Interaction

Most of the programs we write will require some type of interaction with an operator, so it is important to be familiar with the keyboard and mouse, which are the standard ways of interacting with the computer.

In Program 2-1, we can see the recording of data in a console application, of a hypothetical questionnaire of 50 questions with three response options: A, B, and C. This data is necessary to manage the correction and interpretation of any questionnaire. Naturally, there are other ways of entering the answers into the computer, such as optical readers or direct administration of the questionnaire by the computer. However, this method is still the most used today.

Program 2-1.

```
# EnterAnswers.py
import msvcrt


```


J. M. Roig-Fusté, *Python for Psychology, Social Sciences, and Education*,
https://doi.org/10.1007/979-8-8688-2355-8_2

```
# Enter answers
print()
print("                  ------")

print("Enter your answers using the following keys:")
print("    1 for answer 'A'.")
print("    2 for answer 'B'.")
print("    3 for answer 'C', and")
print("    4 for the blank answer.")
print("    - to go back and correct.")
print("               ----------------")
print()
print(" Answers:")

respostes = ""

# ························ 185 respostes
i = 1
while True:
    if i > 185:
        break
    print("    ", i, " : ",  end="")

    key = msvcrt.getch()
    if key != '':

        tecla = key.decode("ANSI")

        if tecla == "1":
            print("A")
            i = i + 1
            respostes = respostes + 'A'
        elif tecla == "2":
            print("B")
            i = i + 1
            respostes = respostes + 'B'

```

```
        elif tecla == "3":
            print("C")
            i = i + 1
            respostes = respostes + 'C'
        elif tecla == "4":
            print("?")
            i = i + 1
            respostes = respostes + '?'
        elif tecla == "-":
            i = i - 1
            print(i)
            if i<1:
                i = 1
            respostes = respostes[:-1] # removes the last character from the string.
            print(respostes)


        else:
            print()
            print("Invalid key. Press only 1 for 'A', 2 for 'B',")
            print("3 for 'C', 4 for blank answer and '-' for")
            print("go back and correct.")
            print()
            print(i, " : ",  end="")

print()

# Variable for correction: MacroC
print(respostes)
```

The program allows one answer for each key press, without the need to press the Return key, and allows you to go back in case of error. The keys used are 1 for answer A, 2 for B, 3 for C, and 4 for a blank answer. If this option is allowed, it is also possible to go back and discount items, in case of error, and to resume recording from the last deleted item.

The program aims to accumulate the answers in a single string that can be saved in a file or processed to correct the test.

A couple of important comments about this program: it does not work if run from the standard Python IDLE and possibly not from other IDLEs either. When running, it enters a loop that does not allow entering the answers. To see how it works, you can compile it or run it from the Windows console prompt, placing yourself in the directory where you saved the file and then call it by typing this:

```
> python enterAnswers.py
```

Some Python installations require typing `python3` or `python3.exe`. The > sign is part of the Windows console and does not need to be typed. A program with the same functionality can be written using the `pynput` or `keyboard` libraries.

Another aspect to keep in mind is that current computing environments are usually graphical, and this is a console application, and therefore text-only, with a somewhat primitive but perfectly functional appearance.

Python has built-in graphics and the possibility of using many libraries to achieve a more modern presentation; however, creating graphical interfaces is more complex and requires knowledge of how the library being used works. We will see some possibilities throughout the book.

Python's built-in graphics, which do not need to be installed, at least in recent versions of the language, are Turtle and Tkinter.

Turtle graphics appeared with the creation of the Logo programming language in 1967 (Wally Feurzeig and Seymour Papert) at MIT to teach programming to children. It meant the introduction of a two-dimensional graphical environment in which a turtle moved via a cursor that was given orders to move forward, backward, or turn, leaving a trace or not on the screen to draw all kinds of shapes (Papert, 1980). Python incorporated a turtle module, a graphical environment that allows interaction with the mouse and keyboard, with the same purpose. With the turtle module, we can program a menu and a screen to enter answers to a questionnaire in a graphical format, as shown in Program 2-2.

Program 2-2.

```
# menuTurtle.py

import time
```

```
import turtle

screen = turtle.Screen()
global key_pressed
global x
global y
global xR # x coordinate of the response
global yR # y coordinate of the response
global responses
global nResponses

key_pressed = False
replies = ''
nResponses = 0

x = -300; y = 275
xR = -300; yR =263

# Function to enter personal data
def enter(x, y):
    nom = turtle.textinput('Enter name', 'name')
    edat = turtle.numinput('Enter age', 'Age', 0, 20, 99)
    sex = turtle.textinput('Enter sex', 'Sex, M for male/F for
    female')
    window2()


def recover(x, y): # select menu option
    turtle.penup()
    turtle.hideturtle()
    turtle.goto(-180,-280)
    turtle.write("Function not available", align="center",
    font=("Arial", 20, "normal"))


```

```
# Exit the program
def exit_program(x, y):
    turtle.bye()


def on_key_press_1(): # ..........................
    turtle.speed(10)
    turtle.penup()
    turtle.course.penup()
    #turtle.curso.clear()
    #turtle.curso.hideturtle()

    global key_pressed
    global x
    global y
    global xR
    global yR
    global responses
    global nResponses

    if nRespostes > 78:
        screen.clear()
        turtle.course.penup()
        turtle.course.pencolor('white')
        #turtle.curso.clear()
        # turtle.course.ht()
        print( responses)
        menu( ) # select main menu

    turtle.goto( xR, yR)
    turtle.write( 'V', align= "center", font=("Arial", 16, "bold"))
    replies = replies + 'V'
    y = y - 30
    nRespostes = nRespostes + 1
    yR = yR - 30

```

```
    key_pressed = False

    if yR < -308: # change column
        xR = xR + 83 # 1st col: -300, 2nd col -220
        yR = 263
        y = 275
        x = x + 83


def on_key_press_2(): # ·························
    turtle.speed(10)
    turtle.penup()
    turtle.course.penup()
    #turtle.curso.clear()
    #turtle.curso.hideturtle()

    #turtle.clear()
    turtle.hideturtle()

    global responses
    global nResponses
    global key_pressed
    global x
    global y
    global xR
    global yR

    if nRespostes > 78:
        screen.clear()
        turtle.course.penup()
        turtle.course.pencolor('white')
        turtle.curso.clear()
        turtle.course.ht()
        print( responses)
        screen.clear()
```

```
            menu() # select main menu

        turtle.goto( xR, yR)
        replies = replies + 'F'
        y = y - 30
        nRespostes = nRespostes +1
        turtle.write( 'F', align= "center", font=("Arial", 16, "bold"))
        yR = yR - 30

        key_pressed = False

        if yR < -308: # change column
            xR = xR + 83
            yR = 263
            y = 275
            x = x + 83


    def window2():
        screen = turtle.Screen()
        screen.setup(770, 690, 50, 50)
        screen.clear()
        screen.title( "Enter responses.")
        global key_pressed
        global response
        global x
        global y

        # place items
        turtle.hideturtle()
        turtle.penup()
        turtle.goto(-330, 260)
        turtle.write( "1. 21. 41. 61.", align="left", font=("Arial", 16, "bold"))
        turtle.goto(-330, 230)
```

```
turtle.write( "2. 22. 42. 62.", align="left", font=("Arial", 16, "bold"))
turtle.goto(-330, 200)
turtle.write( "3. 23. 43. 63.", align="left", font=("Arial", 16, "bold"))
turtle.goto(-330, 170)
turtle.write( "4. 24. 44. 64.", align="left", font=("Arial", 16, "bold"))
turtle.goto(-330, 140)
turtle.write( "5. 25. 45. 65.", align="left", font=("Arial", 16, "bold"))
turtle.goto(-330, 110)
turtle.write( "6. 26. 46. 66.", align="left", font=("Arial", 16, "bold"))
turtle.goto(-330, 80)
turtle.write( "7. 27. 47. 67.", align="left", font=("Arial", 16, "bold"))
turtle.goto(-330, 50)
turtle.write( "8. 28. 48. 68.", align="left", font=("Arial", 16, "bold"))
turtle.goto(-330, 20)
turtle.write( "9. 29. 49. 69.", align="left", font=("Arial", 16, "bold"))
turtle.goto(-343, -10)
turtle.write( "10. 30. 50. 70.", align="left", font=("Arial", 16, "bold"))
turtle.goto(-343, -40)
turtle.write( "11. 31. 51. 71.", align="left", font=("Arial", 16, "bold"))
turtle.goto(-343, -70)
turtle.write( "12. 32. 52. 72.", align="left", font=("Arial", 16, "bold"))
turtle.goto(-343, -100)
turtle.write( "13. 33. 53. 73.", align="left", font=("Arial", 16, "bold"))
turtle.goto(-343, -130)
```

```
turtle.write( "14. 34. 54. 74.", align="left", font=("Arial", 16,
"bold"))
turtle.goto(-343, -160)
turtle.write( "15. 35. 55. 75.", align="left", font=("Arial", 16,
"bold"))
turtle.goto(-343, -190)
turtle.write( "16. 36. 56. 76.", align="left", font=("Arial", 16,
"bold"))
turtle.goto(-343, -220)
turtle.write( "17. 37. 57. 77.", align="left", font=("Arial", 16,
"bold"))
turtle.goto(-343, -250)
turtle.write( "18. 38. 58. 78.", align="left", font=("Arial", 16,
"bold"))
turtle.goto(-343, -280)
turtle.write( "19. 39. 59. 79.", align="left", font=("Arial", 16,
"bold"))
turtle.goto(-343, -310)
turtle.write( "20. 40. 60. 80.", align="left", font=("Arial", 16,
"bold"))

# draw cursor
turtle.course = turtle.Turtle()
turtle.curso.shape("square")
turtle.curso.color("red")
turtle.course.shapesize(1.3, 1, 0)
turtle.curso.goto(-300, 275) # place cursor x, y
turtle.course.penup()
turtle.course.pencolor('white')

turtle.course.pencolor('white')
turtle.course.penup()
turtle.curso.clear()
#turtle.curso.hideturtle()
enterAnswer()
```

```


def enterAnswer():
    global x
    global y

    screen.listen()
    screen.onkey(on_key_press_1, '1')
    screen.onkey(on_key_press_2, '2')
    turtle.curso.goto(x, y) # place cursor x, y
    turtle.course.penup()
    turtle.course.pencolor('white')

    # call window window2 after a short time (100 ms)
    # to scan if there have been any key presses
    screen.ontimer(enterAnswer, 100)
    turtle.listen()


def menu(): # -----------------------------------------------------
    # Display Settings
    screen = turtle.Screen()
    screen.screensize(450, 150)
    screen.setup(550, 550, 100, 100)
    screen.clear()
    screen.title( "Main menu.")
    turtle.speed(10)
    turtle.penup()
    turtle.clear()
    turtle.hideturtle()

    # Creating the first button
    button1 = turtle.Turtle()
    button1.shape("square")
    button1.color("green")
```

```
    button1.shapesize(stretch_wid=4, stretch_len=12)
    button1.penup()
    button1.goto(-100, 200)
    button1.onclick(enter)

    # Create the text of the first button
    label1 = turtle.Turtle()
    label1.hideturtle()
    label1.penup()
    label1.goto(-100, 190)
    label1.color('white') # Change the color of the letter to white
    label1.write("Enter data", align="center", font=("Arial", 20,
    "normal"))

    # Creating the second button
    button2 = turtle.Turtle()
    button2.shape("square")
    button2.color("blue")
    button2.shapesize(stretch_wid=4, stretch_len=12)
    button2.penup()
    button2.goto(-100, 100)
    button2.onclick(recover)

    # Create the text of the second button
    label2 = turtle.Turtle()
    label2.hideturtle()
    label2.penup()
    label2.goto(-100, 90)
    label2.color('white') # Change the color of the letter to white
    label2.write("Recover data", align="center", font=("Arial", 20,
    "normal"))

    # Creating the 3rd button
    button3 = turtle.Turtle()
    button3.shape("square")
    button3.color("red")
```

```
264         button3.shapesize(stretch_wid=4, stretch_len=12)
265         button3.penup()
266         button3.goto(-100, 0)
267         button3.onclick(exit_program)
268
269         # Create the text of the second button
270         label3 = turtle.Turtle()
271         label3.hideturtle()
272         label3.penup()
273         label3.goto(-100, -10)
274         label3.color('white') # Change the color of the letter to white
275         label3.write("Exit", align="center", font=("Arial", 20,
            "normal"))
276
277
278     # Start the main event loop
279     turtle.speed(10)
280     menu()
        turtle.mainloop()
```

This program is shown in Figure 2-1. It starts at line 281, which calls the menu function. This function configures the screen and draws three buttons, the first of which, when clicked with the mouse, directs the action to the response entry screen by drawing `window2`. The second button is not activated and writes an option not available for message to the screen. The third button exits the program.

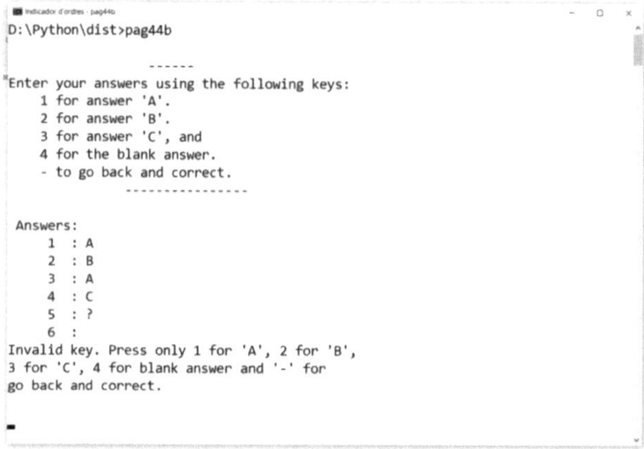

Figure 2-1. *Program 2-2*

More buttons can be added, if desired, in the same way that the three mentioned are designed.

The `window2` function writes the number of all the items in the questionnaire and places a cursor next to the number 1 to enter the first answer. The answers accepted in this case are True and False, which are entered by pressing the 1 and 2 keys. When one of these keys is pressed, the computer writes a T or an F next to the item number, as appropriate, and automatically moves to the next item. When the last item is reached, the program returns to the menu screen. This work is done thanks to the `enterAnswer( )` function, which calls the `on_key_press_1` functions, depending on whether key 1 or key 2 was pressed. These functions accumulate the entered answers in a variable called `respostes` for later processing and check whether the number of items provided has been exceeded to return to the main menu.

Another issue to consider about the keyboard and mouse for collecting responses is their precision and accuracy in collecting responses. In the cases described, an inaccuracy of a few seconds is of no importance because the operator will not notice it. However, in experimental research can be important. Some authors (Damian, 2010; Dalmaijer, 2024) have studied the operation of computer peripherals and have doubts about whether they offer the millisecond precision required for experimental psychology experiments. If we want a guarantee about the collection of information, we will have to resort to software and peripherals built specifically for psychological use, which naturally can be expensive.

Software development, or coding a program that is useful and effective, consists of several phases:

- Analysis
- Design
- Coding
- Testing
- Integration
- Maintenance

For the result to be optimal, each of these stages builds on the previous one and assumes that it has been carried out correctly. Let's look at each of these sections in more detail.

Analysis involves a thorough study of the task that the computer must perform, breaking it down into its most basic parts; it also requires the collection of all the data that will be necessary to create the program.

The design involves the detailed description, in natural language, of all the steps that the program will perform, which is known as an algorithm.

Coding is the writing of a program in a specific programming language. In fact, it can be considered the translation of the previous step, in natural language, into the programming language chosen to create the program that the computer can understand, in our case, Python.

Verification is the testing of the program to ensure, as far as possible, that it works correctly and provides the desired results. It is usually done by comparing known cases, which have been previously processed manually, with the results provided by the computer.

Integration is the sharing and assembly of the program, if it has been carried out by several people, or teams, at the same time, when each of them has dealt with a different part of the task. This is generally necessary in long and complex programs.

Maintenance is the correction of errors discovered throughout the useful life of the program and its improvement or updating, if this proves necessary at some point, due to the characteristics of the task being addressed.

In short programs, or for specific tasks, it is possible for all these phases to be carried out informally and almost simultaneously, by the same person; this is not possible in complex programs, which can take months to develop and in which several people are involved at the same time. Carrying out the program informally has the risk that later it will become difficult to modify or maintain. Therefore, from the beginning, it is important to create program documentation, which includes the objectives, the information necessary to achieve them and the different ways in which it has been decided to approach the tasks within the program itself, the detailed description in natural language of the steps to be carried out, and the codification of this task.

With what we have already learned about Python and considering the procedure mentioned, we can start programming an application that is easy to code and that can adapt well to the computer environment. The first application that we are going to develop will be the core of a program that allows us to manage a simple memory task of number sequences. In this program, we want to present a series of numbers on the screen and then ask the subject to write the numbers presented, first in direct order and then in reverse order. A similar task is part of the Wechsler Intelligence Scale (1939, 1943), a task that Wechsler incorporated from the Stanford-Binet (Roig-Fusté, 2017). This is a task that can be related to attention and working memory. Information about it can be found in Strauss, Sherman, and Spreen (2006) and in Lezak, Howieson, Bigler, and Tranel (2012).

To present a task of this type, we have chosen the Pygame library to achieve a more attractive graphical presentation of the task. Pygame is a graphical library like Turtle but more flexible and with more options. To work with Pygame, it is essential to follow these steps:

1. Import Pygame.
2. Initialize Pygame:

   ```
   pygame.init()
   ```

3. Set the window size:

   ```
   pygame.display.set_ mode( (700, 500))
   ```

4. Set the window title:

   ```
   pygame.display.set_caption ( "Number memory")
   ```

5. It is also possible to place an icon in the window title; this icon must be available in the same directory as the program.

   ```
   # We load the window icon
   icon = pygame.image.load("<icon name>")
   ```

6. We set the icon in the window:

```
pygame.display.set_ icon(icon)
```

7. Create a loop to keep Pygame and the program active:

```
while True:
    for event in pygame.event.get():
        if event.type == pygame.QUIT:
            pygame.quit()
            exit ()
```

If we skip any of these steps, the program will fail or will not work as expected.

The numbers to be remembered will be presented in a predetermined increasing series of 2 to 11 numbers, in two trials for each number quantity, first asking for a response in the same order and in the second part a response in reverse order. The exercise is interrupted after three consecutive failures. The numbers will be presented at a rate of one per second, with a short interval between them. See Program 2-3.

Program 2-3.

```
# Number Memory Test / Dr. Roig, 01.11.2022
# Digit Span version 1.0.0/ DigitSpan.py

import pygame
from pygame import mixer
from pygame.locals import*
from sys import exit
import time

# Constants ······
WHITE = (255, 255, 255)
SCREEN_SIZE = (680, 610)

# initializing pygame
pygame.init()
# Presentation of instructions ---------------------------------
display = pygame.display.set_mode((1100, 600))
```

```
display.fill(WHITE)
pygame.display.set_caption('Digit Span Test / Instructions')
pygame.display.update()
font = pygame.font.SysFont("Arial", 35)
text01 = font.render('Numbers will appear sequentially on the
screen',
0, (0, 0, 255))
display.blit(text01, (100, 100))

text01 = font.render( 'which you must memorize. When prompted
you must
write all the', 0, (0, 0, 255))
display.blit(text01, (100, 150))

text02 = font.render('numbers in the same order as they appeared on
the screen.', 0, (0, 0, 255))
display.blit(text02, (100, 200))

text02 = font.render('Note that each series will only be rendered
once.', 0, (0, 0, 255))
display.blit(text02, (100, 250))

text03 = font.render("When you are ready press the space
bar.", 0, (0,
0, 255))
display.blit(text03, (200, 350))

pygame.display.update()

# wait for test start
key_pressed = False
while not key_pressed:
for event in pygame.event.get():
if event.type == pygame.KEYDOWN:
            key_pressed = True
```

```


# list of number series ·····················
stimul = ['96', '61',
'475', '913',
'8406', '0628',
'46598', '41492',
'248730', '734345',
'1673470', '4050179',
'94391842', '41952485',
'036484935', '9879518640',
            '7105890364', '4104251857',
'98215068107', '13825950724']
resp = ''
points = 0
cErrors = 0 # Error handling
# start test ·························
time.sleep(2)

a=12
font = pygame.font.SysFont("Arial", 250)

for essay in range(18):
pygame.display.set_caption('Digit Span Test / Task')
display.fill(WHITE)
pygame.display.update()


for i in range(len(stimul[trial])):
        font = pygame.font.SysFont( "Arial", 250)

        text = font.render(stimul[test][i], 0, (0, 0, 255))
display.blit(text, (500, 150))
pygame.display.update()
time.sleep(.6)

```

```
display.fill(WHITE)
pygame.display.update()
time.sleep(.4)

resp =''
# admit reply
font = pygame.font.SysFont("Swis", 50)
pygame.display.set_caption('Digit Span Test / Enter Answer')

    txt = font.render("Write your answer: (If you need to correct it,
    delete it", 0, (0, 0, 255))
display.blit(txt, (100, 50))

    txt = font.render("with the backspace key. When finished press
    the", 0, (0, 0, 255))
display.blit(txt, (100, 100))
pygame.display.update()

txt = font.render("'RETURN' key.)", 0, (0, 0, 255))
display.blit(txt, (100, 150))
pygame.display.update()

font = pygame.font.SysFont("Swis", 110)
sort = 0

a = 200
b = 280
cursor = font.render("_", 0, (0, 0, 255))
    display.blit(cursor, (a, b))
pygame.display.update()
# Enter answer ====================================
control = 0
while True:
for event in pygame.event.get():

```

```
if event.type == KEYDOWN:
if event.key == pygame.K_RETURN:
                    # Evaluate the response
if resp == stimul[essay]:
points = points + 1
cErrors = 0
else:
cErrors = cErrors +1

                    sort = 1

if event.key == pygame.K_BACKSPACE and len(resp)>0:
a = a - 42
delete = resp[-1]
resp = resp[:-1]
text = font.render(delete, 0, (255, 255, 255))
display.blit(text, (a, b))
pygame.display.update()

if event.key == pygame.K_0:
                    text = font.render('0', 0, (0, 0, 0))
letter = '0'
control = 1
cursor = font.render("_", 0, (255, 255, 255))
display.blit(cursor, (a, b))

                if event.key == pygame.K_1:
                    text = font.render('1', 0, (0, 0, 0))
letter = '1'
control = 1
cursor = font.render("_", 0, (255, 255, 255))
display.blit(cursor, (a, b))

                if event.key == pygame.K_2:
                    text = font.render('2', 0, (0, 0, 0))
```

```
letter = '2'
control = 1
cursor = font.render("_", 0, (255, 255, 255))
display.blit(cursor, (a, b))

                    if event.key == pygame.K_3:
                        text = font.render('3', 0, (0, 0, 0))
letter = '3'
control = 1
cursor = font.render("_", 0, (255, 255, 255))
display.blit(cursor, (a, b))

                    if event.key == pygame.K_4:
                        text = font.render('4', 0, (0, 0, 0))
letter = '4'
control = 1
cursor = font.render("_", 0, (255, 255, 255))
display.blit(cursor, (a, b))

                    if event.key == pygame.K_5:
                        text = font.render('5', 0, (0, 0, 0))
letter = '5'
control = 1
cursor = font.render("_", 0, (255, 255, 255))
display.blit(cursor, (a, b))

                    if event.key == pygame.K_6:
                        text = font.render('6', 0, (0, 0, 0))
letter = '6'
control = 1
cursor = font.render("_", 0, (255, 255, 255))
display.blit(cursor, (a, b))

                    if event.key == pygame.K_7:
                        text = font.render('7', 0, (0, 0, 0))
```

```
letter = '7'
control = 1
cursor = font.render("_", 0, (255, 255, 255))
display.blit(cursor, (a, b))

                    if event.key == pygame.K_8:
                         text = font.render('8', 0, (0, 0, 0))
letter = '8'
control = 1
cursor = font.render("_", 0, (255, 255, 255))
display.blit(cursor, (a, b))

                    if event.key == pygame.K_9:
                         text = font.render('9', 0, (0, 0, 0))
letter = '9'
control = 1
cursor = font.render("_", 0, (255, 255, 255))
display.blit(cursor, (a, b))

                    if control == 1:
display.blit(text, (a, b))
a = a + 42
pygame.display.update()
resp = resp + letter
control = 0

if sort == 1:
break

     if cErrors > 1:
break

# Test completed ·····························
display.fill(WHITE)
pygame.display.set_ caption( 'Digit Span Test / Test finished.')
```

```
224 pygame.display.update()
225 font = pygame.font.SysFont("Arial", 80)
226 text01 = font.render('Test completed.', 0, (0, 255, 255))
227 display.blit(text01, (100, 80))
228
229 text01 = font.render('Thank you for your participation.', 0, (0, 255,
    255))
230 display.blit(text01, (100, 160))
231
232 p = font.render(str(points), 0, (0, 0, 255))
233 display.blit(p, (100, 450))
234
235 pygame.display.update()
236
237 time.sleep(6)
238
239 pygame.quit()
240 exit()
```

The first two lines of the program contain notes about the name, author, date, and version. When writing many programs, it is important to have them identified and to know the date and version of them to avoid confusion and problems when they are modified, corrected, or extended.

Lines 4 to 8 import the libraries necessary for the correct operation of the program.

Lines 11 and 12 define constants. Python does not differentiate between constants and variables, but it is traditional to write constants in capital letters at the beginning of the program, while variables are written in lowercase letters. These values could be written each time they are needed; however, if we want to make a change once the program is written, it is easier to change a single value, the value of the constant, than to change many values throughout the program each time they are needed.

Line 15 initializes Pygame.

Lines 17 to 37 present the instructions in the form that Pygame accepts: choosing the size of the screen font and the placement of the messages.

Lines 39 to 44 pause the program while the subject reads the instructions until pressing the spacebar.

Lines 47 to 57 contain a list of strings, called `stimul`, which contains the numbers that will be presented to the subject. These stimuli could have been generated randomly, in which case this list would not have been necessary, but in these circumstances not all subjects would have had the same stimuli, and possibly the results would not be comparable. Naturally, if the stimuli are fixed, it is not advisable to repeat the test shortly after having performed it, due to a possible question of memorization or recall of the stimuli that could affect the results. In this program, up to a series of 11 numbers has been included, but if you think that one of your subjects can memorize a greater number of elements, it is possible to continue adding increasingly longer series.

Lines 51 to 53 define variables necessary for the program to function: `resp` will store the series typed by the subject; the variable `points` will accumulate the points earned at a rate of one point per correctly completed series up to a maximum total of 20.

Lines 59 to 61 define the variables necessary for the program to function, the font of the Pygame screen, and its size for the presentation of the stimuli.

Line 60 starts a loop that will present the 20 trials, if the test is not interrupted before due to three consecutive failures, and will collect the subject's response.

Lines 61 to 63 prepare the screen for the presentation of stimuli.

Line 66 breaks each string of the stimulus matrix into elements that are presented sequentially. To do this, a font size is chosen. Line 67 selects the element to be presented. Line 69 presents said element in a specific location on the screen for an agreed upon time, six-tenths of a second. Lines 70 to 72. Lines 74 and 75 constitute the interval of four-tenths of a second between the display of two numbers. Thus, numbers appear every second, which is divided into six-tenths of a second of display time and four-tenths of an interval between numbers. All these values can be changed in the program if necessary.

Starting on line 78, the collection of responses begins. On this line, the variable `resp`, which will have to contain the new response, is emptied. Instructions for responding are given up to line 95.

Lines 107 to 205 record the subject keystrokes on the numbers on the keyboard until the user presses the Return key when finishing the answer. When the subject presses this key, the program scores the answer and moves to the next exercise. While the subject is typing the answer and before pressing the Return key to confirm it, it is possible to correct this answer by deleting one or more numbers with the backspace key.

From lines 213 to 233, the final screen of the test is presented thanking the subject for their collaboration. This occurs after presenting all the stimuli or after three consecutive failures.

When the program is started, the first screen of instructions appears (Figure 2-2).

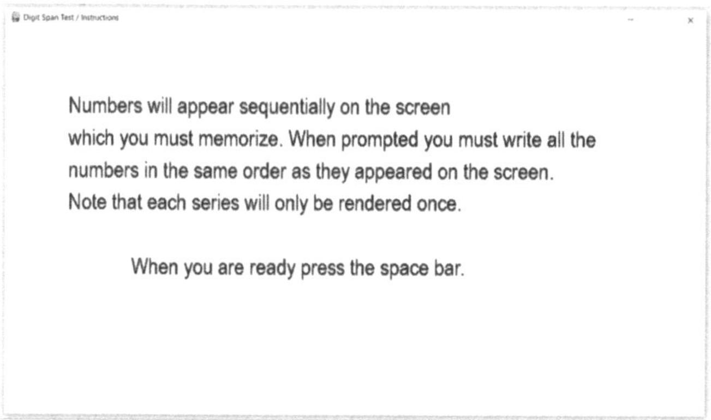

Figure 2-2. *Screen instructions*

Pressing the spacebar will bring up a new screen in which the series of numbers to be remembered will appear sequentially; once all the numbers in the series have been presented, the screen for entering the answer will appear.

After entering the numbers you remember from the series, you must press the Return key so that the program can continue (Figure 2-3). As is traditional, if two series of the same length fail, the program is interrupted, thus ending the task.

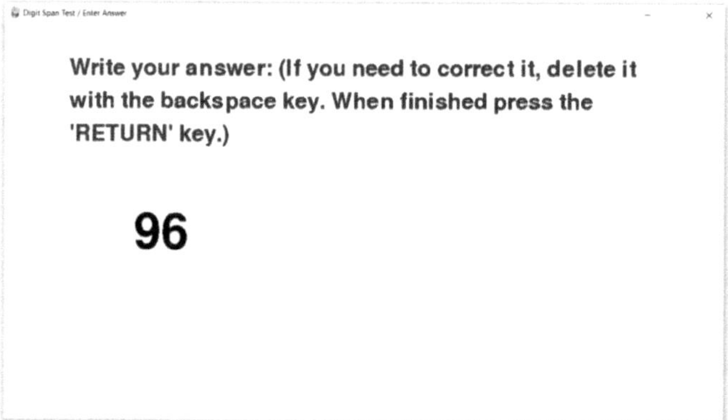

Figure 2-3. *Next screen instructions*

As you can see, the program is not finished because part of the numbers in reverse order is missing. To complete this part, lines 40 to 211 should be repeated, with some modifications, inserting these lines before `# Test finished`. New instructions must be added for this part of the test, warning the subject that, on this occasion, the series of numbers that will be presented must be typed in reverse. That is, if the numbers 6901 appear, the user must answer 1069. The name of some variables must be changed to initialize them at zero without erasing the results of the first part of the test. It is also advisable not to use the same stimulus matrix as in the first part; the new matrix could be called `stimulInvers`. When evaluating the response, it will have to be compared not with the stimulus but with the reverse of the stimulus to credit points. This could be done by storing in the program a new matrix of correct answers or reverses of the stimuli or by adding some lines of code that invert the stimulus before comparing it with the response given by the subject. To know how to do this, consider Program 2-4.

Program 2-4.

```
stimulus = '6093152'
stimulusAux = stimulus
stimulusAux = list(stimulus) # converts a string to a list
stimulusAux.reverse()
stimulusAux = "".join(stimulusAux) # converts the list to a string
# check the operation of the program
print( stimulus)
print( stimulusAux)
```

The correct or incorrect response is established by comparing the subject's response with the Aux stimulus.

In a usable program, it would be convenient to collect, prior to the application of the task, the data of the subject taking the test and decide what to do with the results: display them on the screen or save them to a file on the hard disk. We will see all this in different programs throughout the book.

We have seen a visual presentation of this task, but Python also allows a verbal presentation of the activity and allows it in two different ways. In this case, one way could be to pre-record 10 voice files each with the voiceover of a number from 0 to 9, so instead of presenting the number visually, the voice file, `.waw` or `.mp3`, should be read with a suitable library, such as `pyaudio` or `wave`, as we will see later. Another way would be to transform a text into speech by synthesizing said voice. For an example of this last option, consider Program 2-5.

Program 2-5.

```
1   import pyttsx3
2   import time
3
4   voice = pyttsx3.init()
5   voices = voice.getProperty('voices')
6
7   # Control the speed of speech. The higher the rate, the faster the
8   speed.
9   voice.setProperty("rate", 180)
10
11  # indices for voice[0] - Spanish; [1] English
12  voice.setProperty('voice', voices[0].id)
13
14  # texts to vocalize
15  txt = ['zero', 'one', 'two', 'three', 'four', 'five', 'six',
16         'seven', 'eight', 'nine']
17
18  for i in range(len(txt)):
19  voice.say(txt[i])
20  time.sleep(.6)
21      voice.runAndWait()
```

First, you need to import the `pyttsx3` speech synthesis and `time` libraries and then start using the `pyttsx3` library on line 4. Then, choose the speech speed, on line 8. A rate of around 180 represents a normal speed; you can reach a fast speed with a value of 400 or 500, or slow with a value below 180. On line 11, you choose the voice accent, Spanish or English. Next, there are the texts to be reproduced as voice in the form of a matrix for this program, lines 14 and 15; they could also be sentences. Finally, the 10 digits are vocalized using a loop that starts on line 17. The number is chosen on line 18 with the `say` command. A delay is placed between numbers on line 19, and it is executed on line 20. In this way, the presentation of stimuli could be done in a vocal way, integrating these orders within the loop that presents the numbers. The subject's response could then be collected by having typing the numbers remembered in a suitable window.

Of course, any text, no matter how long, can be synthesized to be broadcast over computer speakers or saved in a file and, as we have mentioned, with different accents.

Graphical Interfaces

We have seen an example of a Python program using some necessary resources without a great deal of knowledge of them. Almost all modern, best-known operating systems work with graphical interfaces, which we have talked little about; that is, a way of interacting between the user and the computer, which is characterized by replacing written orders with events or occurrences.

A graphical interface provides a professional look to programs and makes them more intuitive and easier to use. The different libraries that exist to create graphical environments allow you to add efficient complements in a complicated way to screen presentations. Graphical user interfaces (GUIs, pronounced "gooey") are windows that appear on the screen, with buttons, text fields, and other components that facilitate interaction with the program. As we have already mentioned, there are many libraries that allow you to create graphical environments to interact with programs. Comprehensible consideration of some of them exceeds the objectives of this book; you must find out which one best suit your needs at any given time to learn how to use it. Here we will refer only to some example possibilities that we will use later in the construction of our own programs. Of these libraries, there are some that are more complex in their use and others that are simpler; we will use some of the latter to introduce ourselves to the subject.

We will start by presenting a simplified and easy-to-use library: EasyGUI, which will be the one we will use in our programs to enter personal data, as an alternative to the Python console command `input()`. Before using this library, you should check that you have it installed; if not, you will need to install it. Remember that the following commands can perform these two tasks:

```
pip list
pip install easygui
```

This library can then be used to create the part of the program that allows entering a subject's personal data before starting an experiment or task (Program 2-6). See Figure 2-4.

Program 2-6.

```
# Graphical interface demo 01

import easygui as gui

nom = gui.enterbox(
    msg = "Please enter a name or an identifier.",
title = "Enter personal data",
)
```

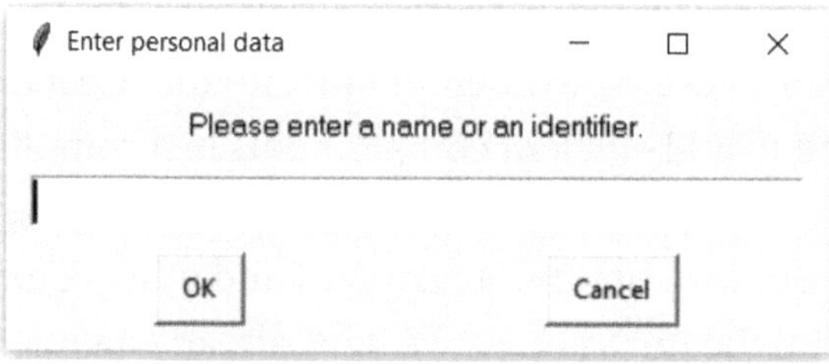

Figure 2-4. *Entering personal data*

To enter different data on the same screen instead of using `enterbox`, you must use `multienterbox`, as shown in Program 2-7.

Program 2-7.

```
# Graphical interface demo 02

from easygui import *
import sys

msg = "Enter a name or identifier and the rest of the requested data"
title = "Personal data"
fieldNames = [" Name", " Age", " Sex (M - Male / F - Female)", " Psychologist in charge"]
fieldValues = multenterbox(msg, title, fieldNames)
if fieldValues is None:
    sys.exit(0)

```

```
13  # to ensure that all fields are filled in
14
15  while 1:
16      errmsg = ""
17      for i, name in enumerate(fieldNames):
18          if fieldValues[i].strip() == "":
19              errmsg += "{} is a required field.\n\n".format(name)
20      if errmsg == "":
21          break # no problems found
22      fieldValues = multenterbox(errmsg, title, fieldNames,
    fieldValues)
23      if fieldValues is None:
24          break
25
26  print("Data collected:{}".format(fieldValues))
```

This gives us a screen like Figure 2-5.

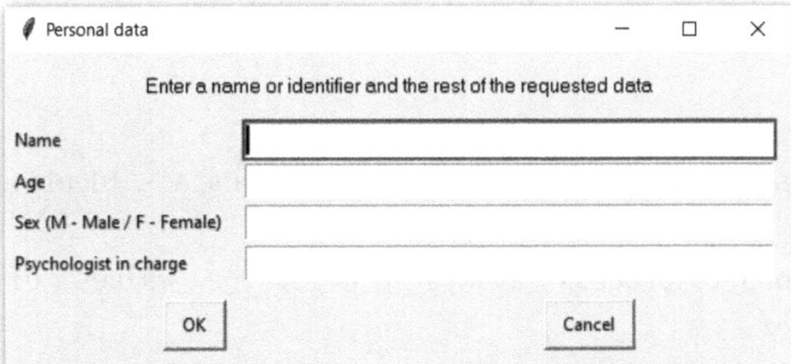

Figure 2-5. *Personal data*

On line 26 the data entered in the text boxes is collected. To manage them, it is better to save them in a variable:

```
collected_data = fieldValues
print ("Data collected:{}".format( data_collected ))
```

Another possibility is to use PySimpleGUI, as we will see in Program 2-8.

Program 2-8.

```
# Enter personal data 05.09.2023

import PySimpleGUI as sg

# Enter identification data with PySimpleGUI as sg -----------

layout = [[sg.Text('Enter the data and press OK when you're
done,',font=("Helvetica", 30))],
[sg.Text('then click Continue to move forward',font=("Helvetica",
30))],
[sg.Text('Name or identifier', font=("Helvetica", 20)),
sg.InputText(size=(50, 2), font=("Helvetica", 20))],
[sg.Text('Age (Valid values between 19 and 99)',font=("Helvetica",
20)), sg.InputText(size=(2, 2),font=("Helvetica", 20) )],
[sg.Text('Gender (Use M for male and F for female)',font=("Helvetica",
20)), sg.InputText(size=(2, 2), font=("Helvetica", 20))],
          [sg.Button('Ok'), sg.Button('Continue')] ]

# Create the window.
window = sg.Window('Questionnaire / Enter data - Identification',
layout)
# Event Loop to process "events" and get the "values" of the inputs
while True:
event, values = window.read()
if event == sg.WIN_CLOSED or event == 'Continue': # if user closes
window or clicks cancel
break
# print('You entered ', values[0], values[1], values[2])
nom = values[0]
age = values[1]
sex = values[2]

window.close()
```

This program will present a window like in Figure 2-6.

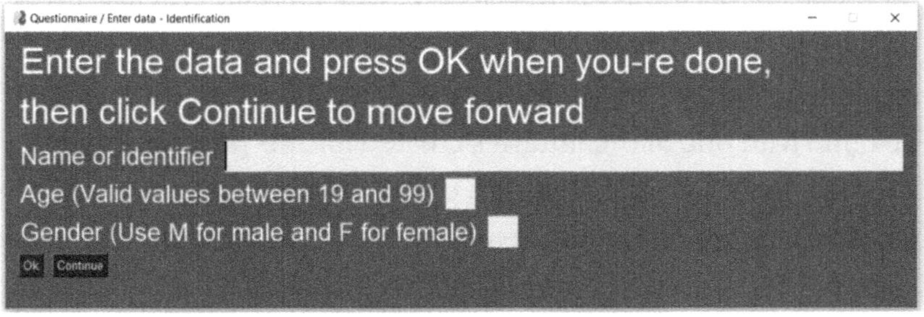

Figure 2-6. *Entering personal data*

This is the start of a Windows program that allows you to process the results of a personality questionnaire. Note that it has a header with the name of the questionnaire, which is assigned on line 12. The instructions, along with the data entry boxes and the buttons to execute the actions, are assigned on lines 5 to 9. As specified in the instructions, you must click the OK button so that the program saves the entered information in a variable and the Continue button to continue with the program's task. If you only click the Continue button, the program will continue but without saving the entered data; you can check this by adding the following command at the end of the program, on line 22:

```
print(name, age, sex)
```

If you have not clicked the OK button, the program will not print anything. If you click it, it will print the data entered on the screen.

If you want to use either of these two libraries, you should download the corresponding documentation that you will find on the Internet to learn about their use and all their possibilities, which are many more than those explained here.

If you want to know more about how to use `easygui` and PySimpleGui, you can consult the following web pages:

```
https://easygui.readthedocs.io/en/master/
https://www.pysimplegui.org/en/latest/
```

When we started working with these libraries, PySimpleGUI was a free and open-source library like most Python libraries. However, nowadays it is a paid library, which makes its use inadvisable due to what it offers. Although it is true that for private use you only must register. If you later want to use the library for commercial use, you will have to pay a fee or expose yourself to claims from the creators. For all these reasons, in our work we have replaced this library with `guizero`, which is equally easy, more complete, and freer.

Creating graphical interfaces can initially be a complex aspect of using Python and has to be done with one of the libraries created for this purpose such as Tkinter, wxPython, pygame, PyQt5, GTK3+, PyGaze, or PsicoPy, among many others available, which we must learn to use before being able to develop a program with a friendly presentation and in line with the graphical environments of current operating systems. To learn more about graphical interfaces, you can consult, for example, Meier (2019), where the use of Tkinter and PyQt5 is explained, or Roseman (2021), who offers a current overview of Tkinter.

A graphical interface will be, as we have seen, the entrance to our program and will give it a professional, modern presentation and a lot of functionality.

Any of the graphical interfaces mentioned must be installed with the pip program before using it. We have already used pygame to obtain a graphical presentation, which was designed to program two-dimensional games and can be adapted to our activities.

Pygame is a free, open-source library designed to program computer games in a simple way and that allows the construction of two-dimensional games with a graphical presentation. It allows the handling of static and moving images, sound, mouse, keyboard, and joystick, as well as establishing an adequate time control. It is based on the SDL 1.2 library (Simple Direct Media Layer), written in C. Pygame is currently in version 2.1.2. It can be useful in psychology if we consider that many of the tasks that we are going to ask the subject of experimentation to do are like those requested in computer games: perceptual discrimination of stimuli and motor responses. A description of its characteristics and operation can be seen in Kinsley and McGugan (2015). We will start by installing the library:

```
>pip install pygame
```

The computer will display installation information and will end up giving a message like the following:

```
>Successfully installed pyGame-2.1.2
```

We have already seen how an application could be created using Pygame for the memory test of number series (Digit Span Test) with this library that we will continue to use later, along with other graphic libraries.

It is advisable to start with the simplest graphical environments such as the one we have already mentioned, guizero, based on Tkinter, whose functionality we will see later, and then continue with the graphical library of choice that best adapts to our specific purpose or our aesthetic taste.

Computer programs usually start with a menu, so we are going to present now an easy environment that allows you to create a menu that can be used for any of the programs we will see; it is the guizero library, which is a Tkinter wrapper and is designed for use by children and young people, so it will be ideal for beginners or people with little technical training, such as professionals in the humanities. It has sufficient documentation, which can be read on the Internet:

`https://lawsie.github.io/guizero/`

Or you can consult the book by Sach and O'Hanlon (2020).

As always, the first step will be to install the library with pip and check that it has been installed correctly. Next, we will present a program that contains a menu with two options: File and Help. The File menu has three submenus: Manage tests, read results, and exit. The Help menu has two submenus: Manual and About (see Figure 2-7).

***Figure 2-7.** Menu with two options*

Designing a Complete Graphic Menu

In this section, we present a program that draws a menu with two entries and various submenus. Of the different windows provided, we have only developed two: Manage Classification Tests and About.

The rest of the submenus when called provide a message indicating that the chosen option is not available now.

Figure 2-8 shows the data entry window.

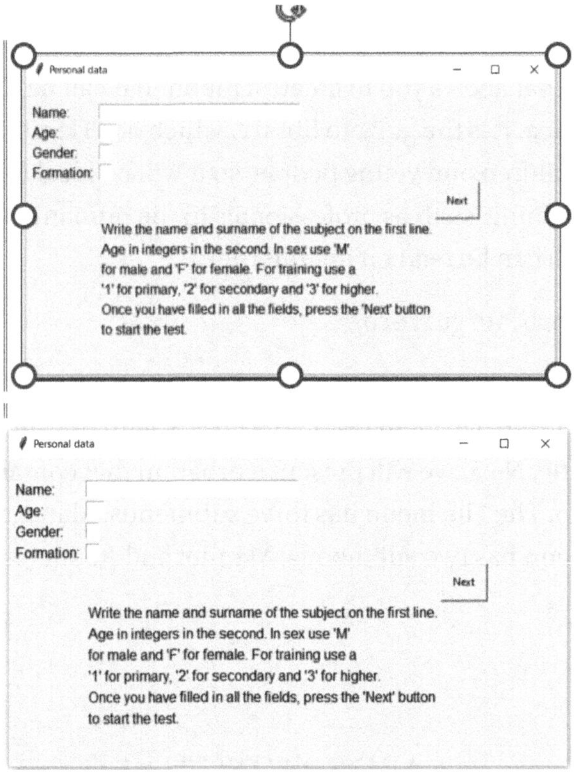

Figure 2-8. *Data entry window*

Figure 2-9 shows the About information window.

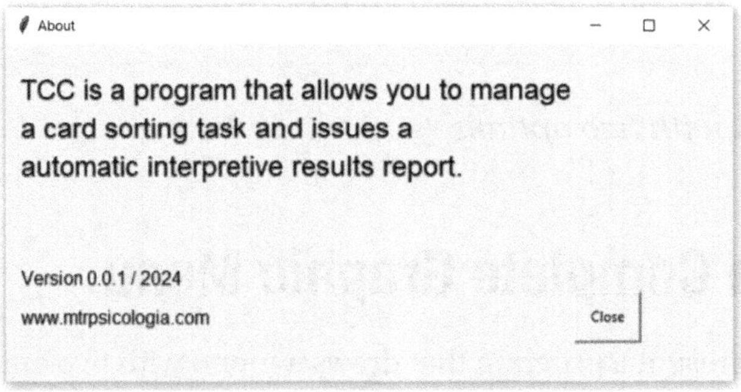

Figure 2-9. *About information window*

This is a menu built to administer a card sorting test, like the Wisconsin Test, which we will discuss later. The File menu consists of three submenus: Administer Sorting Test, Read Results, and Exit. The Help menu consists of two submenus: Manual and About. The manual should describe the use of the test and provide information about the program (see Program 2-9).

Program 2-9.

```
from guizero import App, Text, MenuBar, Window, PushButton, TextBox, info
import sys

# Define variables
global nom
global age
global sex
global form

nom = ""
age = ""
sex = ""
form  = ""

def file_function1(): # Call to manage test -----------------------
    window_1.show()
    boto_1 = PushButton(window_1, text = 'Next', grid=[4,6], align = "bottom", command = execute_boto)

def enter_name ( ):
    global nom
    nom = enter_name.value

def enter_edat():
    global age
    age = enter_edat.value

```

```
def enter_sex():
    global sex
    sex = enter_sex.value

def enter_form():
    global form
    form = enter_form.value

def execute_boto():
    window_1.hide()
    # It is necessary to have this module, which we will see later, in the same directory
    # import TCCWOO.py
    # Check the entered values
    print("Entered values", nom, age, sex, form)

def execute_boto_2():
    window_2.hide()

def file_function2():
    app.info( "info", "Option not available.")

def file_function3():
    if app.yesno("Close", "Do you really want to exit?"):
        app.destroy()
        sys.exit()

def help_function1():
    app.info( "info", "Option not available.")

def help_function2():
    # provides information
    window_2.show()
    text = Text(window_2, text=" ", grid=[0,0], align="left")
```

```
    text = Text(window_2, text="TCC is a program that allows you to manage", size = 18, grid=[1,1], align="left")
    text = Text(window_2, text="a card sorting task and issues a",size = 18,
    grid=[1,2], align="left")
    text = Text(window_2, text="automatic interpretive results report.", size = 18, grid=[1,3], align="left")
    text = Text(window_2, text="", size = 18, grid=[1,4], align="left")
    text = Text(window_2, text="", size = 18, grid=[1,5], align="left")
    text = Text(window_2, text="Version 0.0.1 / 2024", grid=[1,6], align="left")
    text = Text(window_2, text="www.mtrpsicologia.com", grid=[1,7], align="left")
    boto_2 = PushButton(window_2, text = 'Close', grid=[2,7], align = "left", command = execute_boto_2)

# Menu -------------------------------------------------------------
app = App("Card Sorting Test", width=900, height=400)
app.bg = "white"

PreTitl = Text(app,'')
PreTitl.text_size = 70
Title01 = Text(app, "CARD SORTING TEST")
Title01.text_size = 30
Title01.font = "Times New Roman"

Title02 = Text(app, "www.mtrpsicologia.com")
Title02.text_size = 12
Title02.font = "Courier New"


```

```
menubar = MenuBar(app,
                  toplevel=["FILE", "HELP"],
                  options=[
                     [["take the test", file_function1],
                      ["Read results", file_function2],
                      ["Exit", file_function3]],
                     [["Manual", help_function1],
                       ["About...", help_function2]]
                  ])

# Window 1
window_1 = Window(app, layout="grid", title = "Personal data", height=350, width=640)
text = Text(window_1, text="", grid=[0,0], align="left")
text = Text(window_1, text=" Name: ", grid=[0,1], align="left")
enter_name = TextBox(window_1, width=40, grid=[1,1], align="left", command = enter_name)
text = Text(window_1, text=" Age: ", grid=[0,2], align="left")
enter_edat = TextBox(window_1, width = 3, grid=[1,2], align="left", command = enter_edat)
text = Text(window_1, text=" Gender: ", grid=[0,3], align="left")
enter_sex = TextBox(window_1, width = 2, grid=[1,3], align="left", command = enter_sex)
text = Text(window_1, text=" Formation: ", grid=[0,4], align="left")
enter_form = TextBox(window_1, width = 2, grid=[1,4], align="left", command = enter_form)
text = Text(window_1, text="Write the name and surname of the subject on the first line.", grid=[1,11], align="left")
text = Text(window_1, text="Age in integers in the second. In sex use 'M'", grid=[1,12], align="left")
text = Text(window_1, text="for male and 'F' for female. For training use a", grid=[1,13], align="left")
text = Text(window_1, text="'1' for primary, '2' for secondary and '3' for higher.", grid=[1,14], align="left")
```

```
110 text = Text(window_1, text="Once you have filled in all the fields,
    press the 'Next' button", grid=[1,15], align="left")
111 text = Text(window_1, text="to start the test.", grid=[1,16],
    align="left") window_1.hide()
112
    # Window 2 ·················
113 window_2 = Window(app, layout="grid", title = "About", height=290,
    width=630) window_2.hide()
114
115 app.display()
```

The program starts by importing different functions from the `guizero` library.

Lines 4 to 8 define the variables that will contain the personal data entered in the personal data window before starting the test.

From lines 11 to 67, various functions are defined that the menu will use for its purposes.

The menu is designed from lines 69 to 92. The rest of the program defines the windows that will open when clicking the different menu options.

Summary

In this chapter, you were introduced to simple examples of programming for psychology, and you had your first contact with graphic presentations. In the next chapter, you will see how to save data and work with files.

CHAPTER 3

Saving Information to the Hard Drive: Reading and Writing Files

In this chapter, we will see how to save information on the hard drive and how to create and manage databases.

In professional work, it is essential to store information, which can be done in several ways, like plain text, in a binary file, or through a database system.

In Python there are two native types of files: text and binary. Other popular types include CSV files (comma-separated values/comma-separated data) and JSON (JavaScript Object Notation), which can be handled using various libraries.

A plain-text file is a file that contains only text, consisting of a series of lines of information and ending with a carriage return or line feed character. A binary file is a file that contains information of any kind encoded in binary code, ones and zeros, to be stored and processed on a computer. A database file is a file organized into specific, predefined fields.

To work with files, you must follow these steps:

1. Create the file and give it a name (if the file does not exist).
2. Open it.
3. To act on it, writing (w), reading (r), or adding information (a), you must import a Python module or library (io).
4. Close the file when finished.

J. M. Roig-Fusté, *Python for Psychology, Social Sciences, and Education*,
https://doi.org/10.1007/979-8-8688-2355-8_3

The available modes for acting on files are:

- **r**: Read only (default mode).
- **rb**: Read only for binary files.
- **r** +: Reading and writing.
- **rb** +: Reading and writing binary files.
- **w**: Write only. If the file already exists, it is overwritten; otherwise, it is created.
- **wb**: For binary writing. If the file already exists, it is overwritten; otherwise, it is created.
- **w** +: Read and write. If the file exists, it is overwritten; otherwise, it is created.
- **wb** +: Binary reading and writing. If the file already exists, it is overwritten; otherwise, it is created.
- **a**: Adds content to the end of an existing file. If the file does not exist, it is created.
- **ab**: To add content to the end of a binary file. If the file does not exist, it is created.
- **a** +: Adds and reads information. If the file does not exist, it creates it.
- **ab** +: Adds and reads in binary format. If the file does not exist, it creates it.

An open file, for reading or writing, must be closed when you finish interacting with it to avoid problems in the operation of the program and to prevent the information contained in the file from being damaged; this can be done by the programmer, with the `close( )` command, or automatically with the Python `with` statement.

Let's look at an example of a plain text file (see Program 3-1).

Program 3-1.

```
import io

# Open a text file for writing
```

```
dataFile = open("file.txt", "w")
text = "Hello."
dataFile.write (text)
dataFile.close ()

# Open a text file to add
datafile = open("file.txt", "a")
dataFile.write ("\n") #Writes a carriage return
text1 = "How are you?"
dataFile.write ( text1 )
dataFile.close ()

# Open a text file for reading
datafile = open("file.txt", "r")
text2 = dataFile.read ()
dataFile.close ()
print(text2)
```

To save a number in a file, you must first convert it into a string, since this type of file only allows you to save strings. The same will happen when reading a number from a file, which will be considered a string and must be transformed into a number before using it as such.

In all cases, we have indicated only the name of the file; this assumes that the file is in the same directory as the program being executed. If not, the program will throw an error message and stop. If you want to place the file in another directory, you will have to include the pathlib library in the program and explicitly indicate the path. The path can be absolute or relative, the first from the root directory and the second from the directory where you are running the program.

Using `with`, the file would be managed as follows:

```
with open('ElQuijote.txt', encoding = ' utf -8') as f:
    content = f.read ()

words = content.split()
numWords = len (words)
print(f"The file ('ElQuijote.txt') has {numPalabras} words.")
```

To run this program, a text file (`ElQuijote.txt`) was first created from the website `https://www.gutenberg.org/` and contains the contents of the novel. This file was placed in the same directory as the program. On line 1, the file was opened; on line 2, the contents of the file were read and placed in the computer's memory so that it could be worked with. Note that in this case, the `close` command was not necessary; the program managed the file within the block and closed it when it exited the block. On line 4, the content was separated into words; on line 5, the number of words was counted; and on line 6, the number was printed.

The output of this program is as follows:

```
The file ('ElQuijote.txt') has 389641 words.
```

Binary files

To write and read binary files, a `b` will be added to the corresponding letter. `rb` and wb are used for reading or writing. Please note that if a file is opened in write mode and it already exists, it will be overwritten, losing the data from the previous file.

```
f_write = open('data.bin', 'wb')
f_write.write(b'Hello World')
f_write.close()

f_read = open('data.bin', 'rb')
content_bytes = f_read.read()
print(f"Content read (bytes): {content_bytes}")
f_write.close()
```

A file can be deleted in the following way:

```
Import os

If os.path.exists('filename'):
    os.remove('filename')
else:
print('The file does not exist')
```

If you want to delete a directory, you can do so with the following command:

```
os.rmdir("directory name")
```

Be careful when deleting files or directories because once deleted everything in them will be lost and it will be difficult to recover them.

A more elaborate way of working with files is through databases, as covered next.

Databases

Databases are programs designed to store information efficiently, facilitating access and manipulation.

Databases are an important part of computing. They consist of files that contain information in a structured way, which greatly facilitates their management, which basically consists of adding or deleting information and performing queries.

There are two main types of databases: the so-called relational (SQL) and nonrelational (noSQL) databases. SQL databases have a very defined and rigid structure, with tables organized in rows and columns; the rows are the annotations while the columns are previously defined fields in which the information can be entered. Nonrelational databases such as MongoDB are more flexible in their structure.

Databases are necessary to work in any area of activity; we will often find ourselves with the need to save and retrieve data from a database to process it or carry out research. There are public or private databases from which information can be retrieved to obtain knowledge and research. One of the most common type of databases is bibliographical databases that contain information about published books or journal articles. All libraries, whether physical or virtual, have a catalog of their collections that are a database. On the Internet, there are also databases that index the content of a large part of the network so that users can find those pages that interest them most. Google was initially a database for indexing Internet pages, which its creators took advantage of to earn money from the advertising that it inserted, and continues to insert, in its searches or by charging its clients to place their pages at the top of search results.

Working with databases has obvious and immediate advantages, such as saving relevant information permanently or finding the information you are looking for in an efficient and fast way. To do this, you must first create the database you are going to use, from existing libraries or structures. There are many predetermined types of structure, for example: CSV, MySQL, Oracle, PostgreSQL, SQlite3 and SQLServer, among others.

If, for example, we want to create a customer database, we will first have to define the fields, which are the columns that we will need, and specify their type and size. A customer file could include data (Table 3-1) such as name, age, sex, address, etc., for example.

Table 3-1. *Customer File*

Variable	type	Length
Name	character	50
Age(0 to 99)	character	2
Gender (M or F)	character	1
Home	character	40
Phone	character	15
E-mail	character	30
Observations	character	200

The length of the character fields is understood as the maximum length. It is important that this is large so as not to omit any information.

Next, we must choose the database system we want to use to create and manage the files.

Python allows you to create and manage various types of databases. Here we will focus on relational databases using SQL, which allows us to manage all our needs. We will use SQLite3 for our example.

SQLite3 is a relational database management system that uses the SQL language. It is contained in a small library written in the C language. It is a public domain project, and unlike other client-server architecture systems, its search engine is not external but is linked to the program created with Python, becoming part of it. Therefore, it does not need to be installed since it is integrated into the latest versions of Python. SQLite currently allows databases of up to 2 terabytes in size, and its configuration is very simple.

To use a database in a program, you must first create the database file. Import the sqlite3 library, assign the filename `clients.db`, and create a pointer, `myCursor`, to connect to the database. Also, you must define the fields of the table called subjects. Finally, once the action is finished, you must apply the `.comit()` order to confirm the changes and close the connection. See Program 3-2.

Program 3-2.

```
# Create MM result database

import sqlite3

```

```
myConnection = sqlite3.connect ("Customers.db")
myCursor = myConnection.cursor()

myCursor.execute('''CREATE TABLE Subjects
                (id INTEGER PRIMARY KEY AUTOINCREMENT,
                 nom VARCHAR(50),
                 age VARCHAR(2),
                 sex VARCHAR(1),
                 formatio VARCHAR(1),
                 data VARCHAR(8),
                 diagnostic VARCHAR(20),
                 responsible VARCHAR(20),
                 ClientCode VARCHAR(3),
                 obs VARCHAR(200))''')

myConnection.commit()
myConnection.close
```

Next, we must fill out the database with information. This could be done with an infinite `while` loop with several consecutive input commands for name, age, sex, etc.; we exit this loop by entering the word `quit` in the name field, a word that activates a break command. See Program 3-3.

Program 3-3.

```
import sqlite3
from datetime import date
from datetime import datetime


# capture system data
ara = datetime.now()
data = '{}/{}/{}'.format(ara.day, ara.month, ara.year)
a = len(data)
data1 = data[:a-4]
data2 = data[a-2:a]
data = data1 + data2
```

```

nom = ''
age = ''
sex = '' # M - Male , F - Female
training =''
diagnostic = ""
res = '' # Responsible
obs = '' # observations, max 500 characters


# Save information in database --------------------------
con = sqlite3.connect("Clients.db")
cur = con.cursor()

dat = (id, nom, edat, sex, formacio, data, diagnosis, res, obs)
cur.execute('INSERT INTO Subjects VALUES(NULL,?,?,?,?,?,?,?,?)', dat)

con.commit()
con.close
```

Finally, we can retrieve some of the records from our database, which we will do from the record number. See Program 3-4.

Program 3-4.

```
import sqlite3


def read_single_record(id):
conn = sqlite3.connect('Customers.db') # Connect to the database
cursor = conn.cursor()

# Query to select a single record by name
    cursor.execute ("SELECT * FROM subjects WHERE id = ?", (id,))
    print('Number retrieved: ', id)
    record = cursor.fetchone() # Fetch a single record

```

```
        conn.close () # Close the connection
        return record

# Read a single record
name_to_search = input('Record number you want recover: ')
record = read_single_record(name_to_search)
print(' Record :', record)
```

On the Internet you can find a free program called DB Browser for SQLite, currently in version 3.13.1, which can be downloaded from the project page `https://sqlitebrowser.org/` and which will allow you to inspect databases created with Python and the sqlite3 library.

Summary

In this chapter, you learned how to save information on the hard drive and how to create and manage databases. In the next chapter, you will see examples of programming for experimental psychology.

CHAPTER 4

Experimental Psychology

In this chapter, we will look at some topics such as stimulus presentation, response collection, reaction times, and some classic experiments such as the Stroop effect.

Experimental psychology is one of the branches that has benefited most from the emergence of computers, as can be seen from the multitude of developments that aim to make the design of psychological experiments easier: PsychoPy (Peirce, 2007, 2009, 2019; Peirce, Gray, Simpson, Macaskill, Höchenberger, Sogo, Kastman Lindeløv, 2019; Peirce, MacAskill, 2018), OpenSesame (Mathôt, Schreij, Theeuwes, 2012; Mathôt, March, 2022), PEBL (Mueller, Piper, 2014), Psychtoolbox (Misirlisoy, 2017), PsyToolkit (Stoet, 2010), and PyGaze (Dalmaijer, Mathôt, Van Der Stigchel, 2013). Some of them are directly related to Python. They are generally projects promoted by universities and have web pages that can be consulted to find out which experiments have been developed with the help of computer science and programming.

Since the appearance of personal computers, long before Python was developed, they have had uses for psychology (Bird, 1981), and programs were written to interact with subjects and record their behavior, for example Beaumont (1981a, 1981b). On the Internet there are many programs, written in various languages, including Python, that allow the administration of experiments or tests such as the Stroop effect (Stroop, 1935), the Tower of Hanoi, and perhaps the most popular of all, the Wisconsin Card Sorting Test. It should be noted that many of them are written by amateur programmers who are not psychologists, and despite bearing the name of a well-known test or research, they do not adhere to the original requirements, so they can be dangerous. We will talk about this later, when we present a version of the card sorting test.

To design experimental psychology projects to be applied using a computer, it is not enough to know how to program; you must have a good knowledge of the subject and carefully study how computing can help in the proposed activity. If you do not have knowledge of experimental psychology, start with an introductory book to learn the most basic aspects of the subject (Martin, 2008).

J. M. Roig-Fusté, *Python for Psychology, Social Sciences, and Education*,
https://doi.org/10.1007/979-8-8688-2355-8_4

Visual Presentations

Experimental psychologists are the most interested in programming and probably the first to consider a language like Python as valuable for their work (Bertamini, 2018; Dalmaijer, 2017, 2024; Peirce, 2007). Python is ideal for demonstrating perceptual phenomena, such as illusions (Bertamini, 2018; Shapiro, Todorovic, 2017), or presenting stimuli on screen as part of an experiment. Let us look at two simple programs as examples, which present versions of the Ebbinghaus-Titchener and Hering illusions (see Program 4-1 and Program 4-2).

Program 4-1.

```
# Ebbinghaus-Titchener illusion

import matplotlib.pyplot as plt
import matplotlib.patches as patches

def draw_illusion():
    fig, ax = plt.subplots(figsize=(6, 3))

    # Center circle setup
    central_radius = 0.5
    central_position_left = (1.6, 2)
    central_position_right = (5.6, 2)

    # Setting the surrounding circles
    small_radius = 0.25
    large_radius = 0.50

    # Draw the left center circle
    central_circle_left = patches.Circle(central_position_left, central_radius, color='blue')
    ax.add_patch(central_circle_left)

    # Draw the small circles around the left circle
    offsets = [(-1, 0), (1, 0), (0, -1), (0, 1), (-0.7, 0.7), (0.7, 0.7), (-0.7, -0.7), (0.7, -0.7)]
```

```
    for dx, dy in offsets:
        circle = patches.Circle((central_position_left[0] + dx,
        central_position_left[1] + dy), small_radius, color='gray')
        ax.add_patch(circle)

    # Draw the right center circle
    central_circle_right = patches.Circle(central_position_right,
    central_radius, color='blue')
    ax.add_patch(central_circle_right)

    # Draw the big circles around the right circle
    large_offsets = [(-1.4, 0), (1.4, 0), (0, -1.4), (0, 1.4), (-1.1,
    1.1), (1.1, 1.1), (-1.1, -1.1), (1.1, -1.1)]
    for dx, dy in large_offsets:
        circle = patches.Circle((central_position_right[0] + dx,
        central_position_right[1] + dy), large_radius, color='gray')
        ax.add_patch(circle)

    # Configure the axis
    ax.set_xlim(0, 8)
    ax.set_ylim(0, 4)
    ax.set_aspect('equal', adjustable='box')
    ax.axis('off')

    # Show the illusion
    plt.title("Ebbinghaus-Titchener Illusion")
    plt.show()

# Run the function to display the illusion
draw_illusion()
```

Figure 4-1 shows the result of this program.

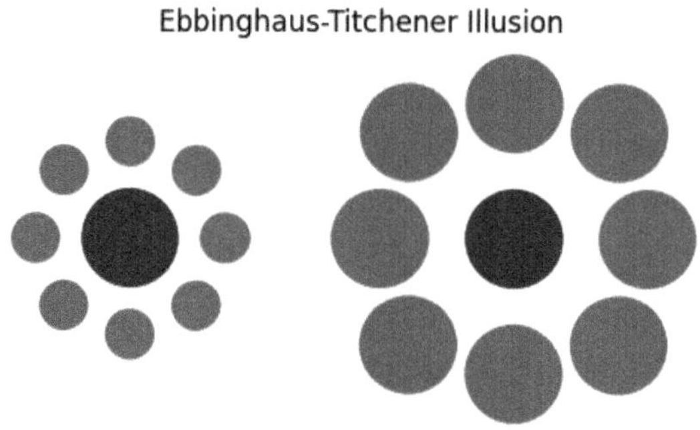

Figure 4-1. *Ebbinghaus-Titchener illusion*

Program 4-2.

```
# Hering Illusion
import matplotlib.pyplot as plt
import numpy as np

def draw_hering_illusion():
    fig, ax = plt.subplots(figsize=(6, 6))

    # Coordinates of the center point between the parallel lines
    center_point = (0, 0)

    # Draw the converging lines from the central point
    for angle in np.linspace(-np.pi / 2, np.pi / 2, 21):
        x_start = -6 * np.cos(angle)
        y_start = -6 * np.sin(angle)
        x_end = 6 * np.cos(angle)
        y_end = 6 * np.sin(angle)
        ax.plot([x_start, x_end], [y_start, y_end], color='black', linewidth=0.8)

    # Draw the horizontal lines
    ax.axhline(y=2, color='red', linewidth=2)
    ax.axhline(y=-2, color='red', linewidth=2)
```

```

    # Configure the axis
    ax.set_xlim(-6, 6)
    ax.set_ylim(-6, 6)
    ax.set_aspect('equal', adjustable='box')
    ax.axis('off')

    # Show the illusion
    plt.title("Hering Illusion")
    plt.show()

# Run the function to display the illusion
draw_hering_illusion()
```

Figure 4-2 shows the result of this program.

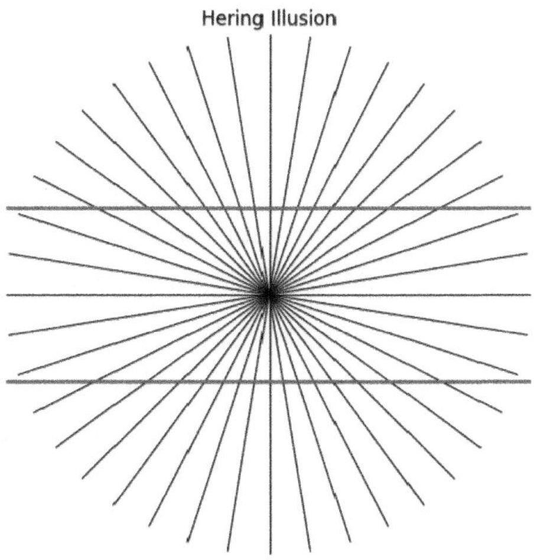

Figure 4-2. *Hering illusion*

Reaction Time

Computerizing a task, in any field, requires understanding it well, knowing what it is that you want to do, and knowing aspects that may affect it (Lu and Proctor, 1995). We have learned something about the language that we are going to use, and we have already seen some applications of it; now we are going to develop a procedure that will meet a new objective. In experimental psychology, this can always have a similar scheme: present some stimuli; collect a response from the subject, controlling the stimuli presented and the response time; and then analyze the information collected.

In experimental psychology, we can propose simple or complicated tasks. For example, we could measure a simple reaction time in which a stimulus is presented, visual or auditory, and a response is collected immediately. When measuring a simple reaction time, the stimulus must be presented with a variable time margin between stimuli so that the subject of the experiment cannot synchronize the response with the presentation time and thus speed up when the next stimulus will appear.

Let us suppose that we want to computerize an experiment. To begin with, we can choose a simple task such as the one mentioned: measuring the reaction time of a subject. However simple this task may be, we must begin by making a series of decisions.

If we have to study the reaction speed of a subject, presenting a single stimulus and recording the time of its response could be sufficient; however, this experiment may be subject to circumstances that do not allow us to ensure that the time obtained is representative of this subject. For this reason, several tests are generally carried out, and statistical data is obtained such as the mean and standard deviation of the times measured. How many tests do we need to achieve greater reliability of the results? Well, the more tests the better. Of course, carrying out a high number of tests could introduce new conditions, such as excessive time devoted to the task, boredom, monotony, or fatigue, which could alter the result. If we were to think that 100 trials is an optimal number needed, it might be better to perform them at different times or with one- or two-minute rest periods between them, for each subject; for example, we might have four trials of 25 trials each, although bear in mind that such an approach might represent about 20 minutes of testing in total.

When starting work, we should first make a diagram, either using pseudocode or using a flowchart. You may think that this planning is not necessary for a simple program like this one, but in the future you may have to deal with much more complex programs than this one. That's when a detailed diagram makes the task easier and usually saves a lot of time; therefore, it is important to get used to working systematically from the beginning, even if this is not strictly necessary in this specific case.

In our work, we will choose to describe the task in pseudocode, because it is more like the final program that we will have to write, although a flowchart certainly presents the ideas in a graphical way that is more visual and intuitive. The pseudocode for a simple reaction task could be as follows:

```
start
enter the subject's identification data
present an instruction screen
Provide some example elements (if deemed necessary)
present a task start warning screen
perform a specified number of tests
      present a stimulus with a time between them of between 3 and 5
      seconds, chosen by the computer at random
      collect a response (time difference between the moment the stimulus
      is presented and the moment the response is given)
report test completion
record the collected data into a file
calculate the mean and standard deviation of the attempts made
print the results
end (exit the program)
```

First, we will assign a name to the program, which will be the name of the file that contains it: `trsimple.py` (simple reaction time encoded in Python). In this file, we will write the code of the program and check that it works correctly, correcting any errors that it may have as they are detected.

Entering the subject's data involves anticipating different variables such as name, age, sex, educational level, who sent the subject, date on which the test is performed, etc. We are not going to develop this part of the program because we have seen it previously, when talking about graphical interfaces.

The instructions must be written, and the stimulus to be presented must be chosen, as well as the way in which the subject will respond to the test. A red dot could be displayed on the screen, and the subject could be expected to press the spacebar on the keyboard. In our case, the stimulus will always be in the same place on the screen, the center, and will be presented, as we have already said, at variable intervals. As a stimulus, we will choose a black cross on a white background, due to its ease of presentation, which in this case will not even require drawing, since we will use the + sign for the text. It could also be a circle, a square, or any other figure that we think is interesting; for example, in the case of children, an image of an animal could be used.

In this case, we are going to work with the Pygame graphic library, which we have seen before. This is how the program could be coded:

```
1   # Simple reaction times / Dr. Roig
2   # trsimple.py / 04.11.2022 / Version 0.0.0
3
4   import random, sys, pygame, statistics
5
6   # Constants ·············································
7   NUM_ESSAYS = 10 # total number of tests
8   MINIMUM_TIMEOUT = 1000 # defines the minimum timeout.
9   MAX_WAIT_TIME = 2000
10  MAX_DELAY_RES = 2000
11  FILE_NOM = 'resultadosTR.txt' # file that will save the data.
12
13  # Define colors
14  BLACK = ( 0, 0, 0)
15  WHITE = (255, 255, 255)
16  RED = (255, 0, 0)
```

Start the program. As always, the program contains some identification data, on lines 1 and 2, such as the name of the program, author, development date, and version.

Lines 4 to 6 import the libraries necessary for the task to run.

Lines 8 through 13 define the constants.

Line 18 starts the Pygame library. Line 20 contains the size of the window in which we are going to work. Line 22 creates a working window. Line 24 presents instructions for the experiment.

Line 30 starts the fundamental loop of the program that will present the stimuli and collect responses.

```
17
18  Pygame.init()
19
20  size = (800, 500)
21
22  screen = pygame.display.set_mode(size) # working window
23
```

```
# Experiment instructions.

while True:
    for event in pygame.event.get():
    if event.type == pygame.QUIT:
            sys.exit()

    # background color
    screen.fill(WHITE)

    # update screen
    pygame.display.flip()
```

The full program is now longer and looks like Program 4-3.

Program 4-3.

```
# Simple reaction times / Dr. Roig
# trsimple.py / 04.11.2022 / Version 0.0.1

import pygame, random, sys, time

# Constants ......................................
NUM_TESTS = 10 # total number of tests
T_ES_MIN = 1000 # defines the minimum waiting time.
T_ES_MAX = 2000 # maximum waiting time

# Define colors
BLACK = ( 0, 0, 0)
WHITE = (255, 255, 255)
RED = (255, 0, 0)

pygame.init()
clock = pygame.time.Clock()
running = True

```

```
size = (990, 600)

screen = pygame.display.set_mode(size) # working window
screen.fill(WHITE)
pygame.display.flip()

# Task instructions.
myfont = pygame.font.SysFont(pygame.font.get_fonts()[0], 40)
pygame.display.set_caption('Simple reaction time / instructions')
txt1 = myfont.render("When a cross (+) appears, press the 'space
bar'", 1, pygame.Color('black'))
txt2 = myfont.render("as fast as you can.", 1, pygame.Color('black'))
txt3 = myfont.render("Press the 'Return / Enter' key to begin.", 1,
pygame.Color('black'))
screen.blit(txt1, (35, 100))
screen.blit(txt2, (35, 150))
screen.blit(txt3, (35, 450))
pygame.display.flip()

# Place the stimulus in the center of the screen
x = 420
y = 150

pygame.display.set_caption('Simple reaction time / exercise')
# press RETURN/ENTER key to start
key_pressed = False
while not key_pressed:
    for event in pygame.event.get():
        if event.type == pygame.KEYDOWN:
            if event.key == pygame.K_RETURN:
                key_pressed = True

# prepare the screen to present the stimuli
myfont = pygame.font.SysFont(pygame.font.get_fonts()[0], 250)
pygame.display.set_caption('Simple reaction time / test')
```

```
screen.fill(WHITE)
pygame.display.flip()

NUM_TESTS = 4
tInitial = 0
tAnswer = 0
tReaction = 0
tsInitial = []
tsWait = []
tsAnswer = []
tsReaction = []

# Main program loop
for essay in range(NUM_ESSAYS):

    # generate waiting time
    tWait = random.randint(T_ES_MIN, T_ES_MAX)
    pygame.time.delay(tWait)

    # clear screen/background color
    screen.fill(WHITE)
    pygame.display.flip()

    # submit stimulus
    txt1 = myfont.render("+", 1, pygame.Color('BLACK'))
    screen.blit(txt1, (x, y))
    pygame.display.flip()
    tInitial = time.time()

    # wait for response
    key_pressed = False
    while not key_pressed:
        for event in pygame.event.get():
            #if event.type == pygame.KEYDOWN:
            if event.type == pygame.KEYUP:
```

```
                if event.key == pygame.K_SPACE:
                    tAnswer = time.time()
                    tReaction = tResponse - tInitial

                    tResponse = round(tResponse,3)
                    tReaction = round(tReaction,3)
                    tsWait.append(tWait)
                    tsResponse.append(tResponse)
                    tsReaction.append(tReaction)

                    key_pressed = True
                    screen.fill(WHITE)
                    pygame.display.flip()

print("wait times: ", tsWait)
print("response times: ", tsResponse)
print("reaction times: ", tsReaction)

screen.fill(WHITE)
myfont = pygame.font.SysFont(pygame.font.get_fonts()[0], 40)
pygame.display.set_caption('Simple reaction time / Test completed')
txt1 = myfont.render("Exercise completed", 1, pygame.Color('black'))
txt2 = myfont.render("Thank you for your collaboration.", 1,
pygame.Color('black'))
txt3 = myfont.render("Press the 'ENTER/RETURN' key to exit.", 1,
pygame.Color('black'))
screen.blit(txt1, (50, 100))
screen.blit(txt2, (50, 150))
screen.blit(txt3, (50, 450))
pygame.display.flip()

pygame.display.set_caption('Simple reaction time / test completed')
# press RETURN/ENTER key to exit
key_pressed = False
while not key_pressed:
```

```
125         for event in pygame.event.get():
126             if event.type == pygame.KEYDOWN:
127                 if event.key == pygame.K_RETURN:
128                     key_pressed = True
129
130     pygame.quit()
131     sys.exit()
```

At the end, the program displays the following data on the screen:

```
wait times: [1708, 1159, 1161, 1580]
response times: [1693675040.418, 1693675042.018, 1693675043.594,
1693675045.618]
reaction times: [0.416, 0.44, 0.413, 0.443]
```

Of these, we are interested in the reaction times, expressed in thousandths of seconds, of the four tests carried out, which are read on the last line. The other data is not necessary but can be printed to check and ensure that everything is correct. This data can also be saved in a file.

As we have seen, the program works correctly and performs the task we had planned; however, no professional programmer would write a program in this way. The correct way to do it is through functions. That is, for each task of the program, a function is created, which is then called from the main program. This makes it easier to write the program itself and to debug it if difficulties arise or to modify it later if necessary. For example, in this program, lines 46 to 52 and lines 128 to 133 do the same thing: wait for the Enter key to be pressed to continue. If we program a function with this content, we will only have to write this section once instead of twice, and we will call the function that contains the code at the points in the program where it is necessary to wait for this key to be pressed to continue.

Let's see how the same program should be written using functions to appreciate the advantages of this method; see Program 4-4.

Program 4-4.

```
# Simple reaction times / Dr. Roig
# trsimple.py / 04.11.2023 / Version 0.0.1

import random
```

```
import pygame
import statistics

# Constants ·····································
NUM_ESSAYS = 10 # total number of tests
MINIMUM_WAIT_TIME = 1000
MAXIMUM_WAIT_TIME = 2000
MAX_DELAY_RES = 2000
FILE_NAME = 'resultadosTR.txt'

def create_window():
    screen = pygame.display.set_mode((900, 500))
    screen.fill(pygame.Color('white'))
    pygame.mouse.set_visible(False)
    return screen

def clear_screen(screen):
    screen.fill(pygame.Color('white'))
    pygame.display.flip()

def instructions(screen, x, y):
    myfont = pygame.font.SysFont(pygame.font.get_fonts()[0], 40)
    pygame.display.set_caption('Simple reaction time / instructions')
    txt1 = myfont.render("When a cross (+) appears, press the 'space bar'", 1, pygame.Color('black'))
    txt2 = myfont.render("as fast as I can.", 1, pygame.Color('black'))
    txt3 = myfont.render("Press 'spacebar' to start.", 1, pygame.Color('black'))
    screen.blit(txt1, (x, y - 200))
    screen.blit(txt2, (x, y - 150))
    screen.blit(txt3, (x, y + 90))
    pygame.display.flip()

```

```
def stimulus():
    myfont = pygame.font.SysFont(pygame.font.get_fonts()[0], 250)
    x = 370
    y = 90
    pygame.display.set_caption('Simple reaction time / test')
    txt1 = myfont.render("+", 1, pygame.Color('black'))
    screen.blit(txt1, (x, y))
    pygame.display.flip()

def wait_response():
    key_pressed = False
    while not key_pressed:
        for event in pygame.event.get():
            if event.type == pygame.KEYDOWN:
                key_pressed = True

def finalize(screen, x, y):
    myfont = pygame.font.SysFont(pygame.font.get_fonts()[0], 40)
    pygame.display.set_caption('Simple/Final Reaction Time')
    txt1 = myfont.render("Exercise completed", 1,
pygame.Color('black'))
    txt2 = myfont.render("Thank you for your collaboration.", 1,
pygame.Color('black'))
    txt3 = myfont.render("Press 'spacebar' to exit.", 1,
pygame.Color('black'))
    screen.blit(txt1, (x, y - 200))
    screen.blit(txt2, (x, y - 150))
    screen.blit(txt3, (x, y + 90))
    pygame.display.flip()

def reaction_time_measurement(MAX_DELAY_RES=2000):
    button_pressed = False
    escape = False
    response_delay_elapsed = False
    reaction_time = 2
```

```
    pygame.event.clear() # lookaheads will be ignored
    t0 = pygame.time.get_ticks()

    while not button_pressed and not escape and not
response_delay_elapsed:
        for ev in pygame.event.get():
            if ev.type == pygame.KEYDOWN and ev.key ==
            pygame.K_ESCAPE:
                escape = True
                break
            if ev.type == pygame.QUIT:
                escape = True
                break
            if ev.type == pygame.MOUSEBUTTONDOWN or ev.type ==
pygame.KEYDOWN:
                reaction_time = pygame.time.get_ticks() - t0
                button_pressed = True

            if pygame.time.get_ticks() - t0 > MAX_DELAY_RES:
                response_delay_elapsed = True

    if escape:
        return None
    else:
        return reaction_time

def save(wait_time, reac_time, filename=FILE_NAME):
    with open(filename, 'wt') as f:
        f.write('Wait,TR\n')
        for wt, rt in zip(wait_time, reac_time):
            f.write(f"{wt},{rt}\n")

        a = str(round(statistics.mean(reac_time), 3))
        b = str(round(statistics.stdev(reac_time), 3))
        f.write("\n")
```

```
        f.write("Media / SD\n")
        f.write(a)
        f.write('/')
        f.write(b)

# Program ------------------------------------------------------------
pygame.init()
screen = create_window()
r = screen.get_rect()
W, H = r.width, r.height
center_x = W // 2
center_y = H // 2

wait_time = []
reac_time = []

instructions(screen, 20, center_y)
wait_response()
clear_screen(screen)

pygame.time.delay(1000)

for trial in range(NUM_ESSAYS):
    clear_screen(screen)

    waiting_time = random.randint(MINIMUM_WAIT_TIME, MAXIMUM_
    WAIT_TIME)
    pygame.time.delay(waiting_time)

    stimulus()

    reaction_time = reaction_time_measurement()
    if reaction_time is None: # Escape pressed
        break

```

```
        wait_time.append(waiting_time)
        reac_time.append(reaction_time)
        print(trial, wait_time, reac_time)

    clear_screen(screen)
    finalize(screen, 20, center_y)
    save(wait_time, reaction_time)
    wait_response()

    pygame.quit()
```

When running the program, we get the instruction screen shown in Figure 4-3.

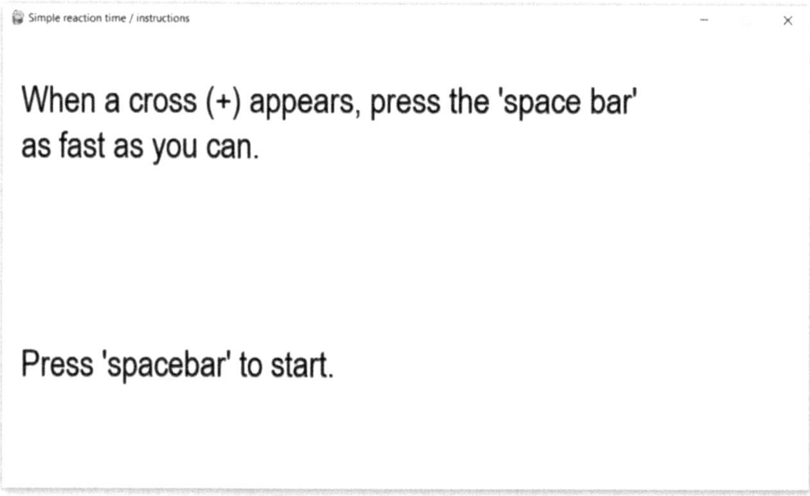

Figure 4-3. *Instructions regarding the cross and spacebar*

Once the spacebar is pressed, the stimuli appear successively, as shown in Figure 4-4.

***Figure 4-4.** Instruction showing cross appearing after hitting spacebar*

Once the exercise is finished, the screen shown in Figure 4-5 appears.

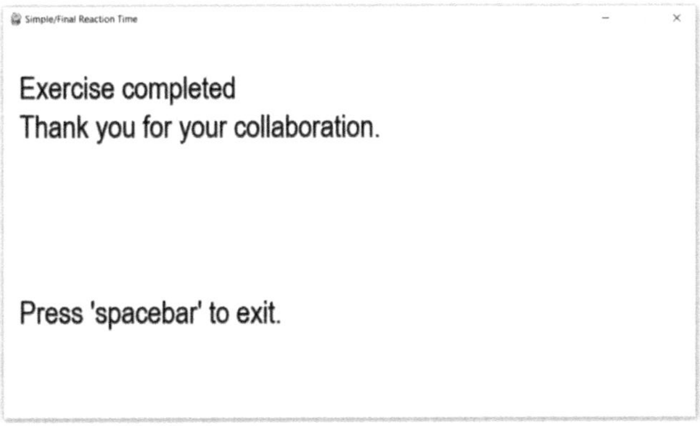

***Figure 4-5.** Completion screen*

Let's look at the content of the program:

- Lines 1 and 2 are program identification.
- Lines 4 to 6 import the libraries we will need for the program to work.
- Lines 9 to 13 contain the program constants.
- Line 16 defines the window in which we will work.
- Line 23 contains the function that clears our screen.
- Line 28 starts the function that will display the task instructions.

The function starting on line 40 presents the stimulus.

Lines 50 to 55 contain the function that waits for the subject's response and notes the times.

Lines 58 through 67 present the completion screen, informing the subject that the task is over.

The `measured_reaction_time` function, lines 70 to 96, is responsible for timing the time it takes the subject to give the response.

The program itself begins on line 112 and will call the different functions to carry out its task. First, it will prepare the screen and define the variables necessary to store the results (lines 120 to 121), and then call the instructions function, wait for the subject's start response, and clear the screen to display the stimuli (lines 123 to 125).

In line 127, a first delay is applied before presenting the first stimulus.

The stimuli are presented in a loop from lines 129 to 143, which allows reaction times to be recorded.

Finally, the task completion information screen is cleared, and the results are saved.

The save function saves the data to the hard disk in a file called `resultadosTR.txt`. This file looks like the following table, and the values are in milliseconds. Note that there are two values. The first represents the moment in which the stimulus was presented from the second zero, when the test starts; the second value is the time taken by the subject to respond to this stimulus. The values in the first column are used to calculate the presentation intervals, so between the start and the appearance of the first stimulus, 1,110 milliseconds pass; between the first stimulus and the second, 1,239 milliseconds pass; between the second and the third, 1,023; and so on.

Waiting Time	TR
1110	334
1239	316
1023	291
1528	290
1946	297
1471	321
1160	317

(*continued*)

Waiting Time	TR
1962	280
1182	316
1820	285
	Media 304.7 0
	SD 18.23

When programming with functions, you have to take into account the scope of the variables. In Python these are local. That is, they exist in the body of the program or within the function, and they do not interfere with each other even if they have the same name, so the value of a variable in the program cannot be modified within a function, and the value of a variable in a function cannot be modified in the program. If we want to pass a value from the program to the function, we must specify it when calling the function, and if we want to pass a value from the function to the program, we will do so with the return command at the end of the function.

There are global variables in Python, but their use is discouraged because an accidental modification of their value in some part of the program or its functions is difficult to trace. Global variables are normally defined at the beginning of the program. Then when they are used within a function, it is specified at the beginning of the function that it is global, always with the command `global <variable name>`; from here on it can be used normally within the function, taking into account that what is done with it will affect the variable throughout the program.

A reaction time task can be programmed in many ways, each with its own particularities. For example, various stimuli could be presented, such as a red dot and a green dot, and the subject could be asked to press the right Ctrl key when the red dot appears and the left Ctrl key when the green dot appears. A third yellow dot could also be added to which the subject would not have to respond. In this case, the stimuli could be presented at equal intervals, for example, every three seconds, and we could study various variables in addition to reaction time, which would have to be recorded separately for each of the stimuli presented. The other variables would be errors and omissions.

Working with two different stimuli, for example a + and a -, or two dots of different colors, it is possible to study the subject's reaction based on the percentage of each stimulus. For example, at first, we could assume that these two stimuli, which have to be generated at random, appear with a 50% probability, but what would happen if one of the stimuli had a much lower probability than the other, for example, in a proportion of 90 to 10? In this case, the speed of response to the more frequent stimulus would surely increase, but errors would also increase due to the subject's inability to inhibit the response when it is not required.

We have given an example with only 10 trials. Naturally a useful test could contain many more trials, such as 20, 50, 100, or more. This, as we have already said, introduces other elements into the results. For example, it makes the activity boring and monotonous, although theoretically it allows to increase the reliability of the test and to study aspects such as motivation or the work curve and the appearance of fatigue. For this, the responses should be collected in defined time intervals, for example every minute, with which an efficiency curve could be drawn throughout the test.

Is the program presented the perfect program for this task? Surely not, and with our use we can discover errors or possibilities for improvement, which will have to be corrected over time, if possible. Some of the problems could come from the computer itself, since it has latency times that could make it difficult to accurately measure the results, which in experimental psychology should be in milliseconds, due to the use of a standard keyboard. This limitation of some computer peripherals can introduce error variance in the results (Damian, 2010). Other problems can come from unforeseen behaviors of the experimental subject. For example, what would happen if the test subject kept the spacebar pressed for the duration of the experiment? Testing it in the simple reaction time program, our result is as follows:

Waiting Time	TR
1317	0
1271	0
1491	0
1465	0
1225	0
1234	0

(*continued*)

Waiting Time	TR
1583	0
1267	0
1196	0
1867	0
	Average 0.00
	SD 0.00

We see that it gives us an aberrant result with a reaction time that is always zero, which leads us to classify the exercise performed as an invalid test. This could and should be fixed; we cannot allow unforeseen behavior to go undetected by the program. One way to fix this problem is to consider not only the pressure on the target key but also the release of it. The keyboard collects information about the moment in which the key is pressed and the moment in which it is released. We should take advantage of this information to prevent the test from malfunctioning due to misuse by the subject of experimentation.

Complex Reaction Time

As an example, in this chapter, I have studied a single case to present the experiments considered and the corresponding programs to apply them. In a real situation it could be interesting to carry out the same investigations in a large group of subjects to know the individual differences between the results obtained. In any case, let us not lose sight of the fact that experimental psychology attempts to investigate the mechanisms by which a response is produced, and for this purpose research on a single subject could be sufficient; the individual differences that interested J. McKeen Cattell and Binet, and that were the basis of applied and clinical psychology, were a nuisance for Wundt, the creator of experimental psychology (Roig-Fusté, 2017).

Now we will design a more complex reaction time experiment that has two conditions: a red cross and a black cross. When the black cross appears, the subject must press the spacebar, and when the red cross appears, he does not have to do anything but wait. This will allow the stimuli to be shown at constant intervals, since the subject does not know in advance if the cross will be red or black. It will also introduce other variables such as the possibility of making mistakes, that is, pressing when one should not press or stop pressing when one should. In this case, we wonder if the reaction time for a person will remain the same as in the previous case, of simple reaction time, or if it will suffer some variation. Logically we can think that the reaction time will increase, because the subject will have to pay attention to more things to give the correct answer.

Whether the cross is black or red in our program will depend on chance, but we will have to make a decision when writing the program. This decision will be the percentage of black and red crosses in the exercise. To see how this percentage influences the result, we will consider three different cases: 10% black crosses and 90% red crosses; 50% black crosses and 50% red crosses; finally, 90% black crosses and 10% red crosses. There will be some important differences with the previous program, but first let's look at Program 4-5.

Program 4-5.

```
# Complex reaction time / Dr. Roig
# trcomplex005.py / 03.09.2023 / Version 0.0.5

import random
import pygame
import statistics

# Constants ......................................
NUM_ESSAYS = 10 # total number of tests
TIME_WAIT = 1500 # time between trials
FILE_NAME = 'resultsTRcomplex.txt'

def create_window():
    screen = pygame.display.set_mode((900, 500))
    screen.fill(pygame.Color('white'))
    pygame.mouse.set_visible(False)
    return screen

def clear_screen(screen):
    screen.fill(pygame.Color('white'))
    pygame.display.flip()

```

```
def instructions(screen, x, y):
    myfont = pygame.font.SysFont(pygame.font.get_fonts()[0], 40)
    pygame.display.set_caption('Complex reaction time /
instructions')
    txt0 = myfont.render("In this exercise a cross (+) will appear
    on the screen", 1, pygame.Color('black'))
    txt1 = myfont.render("which can be red or black, When the cross
    is", 1, pygame.Color('black'))
    txt2 = myfont.render("black, press 'spacebar' as fast as you
    can", 1, pygame.Color('black'))
    txt3 = myfont.render( "If it's red, do nothing, wait next cross
    appears", 1, pygame.Color('black'))
    txt4 = myfont.render("", 1, pygame.Color('black'))
    txt5 = myfont.render("Press 'spacebar' to start.", 1,
pygame.Color('black'))
    screen.blit(txt0, (x, y - 200))
    screen.blit(txt1, (x, y - 160))
    screen.blit(txt2, (x, y - 120))
    screen.blit(txt3, (x, y - 80))
    screen.blit(txt4, (x, y - 40))
    screen.blit(txt5, (x, y + 120))
    pygame.display.flip()

def stimulus(current_color):
    myfont = pygame.font.SysFont(pygame.font.get_fonts()[0], 250)
    x = 370
    y = 90

    if current_color < 8:
        color = 'black'
        txt1 = myfont.render("+", 1, pygame.Color('black'))
    else:
        color = 'red'
        txt1 = myfont.render("+", 1, pygame.Color('red'))

```

```
        screen.blit(txt1, (x, y))
        pygame.display.flip()
        return color

    def wait_response():
        key_pressed = False
        while not key_pressed:
            for event in pygame.event.get():
                if event.type == pygame.KEYDOWN:
                    key_pressed = True

    def finalize(screen, x, y):
        myfont = pygame.font.SysFont(pygame.font.get_fonts()[0], 40)
        pygame.display.set_caption('Simple/Final Reaction Time')
        txt1 = myfont.render("Exercise completed", 1,
    pygame.Color('black'))
        txt2 = myfont.render("Thank you for your collaboration.", 1,
    pygame.Color('black'))
        txt3 = myfont.render("Press 'spacebar' to exit.", 1,
    pygame.Color('black'))
        screen.blit(txt1, (x, y - 200))
        screen.blit(txt2, (x, y - 150))
        screen.blit(txt3, (x, y + 90))
        pygame.display.flip()

    def measure_reaction_time(MAX_DELAY_RES=2000):
        button_pressed = False
        escape = False
        response_delay_elapsed = False
        reaction_time = None
        pygame.event.clear() # lookaheads will be ignored
        t0 = pygame.time.get_ticks()

        while not button_pressed and not escape and not
```

```
response_delay_elapsed:
        for ev in pygame.event.get():
            if ev.type == pygame.KEYDOWN and ev.key ==
pygame.K_ESCAPE:
                escape = True
                break
            if ev.type == pygame.QUIT:
                escape = True
                break
            if ev.type == pygame.MOUSEBUTTONDOWN or ev.type ==
pygame.KEYDOWN:
                reaction_time = pygame.time.get_ticks() - t0
                button_pressed = True

            if pygame.time.get_ticks() - t0 > TIME_WAIT:
                response_delay_elapsed = True

    if escape:
        return None
    else:
        return reaction_time

def save(colors, reaction_times, filename=FILE_NAME):
    matrix_aux = [] # matrix to store tr values for mean and sd
calculation
    errors = 0 # variable to count errors
    with open(filename, 'wt') as f:
        f.write('Color,TR\n')
        for wt, rt in zip(colors, reaction_times):
            f.write(f"{wt},{rt}\n")

        # prepare data to calculate average time and errors
        for i in range(len(colors)):
            if colors[i] == 'black' and reaction_times[i] is not
```

```
None:
                matrix_aux.append(reaction_times[i])
            if colors[i] == 'red' and reaction_times[i] is not
None:
                errors = errors + 1

        mean = str(round(statistics.mean(matrix_aux), 3))
        sd = str(round(statistics.stdev(matrix_aux), 3))
        errors = str(errors)

        f.write("\n")
        f.write("Mean / SD\n")
        f.write(mean)
        f.write('/')
        f.write(sd)
        f.write("\n")
        f.write("Errors: ")
        f.write(errors)

# Program ------------------------------------------------------
pygame.init()
screen = create_window()
r = screen.get_rect()
W, H = r.width, r.height
center_x = W // 2
center_y = H // 2

colors = []
reaction_times = []
red_stimulus = []
black_stimulus = []

instructions(screen, 20, center_y)
wait_response()
clear_screen(screen)
```

```
pygame.time.delay(1000)
pygame.display.set_caption('Complex reaction time/test')
for essay in range(NUM_ESSAYS):
    clear_screen(screen)
    pygame.time.delay(TIME_WAIT) # fixed wait time between trials
    color = random.randint(1, 10)
    color = stimulus(color)
    reaction_time = measure_reaction_time()
    # save color ----------------------------------
    reaction_times.append(reaction_time)
    colors.append(color)
clear_screen(screen)
finalize(screen, 20, center_y)
save(colors, reaction_times)
wait_response() # to exit the last thank you screen
pygame.quit()
```

Figure 4-6 shows the result of the program.

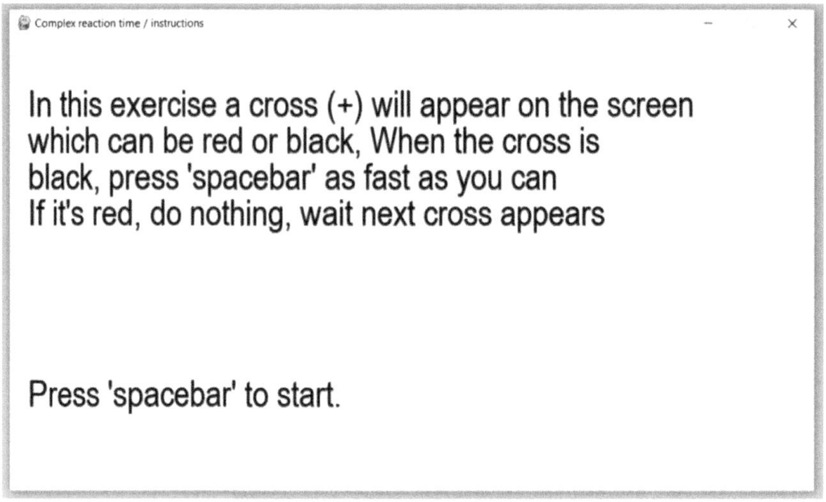

Figure 4-6. *Instruction screen regarding red or black cross, resulting from program*

This program is like the previous one and works in the same way, with the same functions. First, the appearance of a red or black cross is generated in line 158 to call the stimulus function in line 159. The choice of the color of the cross is done by generating 10 random numbers and assigning each number a color. This gives more flexibility of choice since each number represents 10% of the total, so if we assign 5 numbers to red and 5 to black, a total of 50% red crosses and 50% black crosses should appear. In the same way, if we assign a number to red and 9 to black, 10% red crosses and 90% black crosses should appear.

When calculating the results, the mean, and the standard deviation, it cannot be done on the reaction times matrix (`reaction_times[]`), since it accumulates None values, when there is no response in the red crosses, which give an error when requesting the mean and standard deviation. For this reason, we have created an auxiliary matrix that eliminates the None values and the reaction times of the errors, in lines 116 and 117. In lines 118 and 119, the errors are counted.

The Stroop Effect

J. Ridley Stroop (1935) designed an experiment to demonstrate the interference between various mental mechanisms, specifically between the naming of a color and the reading of color names, in literate subjects. Thus, when a subject is asked to name the color of the ink in which some color names are written, interference occurs, since the subject must inhibit the meaning of the written word if it is the name of a color other than the ink. This process is manifested in a lengthening of the reaction time. To study this phenomenon, we can design an experiment in two phases: one for naming colors and another for naming colors in words that refer to colors. We will do a simple experiment using only three colors: red, green, and blue. The instructions will always be to recognize the color with which the letters are written. We will need a screen that displays letters, for example "XXXX," written in one of the three chosen colors, along with three response buttons, each one in a different color. In the second part of the screen will be the names of the colors written in various colors and the same buttons to give the response, carrying out a repeated number of trials in each part.

The program includes only instructions and task administration; it does not include the collection of data from the subject or the presentation of results in a report, since these aspects will be discussed elsewhere. See Program 4-6.

Program 4-6.

```
# Stroop version 0.0.4 / Stroop004.py
# Dr. Josep M. Roig / 4.11.2024


import sys
import pygame
import time
import random
import statistics
from datetime import date
from datetime import datetime


# get system date
ara = datetime.now()
date = '{}/{}/{}'.format(ara.day, ara.month, ara.year)

pygame.init()

```

```
# Define colors
white = (255, 255, 255)
green = (66, 245, 108)
blue = (66, 81, 245)
red = (245, 66, 144)

essays = 10


# Instruction screen ---------------------------------------------
screen = pygame.display.set_mode((950, 650))
pygame.display.set_caption('Stroop Effect / Instructions Part 1.')
textFont = pygame.font.SysFont("Calibri", 40)


running = True
while running:

    screen.fill((255,255,255))
    text = textFont.render("PART 1.", True, (0, 0, 0))
    screen.blit(text,(50,50))

    text = textFont.render("", True, (0, 0, 0))
    screen.blit(text,(50, 75))

    text = textFont.render("On the next screen the letters 'XXXX' will appear", True, (0, 0, 0))
    screen.blit(text,(50, 150))

    text = textFont.render("written in red, green or blue, will have to ", True, (0, 0, 0))
    screen.blit(text,(50, 200))
    text = textFont.render("identify the color and press the corresponding button", True, (0, 0, 0))
    screen.blit(text,(50, 250))
```

```

    text = textFont.render("from the bottom, as fast as possible.
    When ", True, (0, 0, 0))
    screen.blit(text,(50, 300))

    text = textFont.render("ready press the 'START' button.",
    True, (0, 0, 0)) screen.blit(text,(50, 350))

    rectangle = pygame.draw.rect(screen, (70, 180, 20),
    (670,450,220,60), 0)
    text = textFont.render("START", True, (255, 255, 255))
    screen.blit(text,(702,465))
    pygame.display.flip()

    for event in pygame.event.get():
        if event.type == pygame.QUIT: sys.exit()

        if event.type == pygame.MOUSEBUTTONDOWN:
            x, y = pygame.mouse.get_pos() # Get click position
            if rectangle.collidepoint(x, y):
                running = False

t1 = 0.0
t2 = 0.0
resp = [] # accumulates the response time
hits = [] # accumulates the score 1 - hit, 0 - miss
color = [] # records the color to which the response was to be made


#Exercise ---------------------------------------------------------
screen = pygame.display.set_mode((750, 450))
pygame.display.set_caption( 'Stroop Effect / Exercise 1.')

# Fill screen with white
```

```
screen.fill(white)
pygame.display.flip()

currentColor = 0
TIME_DELAY = 2
II = 0

running = True
while running:

    textFont = pygame.font.SysFont("Calibri", 120)
    # check break conditions -------------
    if II > essays - 2:
        running = False

    # submit stimulus ------------------
    currentColor = random.randint(1, 3)

    if currentColor == 1:
        colorLetters = red
    if currentColor == 2:
        colorLetters = green
    if currentColor == 3:
        colorLetters = blue


    text = textFont.render("XXXX", True, (colorLetters))
    screen.blit(text,(250,110))

    # take presentation time
    t1 = time.time()


    # buttons
```

```
    labelA = pygame.draw.rect(screen, (red), (145,300,50,40), 0)
    labelB = pygame.draw.rect(screen, (green), (345,300,50,40), 0)
    labelC = pygame.draw.rect(screen, (blue), (545,300,50,40), 0)

    pygame.display.flip()

    # Accept response ······················
    pressed = ''
    WaitResponse = True
    while WaitResponse:
        for event in pygame.event.get():
            if event.type == pygame.QUIT:
                pygame.quit()
                sys.exit()


            if event.type == pygame.MOUSEBUTTONDOWN:
                x, y = pygame.mouse.get_pos() # Get click position

                color.append(currentColor)
                if labelA.collidepoint(x, y): # A red 141········
                    pressed = 'A'

                    # note and evaluate response
                    t2 = time.time()
                    resp.append( round(t2 - t1, 3))

                    if currentColor == 1:
                        hits.append(1)
                    else:
                        hits.append(0)

                    II = II + 1
                    WaitResponse = False

                if labelB.collidepoint(x, y): # B green···········
```

```
                    pressed = 'B'

                    # note and evaluate response
                    t2 = time.time()
                    resp.append( round(t2 - t1, 3))

                    if currentColor == 2:
                        hits.append(1)
                    else:
                        hits.append(0)

                    II = II + 1
                    WaitResponse = False

                if labelC.collidepoint(x, y):# C blue················
                    pressed = 'C'

                    # note and evaluate response
                    t2 = time.time()
                    resp.append( round(t2 - t1, 3))

                    if currentColor == 3:
                        hits.append(1)
                    else:
                        hits.append(0)

                    II = II + 1
                    WaitResponse = False


    pygame.draw.rect(screen, (255, 255, 255), (250,80,400,150))
    pygame.display.flip()
    screen.blit(text,(250,110))
    time.sleep(1)

# part 2 -----------------------------------------------------------
```

```
screen = pygame.display.set_mode((1050, 650))
pygame.display.set_caption('Stroop Effect / Instructions Part 2.')
textFont = pygame.font.SysFont("Calibri", 40)

running = True
while running:

    screen.fill((255,255,255))
    text = textFont.render("PART 2.", True, (0, 0, 0))
    screen.blit(text,(50,50))

    text = textFont.render("", True, (0, 0, 0))
    screen.blit(text,(50, 75))

    text = textFont.render("The words 'RED', 'GREEN' or 'BLUE'will
    appear on
    the ", True, (0, 0, 0)) screen.blit(text,(50, 150))

    text = textFont.render("next screen. written in red, green or
    blue,", True,    (0, 0, 0))
    screen.blit(text,(50, 200))

    text = textFont.render("will have to identify the color in which
    each one    is written", True, (0, 0, 0))
    screen.blit(text,(50, 250))

    text = textFont.render("word, regardless of the meaning of the
    word and
press", True, (0, 0, 0))
    screen.blit(text,(50, 300))

    text = textFont.render(" the button of the corresponding
    color of the
bottom of the", True, (0, 0, 0))
```

```
        screen.blit(text,(50, 350))

        text = textFont.render("screen, as fast as I can. When ready",
        True, (0, 0,
        0))
        screen.blit(text,(50, 400))
        text = textFont.render("press the 'START' button.", True,
        (0, 0, 0))
        screen.blit(text,(50, 450))

        rectangle = pygame.draw.rect(screen, (70, 180, 20),
        (670,550,220,60), 0)
        text = textFont.render("START", True, (255, 255, 255))
        screen.blit(text,(702,565))
        pygame.display.flip()
        for event in pygame.event.get():
            if event.type == pygame.QUIT: sys.exit()

            if event.type == pygame.MOUSEBUTTONDOWN:
                x, y = pygame.mouse.get_pos() # Get click position

                if rectangle.collidepoint(x, y):
                    running = False

t1 = 0.0
t2 = 0.0
resp2 = []
hits2 = []
color2 = []
currentColor = 0

# Exercise -----------------------------------------------------
screen = pygame.display.set_mode((750, 450))
pygame.display.set_caption('Stroop Effect / Exercise 2.')
```

```
screen.fill(white)
pygame.display.flip()


green = (66, 245, 108)
blue = (66, 81, 245)
red = (245, 66, 144)
TIME_DELAY = 2
II = 0

running = True
while running:
    textFont = pygame.font.SysFont("Calibri", 120)
    # check break conditions -------------
    if II > essays-2:
        running = False

    # submit stimulus -------------------
    currentColor = random.randint(1, 3) # color of the word
    currentWord = random.randint(1, 3) # word written

    if currentColor == 1:
        colorLetters = red
    elif currentColor == 2:
        colorLetters = green
    elif currentColor == 3:
        colorLetters = blue


    if currentWord == 1:
        word = "GREEN"
        width = 200
    elif currentWord == 2:
```

```
        word = "BLUE"
        width = 250
    elif currentWord == 3:
        word = "RED"
        width = 250


    text = textFont.render(word, True, (colorLetters))
    screen.blit(text,(width,110))

    # take presentation time
    t1 = time.time()

    # draw buttons
    labelA = pygame.draw.rect(screen, (red), (145,300,50,40), 0)
    labelB = pygame.draw.rect(screen, (green), (345,300,50,40), 0)
    labelC = pygame.draw.rect(screen, (blue), (545,300,50,40), 0)


    pygame.display.flip()

    # Accept response 308·········································
    pressed = ''
    WaitResponse = True
    while WaitResponse:
        for event in pygame.event.get():
            if event.type == pygame.QUIT:
                pygame.quit()
                sys.exit()


            if event.type == pygame.MOUSEBUTTONDOWN:
                x, y = pygame.mouse.get_pos() # Get click position

                color2.append(currentColor)
```

```
if labelA.collidepoint(x, y): # A red
323·················
    pressed = 'A'

    # note and evaluate response
    t2 = time.time()
    resp2.append( round(t2 - t1, 3))

    if currentColor == 1:
        hits2.append(1)
    else:
        hits2.append(0)

    II = II + 1
    WaitResponse = False

if labelB.collidepoint(x, y): # B green·······
    pressed = 'B'

    # note and evaluate response
    t2 = time.time()
    resp2.append( round(t2 - t1, 3))

    if currentColor == 2:
        hits2.append(1)
    else:
        hits2.append(0)

    II = II + 1
    WaitResponse = False


if labelC.collidepoint(x, y):# C blue 355······
    pressed = 'C'

    # note and evaluate response
```

```
                    t2 = time.time()
                    resp2.append( round(t2 - t1, 3))

                    if currentColor == 3:
                        hits2.append(1)
                    else:
                        hits2.append(0)

                    II = II + 1
                    WaitResponse = False

    pygame.draw.rect(screen, (255, 255, 255), (190,80,400,150))
    pygame.display.flip()
    text = textFont.render("", True, (255,255,255))
    screen.blit(text,(250,110))
    time.sleep(1)

# Print results ---------------------------------------------
print ('Part 1.')
print('Time: ', resp)
print('Hits: ', hits)
print('Colors: ', color)
print('N:', len(resp), ', Mean times: ', round(statistics.mean(resp), 3))

print()
print ('Part 2.')
print('Time: ', resp2)
print('Hits: ', hits2)
print('Colors: ', color2)
print('N:', len(resp2), ', Mean times: ', round(statistics.mean(resp2), 3))

# Go out ----------------------------------------------------
pygame.quit()
sys.exit()
```

The program starts with its identifier, in lines 1 and 2. Lines 5 to 11 import the libraries necessary for the program to run. Line 18 starts Pygame. Lines 21 to 24 define the colors. Line 26 defines the number of trials, which will be the same for parts 1 and 2.

From lines 30 to 70, the instructions screen for part 1 is presented, and a mechanism is established to follow when the user confirms they have read and understood the instructions.

From lines 71 to 75, the variables that will be necessary to record the subject's results are started. `t1` and `t2` are auxiliary variables to record the moment in which the stimulus is presented and the moment in which the response is given. `resp[]` is an empty matrix to which the response times are added; `hits[]` contains for each response a 1 if it is correct or a 0 if it is not; and color contains the target color for each stimulus, 1 for red, 2 for green, and 3 for blue.

From lines 79 to 84, the screen for exercise 1 is displayed, which starts on line 90. Within the exercise loop, the font size is defined, in line 93. A check is made to see if the number of trials has been exceeded, in lines 95 and 96. The color of the trial is randomly generated, in lines 99 to 106. Then the stimulus is presented: the letters with the appropriate color, in lines 109 to 110. The start time is taken, and the buttons for the response are presented, in lines 117 to 121.

On line 123, the response of admission begins with the definition of the variable pressed, which will be used to identify the button that was pressed and with a loop that waits for the subject to press one of the buttons.

If the interaction is of the exit type, the program will end, in lines 128 to 130; if the event is a press of the left mouse button, the position of the mouse pointer will be identified to know which of the buttons has been pressed, in lines 133 to 134.

In line 136, the color of the current test is saved. Next, it analyzes which button was pressed, and the results are saved for button A (137–147), B (152–165), or C (167–180).

To prepare the screen for the next trial, within the loop, the current stimulus (183–185) must be erased and a dead time allowed between stimuli (186), which in this case is one second.

Part two has two minor differences: two random values must be generated for the ink color of the stimulus and for the word presented. The results are printed on lines 370–383, and the program ends on lines 386–387.

Other Possibilities for Writing Programs for Experimental Psychology

Many libraries are specifically designed for programming experimental psychology tasks, such as Expyriment (Krause & Lindemann, 2014), neurokit2 (Makowski, Pham, Lau, Brammer, Lespinasse, Pham, Schölzel, & Chen, 2021), neuropsidia,[1] OpenSesame (Mathôt, Schreij, & Theeuwes, 2012), PsychoPy2 (Peirce, Gray, Simpson, Macaskill, Höchenberger, Sogo, Kastman, & Lindeløv, 2019), Ratcave (Del Grosso & Sirota, 2019), PsyToolKit (Stoet, 2011), PyGaze (Dalmaijer, Mathôt, & Van Der Stigchel, 2013), etc. Look for documentation for these libraries on the Internet to see the examples and possibilities they offer and to expand your knowledge.

In summary, Python is a useful programming language in the field of experimental psychology, as it offers many libraries and tools for performing data analysis, visualizations, and experiments. Here are some ways in which Python can be used in experimental psychology.

Data Analysis and Statistics:

- **NumPy and Pandas:** These libraries are essential for handling and analyzing numerical and tabular data.
- **SciPy:** This offers a wide range of statistical functions and tools for data analysis.
- **statsmodels:** This is specialized in statistical model analysis and hypothesis testing.

Data Visualization:

- **Matplotlib:** This is a popular library for creating static 2D visualizations.
- **Seaborn:** This is based on Matplotlib but simplifies the creation of attractive statistical graphs.
- **Plotly:** This is ideal for interactive visualizations and 2D/3D graphics.

[1] Dominique Makowski, 2017 (`https://github.com/DominiqueMakowski`)

Experiments and Stimuli:

- **PsychoPy:** This is a complete tool for designing and running psychological experiments, including stimulus presentation and data collection.
- **OpenSesame:** This is another tool for creating experiments with an easy-to-use graphical interface.

Text Analysis:

- **NLTK (Natural Language Toolkit):** This is for text analysis and natural language processing in research involving content analysis.

Machine Learning and Sentiment Analysis:

- **scikit-learn:** This library is for applying machine learning techniques.
- **TextBlob:** This library is for sentiment analysis and simple text processing.

Data Recording and Automation:

- **SQLite or MySQL:** This is to manage databases of participants and results.
- **Task Automation:** Python can be used to automate repetitive processes, such as organizing data or generating reports.

Image Analysis:

- **OpenCV (Open Source Computer Vision Library):** If your research requires image analysis, this library is ideal for image processing and computer vision.

Integration with Devices and Sensors:

- **pySerial:** This library can communicate with serial devices, such as sensors or laboratory equipment.
- **Python-MIDI:** This specifies whether the integration of auditory stimuli or control of MIDI devices is required.

Social Media Analysis:

- **Tweepy:** This is for Twitter data collection and analysis.
- **NetworkX:** This is for network and graph analysis.

Remember that the choice of tools will depend on your specific needs and the nature of your research. Python offers great flexibility and is apparently already widely used in the experimental psychology research community.

A technique that has become popular in experimental psychology and cognitive neuroscience is eye tracking (Dalmaijer, Mathôt, van der Stigchel, 2013; Dalmaijer, 2024; Duchowski, 2017; Peirce, Hirst, Macaskill, 2022; Wang, 2021), which can also be used in experimental psychology although it has the disadvantage that it requires special devices to connect to the computer.

Summary

In this chapter, you learned about topics such as stimulus presentation, response collection, reaction times, and some classic experiments such as the Stroop effect. In the next chapter, you will see applications for clinical psychology.

CHAPTER 5

Clinical Psychology

In this chapter, you will administer some classic tests and manage personality questionnaires.

The applications of computer science, and therefore of Python, to clinical psychology are various (Roig-Fusté, 2018), including the application, correction, and assessment of psychological tests; preparation of results reports; the collection and storage of data from clinical histories, obtaining the clinical history directly from the patient by computer; the development of theoretical models; and the development and monitoring of therapy programs. All these applications were already tested some time ago (Apter, 1973; Bird, 1981), but nowadays computers offer better features and a very low cost to carry them out. The introduction of virtual reality for treating phobias also seems to be a promising field, and Python allows programming virtual reality environments (Eichenberg, 2012; Manolas, Xanthidou, and Xanthidis, 2022).

Psychological Assessments

Any task that requires exhaustive control of the subject's behavior is ideal for programming; for example, attention tests that require exact control of time, successes, errors (due to distraction or inability to inhibit response), and omissions can be adapted easily and reused repeatedly.

As an example, we are going to develop a finger-tapping speed program (the Finger Tapping Test) to study all these benefits.

A simple neuropsychological test, the Finger Tapping Test (FTT), is considered an accurate indicator of the health of the central nervous system. It consists of tapping on a surface with a finger, usually the index finger, as quickly as possible. This activity is related to the general functioning of the nervous system and manual dexterity, which is why it can be a powerful psychological test (Strub & Black, 1983; Strauss, Sherman, & Spreen, 2006; Lezak, Howieson, Bigler, & Tranel, 2012).

J. M. Roig-Fusté, *Python for Psychology, Social Sciences, and Education*,
https://doi.org/10.1007/979-8-8688-2355-8_5

This test can be applied without apparatus, as part of a routine neurological clinical examination, or with some type of apparatus, mechanical or electromechanical, consisting of a push button that is similar to that used by old telegraph operators and incorporating a counting system, which can be mechanical or electrical, to record the number of blows given during a fixed period of time. The time in this case is measured by the examiner with a stopwatch.

As a psychological test, this task is part of well-known neuropsychological batteries such as those of Halstead (1947) and Reitan (1969). Technical information on it can be found, for example, in Lezak, Howieson, Bigler, and Tranel (2012), or in Strauss, Sherman and Spreen (2006). The characteristics of this task make it easy to adapt it to any type of computer; for this purpose, we will use a standard screen and keyboard. On the screen we will present the instructions and obtain the results; the results obtained can be presented on the screen or saved on the computer disk with the data about who performed the test. With the standard keyboard of the computer, we can record the answers about the subject.

On the keyboard, a large key is chosen, usually the spacebar, and the program is configured to react only to this key. The keyboard can be set to leave only the key that we are going to use visible, by covering the rest of the keys with a piece of cardboard, the edges of which are inserted into the slots left at the ends of the keyboard, and which has a hole that leaves the key chosen for the test exposed. Of course, a special key device can also be used, which we will discuss later.

Let's look at a possible computer solution for this task.

The task is simple; it begins with the presentation of instructions, for the time necessary for the subject to understand them, and it will end when the subject agrees to start the test. From this moment on, each time the subject presses the spacebar, we will add a unit to a counting variable that we have started at 0. The task can allow a training stage, and its duration must be determined, which can be integrated into the program or be another variable of the data entry. As with the measurement of reaction time, in this case short times of 10 or 20 seconds are generally applied. Very short times do not allow the subject's performance to be evaluated accurately, and long times predispose to fatigue or boredom, which could alter the results. Bear in mind that fatigue can be an interesting neurological indicator, but it probably is only a problem if it occurs during short periods of activity.

It is also possible to make the program more complex by enabling several tests for each hand in order to compare results to each other to establish a lateral dominance index or to improve the reliability of the measurement.

Unfortunately, Python does not have a specific command to identify an individual key press, as other programming languages do, so we will have to resort to a library. Here we encounter the first problem. There are several libraries that can carry out this task (msvcrt, getchar, pynput), which poses the dilemma of which one to choose. You will probably have to try several to see which one best suit your needs. See Program 5-1.

Program 5-1.

```
# FingerTappingTest.py, Dr. JM Roig-Fusté
# Finger Tapping Test / 7.07.22

import sys
import msvcrt
import time

# variable initialization ---------------------------
hits = 0
tInitial = 0 # start time
tTest = 0 # time that will control the end of the test
tAllowed = 10 # 10 seconds, duration of the test

# Submit instructions
print("Press the space bar with your index finger.")
print ("from the keyboard, as fast as I can.")
print ("When you are ready, you can begin.")

key = "x"
# The first hit on the space bar starts the time counter
while key != "":
    key = msvcrt.getch()
    key = key.decode("ANSI")
    if key ==" ":
        break
```

```
25        else:
26            print("You can only use the space bar,")
27            print ("try again.")
28
29    tInitial = time.time()
30    print("Initial time: " + str(tInitial))
31    tTest = tInitial + tAllowed
32    print("Final time: " + str(tTest))
33
34    while tTest > time.time():
35        key = msvcrt.getch()
36        key = key.decode("ANSI")
37        if key == " ":
38            if tTest > time.time():
39                hits = hits + 1
40                print(beats, round(time.time(),3))
41
42    print()
43    print("Total number of keystrokes: " + str(hits))
44    print("The test is finished, thank you for your cooperation.")
45
46    exit = input("press the 'Return' key")
```

The first two lines contain program identification. Lines 4, 5, and 6 import the libraries that are necessary for the program to work correctly. Lines 9 to 12 define the variables that we will use in the program; the variable `tAllowed` has a value of 10 seconds; this value can be changed to make the test longer or shorter. Lines 15 to 17 present the instructions on the screen. Lines 18 to 27 create a waiting loop until the subject presses the spacebar; if the subject presses any other key, they are warned that they should only use the spacebar. When the subject presses the space bar, this loop is exited, and the test times are assigned, in this case 10 seconds of task. Lines 31 and 33 print the moment when the test starts and when it should end. This information does not need to be printed, but it is done so that the programmer knows the values while writing and testing the program. Once the program is fully functional, these lines can be deleted. It is common that at some point in a program the value of one or more variables is printed to check that everything works as expected. When the program has finished and all the necessary checks have been made, these printing orders are canceled or deleted.

Next, on line 35, another loop is starting to collect the subject's keystrokes. The loop also prints out, on line 41, the number reached, and the time at which the keystroke occurred. It is not necessary to give this information to the client, so this line can be omitted if desired. However, it should be considered whether giving this information, in one way or another, can be a motivating element for the subject, which encourages the subject to give their best performance, or whether it is simply a distracting element, which will slow down their performance. This information, whether given or not, can be saved in a list and recorded in a file, which will allow the subject's work to be analyzed later. Finally, the total number of strokes performed is printed on line 44. It is also not necessary to give this information if it is not desired, and the results must then be saved in a file on the computer disk or presented on a screen that can only be accessed with a password.

Line 45 thanks for participating in the task and informing us of the end of the test.

Overall, the program is simple and seems like we can use it with our clients; however, this program as written has some major problems.

If you try to run this program in Python IDLE, as we have seen on a previous occasion, it works badly. The first loop does not wait for the subject to press the spacebar to start the task and enters an infinite repetition in which it prints the error message informing that only the spacebar can be used to perform the exercise. For the program to work as we have planned, it must be run directly from the interpreter or compiled with pyinstaller, before using it, as we have explained previously. Once compiled, the program works as expected.

There is another, more serious problem, which you may have already discovered by now if you have used the program and which we have already discussed in previous programs: the keys on the computer keyboard are self-repeating, including the spacebar. This means that if the key is held down instead of being pressed, the computer counts responses at high speed without the subject doing anything and can reach more than 280 responses in 10 seconds, when hitting it alone can reach 60 or 70 at most, in the best of cases. This problem should be solved either by supervising the subject being examined to ensure they key is not being held down, or by checking for each keystroke not only that the key has been pressed but also that it has been released, so that if the complete cycle does not occur, the program does not count a new keystroke. In fact, the action of releasing a key cannot be repeated; it requires that the key has been previously pressed. Therefore, a simple way of coding the program would be to consider only the action of releasing the key. Not doing so would mean that the experimenter would have to closely monitor the subjects to ensure that they do not act incorrectly by constantly pressing the key. However, this is not what we want when we think about automating an experiment like this, so control must be carried out from the program itself as we have explained.

Another easier way to solve this problem, as we will see later, is to use Pygame to collect keystrokes, a library in which the keys are not automatically repeated.

You should also consider that this would be the core of the program, but naturally a complete program would have a start menu that would allow you to indicate the number of trials to be performed and the time of each trial. The program should allow you to enter the test subject's identification data and allow you to enter a practice period, or perhaps the possibility of performing trials with the right hand and the left hand. The identification data and other demographic information should be automatically saved at the end of the test with the results obtained, in a file on the computer's hard drive.

Keystroke recognition can be applied to many other specific purposes, as we will see later, so it is also important to know how the computer works and about any possible problems that may arise from this operation. Research into mental functioning recognizes the need for millisecond sensitivity in research instruments (Luce, 1986), which is why various researchers working with computers have asked themselves whether the standard configurations of these devices meet the stated requirement (Dalmaijer. 2017; Damian, 2010; Plant, Hammond and Turner, 2004; Plant, Turner, 2009; Shimizu, 2002). The computer controls all its peripherals from the operating system. This means that a response given by the keyboard or mouse is not immediately considered by the device, remaining in the device until the computer checks to see if an event has occurred in the peripherals. This check occurs approximately every 20 milliseconds, depending on the quality of the peripherals and the way they are connected to the computer. Therefore, if a subject presses the keyboard one millisecond after the last check, this keystroke will not be recorded by the computer until 19 milliseconds later. This error is not fixed, and for each keystroke it can vary between 0 and 19 milliseconds on standard equipment, possibly one or two milliseconds more due to the operations that the operating system must perform. Keyboards and mice connected to the computer via a USB port seem to slightly reduce this time. If this level of error cannot be assumed, specific peripherals must be used, connected in a different way to the computer, and with special software configurations that can be very expensive.

Having seen these problems, we are now going to write the same program to avoid the problem of key repetition when the keys are held down. We have seen how the FTT could be developed in a console environment. Now Program 5-2 shows the same application for a Windows graphical environment.

Program 5-2.

```
# Tapping test 20.06.2020

import pygame
from pygame.locals import *
from sys import exit

# Constants
WHITE = (255, 255, 255)
BLACK = (0, 0, 0)

# Assign variables
cops = 0 # hits
chrono = 0 # clock
allocatedTime = 0 # total time allowed
ticks = 0 # select milliseconds

pygame.init()

screen = pygame.display.set_mode((840, 480), 0, 32)
screen.fill(WHITE)
pygame.display.set_caption('Finger Tapping Test') # Set a caption to the window

my_font = pygame.font.SysFont("Arial", 55)
text_screen = my_font.render("Instructions.", 0, (0, 0, 0))
screen.blit(text_screen, (60, 45))

my_font = pygame.font.SysFont("Arial", 40)
text_screen = my_font.render("Press the space bar with your index
```

```
finger", 0, (0, 0, 0))
screen.blit(text_screen, (60, 150))
text_screen = my_font.render("as fast as you can. When you're
ready", 0, (0, 0, 0))
screen.blit(text_screen, (60, 200))
text_screen = my_font.render("you can start.", 0, (0, 0, 0))
screen.blit(text_screen, (60, 250))

pygame.display.update()

# Enter the first answer and start timings
while cops == 0:
    for event in pygame.event.get():

        if event.type == QUIT: # Exit the program
            pygame.quit()
            exit()

        if event.type == KEYDOWN:
            if event.key == K_SPACE:
                crono = pygame.time.Clock()
                crono.tick(10)
                ticks = pygame.time.get_ticks()
                allocatedTime = ticks + 10000
                cops = cops + 1
                screen.fill(WHITE)
                my_font2 = pygame.font.SysFont("Arial", 100)
                cops_texte = my_font2.render("Keystrokes: " +
                str(cops), True, BLACK)
                screen.blit(cops_texte, (150, 150))
                pygame.display.update()
                print(str(cops), str(ticks))

while allocatedTime > ticks:

```

```
    for event in pygame.event.get():
        if event.type == QUIT:
            pygame.quit()
            exit()

        if event.type == KEYDOWN:
            if event.key == K_SPACE:
                crono = pygame.time.Clock()
                crono.tick(10)
                ticks = pygame.time.get_ticks()
                cops = cops + 1
                my_font2 = pygame.font.SysFont("Arial", 100)

                print(str(cops), str(ticks))

            # Write text
            screen.fill(WHITE) # doesn't work
            cops_texte = my_font2.render("Keystrokes:
            " +str(cops), True, BLACK)
            screen.blit(cops_texte, (150, 150))
            pygame.display.update()

            if event.key == K_ESCAPE: # sort press escape
                pygame.quit()
                sys.exit()

my_font3 = pygame.font.SysFont("Arial", 40)
message = my_font3.render('Test completed.', True, BLACK)
screen.blit(message, (150, 320))
message2 = my_font3.render('Thank you for your collaboration.',
True, BLACK)
screen.blit(message2, (150, 360))
pygame.display.update()
print(str(cops), str(ticks))
```

Figure 5-1 shows the test instructions.

Figure 5-1. *Text instructions*

While the test is in progress, information can be provided on the number of pulses performed. The message at the end of the test appears in Figure 5-2.

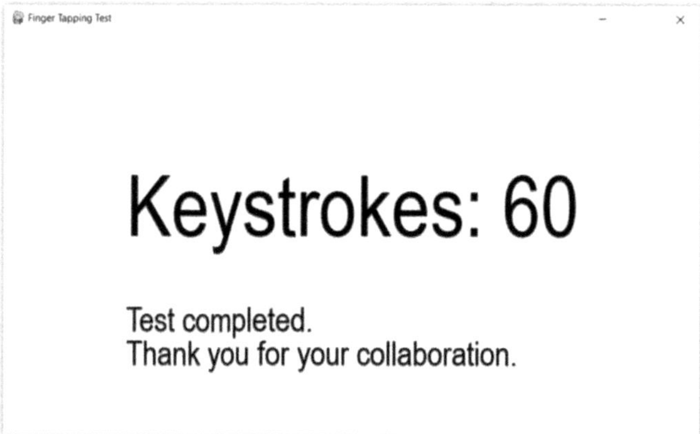

Figure 5-2. *Message at end of test*

We start the program with an identification comment on line 1. Lines 3, 4, and 5 import libraries for the program to work. Lines 8 and 9 define constants for color assignment. Lines 12 to 15 initialize the variables that we will need for the program. Line 17 is necessary to start the pygame library; it must be written at the beginning of the program, and if it is omitted, the interpreter will give a runtime error. Line 19 creates a work screen with a size of 840x480 pixels. In line 20 a background color is assigned, and in line 21 a title is given to the screen.

On lines 23 to 28, the test instructions are written in the body of the window; this screen will not change until the subject presses the spacebar for the first time.

When the subject presses the spacebar for the first time, a press and the start time are recorded, to which 10,000 milliseconds (10 seconds) are added, and the test is started (lines 36 to 56).

The keystrokes are collected through line 43, which is `'if event.type == KEYDOWN:'`, and here the only key that is recognized is the spacebar (line 44).

Lines 57 to 62 are the loop that constitutes the core of the program. While the time has not elapsed, the responses and the times for each of them are collected, while the subject's progress is displayed on the screen. One might consider whether displaying the response is a stimulus or would constitute providing information to the subject that is not convenient. Therefore, when building the program, one could consider various ways of administering the test: showing and not showing the progress of the test.

With this we finish the core of the test, naturally for it to be useful, some things are missing. Specifically, before starting, the subject identification data should be entered (name, age, sex, education...); an easy way to do this would be using a library such as guizero or the dialogs of the PsychoPy library, as shown here:

```
from psychopy import core, event, visual, gui

info={'a. name':'','b. age':'', 'c. sex':''}
dlg = gui.DlgFromDict(dictionary=info,title='Personal data.')
if dlg.OK==False:
core.quit() #user pressed cancel

name = info['nom']
age = info['age']
sex = info['sex']
```

The test could be organized in such a way that it allows for a first test trial and then several trials for each hand; once the test is finished, the results should be managed and stored in a permanent file so that they can be studied. We will look at some of these things later.

Finally, we must mention another problem: is the data obtained reliable and accurate? As regards to the number of strokes, that is certainly accurate, but the time between each stroke is not entirely accurate if standard devices such as a keyboard or mouse are used, which must be taken into account in case it may represent a problem in the experiment. The computer is a general-purpose device and is designed to provide acceptable performance at a minimum cost. As we have already explained, computer peripherals, such as a keyboard or mouse, are connected to the operating system, and the latter performs a cyclical check to collect the information they provide, which is not collected instantly but is collected in the first check that the computer performs after the action has occurred, such as pressing a key, for example. These checks occur every 10 or 20 milliseconds, meaning that if a keystroke occurs one millisecond after a check, the time of the keystroke recorded by the computer may be up to 19 milliseconds behind the real time. This is not a problem for word processing, where the operator will not notice the delay, but it can be a serious problem for a psychological experiment (Dalmaijer, 2017, Damian, 2010).

In our program, we have planned 10-second trials. For this we add 10 seconds to the initial time, that of the first keystroke, and we check that this allowed time is not exceeded while the task is being carried out. When it is exceeded, the test is interrupted. The time check is done within the loop that records the keystroke, so that if this keystroke does not occur, the check is not carried out, and the test is not interrupted. In practice, this means the time is never exactly 10 seconds, that is, 10,000 milliseconds, but is between 10,000 and 10,020 milliseconds, and this discrepancy is distributed randomly, benefiting some subjects and harming others.

Tower of Hanoi

Of course, it is possible to administer more complex psychological tests than those seen so far; let us look at an example of a problem-solving test called the Tower of Hanoi (Figure 5-3) (Ahonniska, Ahonen, Aro, & Lyytinen, 2000; Hinz, 1989; Hinz, Klavzar, Milutinovic, & Petr, 2013; Lezak, Howieson, Bigler, Tranel, 2012; Welsh and Huizinga, 2001), which has been used in neuropsychological exploration.

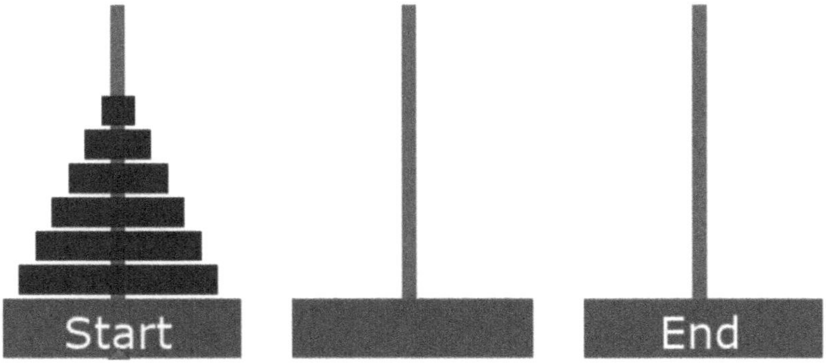

Figure 5-3. *Tower of Hanoi*

This puzzle was proposed by the French mathematician Edouard Lucas in 1883 (Lucas, 1893: Hinz, Klavzar, Milutinovic and Petr, 2013). It consists of three rods that accumulate a certain number of disks stacked in a pyramidal shape, that is, ordered by size from largest to smallest. The exercise requires moving all the disks from the first rod, from the beginning, to the last or final one. These are the rules:

a) Only one disk can be moved at a time.

b) The disk that is moved must be smaller than the last disk in the stack where it will land.

c) You can only move the disk that is on top of each rod.

The minimum number of moves required to complete the task depends on the number of disks and is calculated using the formula $2^n - 1$, where n is the number of disks.

The official Python IDLE shows an example of how the Tower of Hanoi works, made from the turtle library. This is not suitable for exploring patients, since it does not allow interactions with an operator, so let's look at a simple version, prepared for interaction with the explored subject (Program 5-3).

Program 5-3.

```
# Tower of Hanoi
# Dr. Roig / 11.10.2023 / Hanoi.py / TorreDeHanoi03.py

import pygame, sys, time
from pygame.locals import QUIT
```

```
# test variables
fin_test = False
n_disks = 3 # default number of disks
disks = []
towers_midx = [120, 320, 520] # posición del indicador
pointing_at = 0
floating = False
floater = 0
movimientos = 0

# color constants ------------
black = (  0,   0,   0)
blue =  (  0,   0, 255)
green = (  0, 128,   0)
grey =  (128, 128, 128)
red =   (255,   0,   0)
white = (255, 255, 255)

# pygame initialization ---------
pygame.init()
screen = pygame.display.set_mode((840, 490))
pygame.display.set_caption("Tower of Hanoi")
clock = pygame.time.Clock()

# program functions -----------
def blit_text(screen, text, midtop, aa=True, font=None, font_name = None,
size = None, color=(255,0,0)):
    if font is None:   # font not found option
        font = pygame.font.SysFont(font_name, size)
    font_surface = font.render(text, aa, color)
    font_rect = font_surface.get_rect()
    font_rect.midtop = midtop
    screen.blit(font_surface, font_rect)
```

```

def menu_inicio():  # start menu
    global screen, n_disks, fin_test
    menu_done = False
    while not menu_done:
        screen.fill(white)
        blit_text(screen, 'Tower of Hanoi', (400,75),
        font_name='comicsansms', size=92, color=black)
        blit_text(screen, 'Use the arrow keys to choose the
        difficulty level', (420, 220), font_name='veraserif',
        size=30, color=black)
        blit_text(screen, str(n_disks), (420, 260),
        font_name='verdana', size=40, color=blue)
        blit_text(screen, 'Press ENTER to continue', (420, 320),
        font_name='verdana', size=30, color=black)
        for event in pygame.event.get():
            if event.type==pygame.KEYDOWN:
                if event.key == pygame.K_q:
                    menu_done = True
                    fin_test = True
                if event.key == pygame.K_RETURN:
                    menu_done = True
                if event.key in [pygame.K_RIGHT, pygame.K_UP]:
                    n_disks += 1
                    if n_disks > 6:
                        n_disks = 6
                if event.key in [pygame.K_LEFT, pygame.K_DOWN]:
                    n_disks -= 1
                    if n_disks < 1:
                        n_disks = 1
            if event.type == pygame.QUIT:
                menu_done = True
                fin_test = True
        pygame.display.flip()
        clock.tick(60)
```

```


def draw_towers():
    global screen
    for xpos in range(40, 460 + 1, 200):
        pygame.draw.rect(screen, green, pygame.Rect(xpos, 400, 165 , 40)) # base of the towers
        pygame.draw.rect(screen, grey, pygame.Rect(xpos + 75, 200, 10, 200)) # axis of the towers
        blit_text(screen, 'Start', (towers_midx[0], 403), font_name='verdana', size=30, color=white)
        blit_text(screen, 'End', (towers_midx[2], 403), font_name='verdana', size=30, color=white)


def make_disks():
    global n_disks, disks
    disks = []
    height = 20
    ypos = 397 - height
    width = n_disks * 23
    for i in range(n_disks):
        disk = {}
        disk['rect'] = pygame.Rect(0, 0, width, height)
        disk['rect'].midtop = (120, ypos)
        disk['val'] = n_disks-i
        disk['tower'] = 0
        disks.append(disk)
        ypos -= height+3
        width -= 23


def draw_disks():
    global screen, disks
    for disk in disks:
```

```
        pygame.draw.rect(screen, blue, disk['rect'])
    return

def draw_ptr(): # indicator pointer
    ptr_points = [(towers_midx[pointing_at]-7 ,440),
    (towers_midx[pointing_at]+7, 440), (towers_midx[pointing_at], 433)]
    pygame.draw.polygon(screen, red, ptr_points)
    return

def check_won():
    global disks
    over = True
    for disk in disks:
        if disk['tower'] != 2:
            over = False
    if over:
        time.sleep(0.2)
        test_over()

def reset():
    global movimientos,pointing_at,floating,floater
    movimientos = 0
    pointing_at = 0
    floating = False
    floater = 0
    menu_inicio()
    make_disks()


def test_over(): # pantalla de fin de tarea
    global screen, movimientos
    screen.fill(white)
    blit_text(screen, 'Task Completed', (420, 100),
    font_name='verdana', size=52, color=black)
```

```
    blit_text(screen, 'Movements: '+str(movimientos), (420, 200), font_name='verdana', size=40, color=black)

    pygame.display.flip()
    time.sleep(5) # wait for 15 seconds
    pygame.quit() # exit pygame
    sys.exit()


if __name__ == "__main__":
    menu_inicio() # call the start menu

    make_disks()  # draw discs on the screen

    while not fin_test:  # main loop
        for event in pygame.event.get():
            if event.type == pygame.QUIT:
                fin_test = True
            if event.type == pygame.KEYDOWN:
                if event.key == pygame.K_ESCAPE:
                    reset()
                if event.key == pygame.K_q:
                    fin_test = True
                if event.key == pygame.K_RIGHT:
                    pointing_at = (pointing_at+1)%3
                    if floating:
                        disks[floater]['rect'].midtop = (towers_midx[pointing_at], 100)
                        disks[floater]['tower'] = pointing_at
                if event.key == pygame.K_LEFT:
                    pointing_at = (pointing_at-1)%3
                    if floating:
                        disks[floater]['rect'].midtop = (towers_midx[pointing_at], 100)
                        disks[floater]['tower'] = pointing_at
```

```
                if event.key == pygame.K_UP and not floating:
                    for disk in disks[::-1]:
                        if disk['tower'] == pointing_at:
                            floating = True
                            floater = disks.index(disk)
                            disk['rect'].midtop =
                            (towers_midx[pointing_at], 100)
                            break
                if event.key == pygame.K_DOWN and floating:
                    for disk in disks[::-1]:
                        if disk['tower'] == pointing_at and
                        disks.index(disk)!=floater:
                            if disk['val']>disks[floater]['val']:
                                floating = False
                                disks[floater]['rect'].midtop =
                              (towers_midx[pointing_at], disk['rect']
                              .top-23)
                                movimientos += 1
                            break
                    else:
                        floating = False
                        disks[floater]['rect'].midtop =
(towers_midx[pointing_at], 400-23)
                        movimientos += 1
        screen.fill(white)
        draw_towers()
        draw_disks()
        draw_ptr()
        blit_text(screen, 'Movements: '+str(movimientos), (320, 50),
        font_name='verdana', size=30, color=black)
        pygame.display.flip()
        if not floating:check_won()
        clock.tick(60)  # screen refresh rate

    pygame.QUIT
```

Lines 1 and 2 contain the program ID.

Lines 4 and 5 import the libraries needed for operation: pygame, sys, and time.

Lines 8 through 15 initialize the variables to control the test. Lines 18 through 23 indicate the color constants to be used on the screen.

Line 26 starts pygame, line 27 defines the test screen width and height in pixels, line 28 writes the title of the pygame screen, and line 29 starts the clock that controls the screen refresh.

Following lines 32 to 137, the functions necessary for the program are defined:

- `blit_text`
- `menu_screen`
- `draw_towers`
- `make_disks`
- `draw_disks`
- `draw_ptr`
- `check_won`
- `reset`
- `test_over`
- `home_menu`

The program starts on line 140; on 141 it calls the `start_menu` function. Once the `start_menu` has been accepted, it moves on to drawing the towers in the `make_disks` function. Lines 145 to 190 contain the loop that accepts the movements, makes the appropriate changes to the screen, and checks whether the task has finished, in which case it displays the results.

Managing a Personality Questionnaire

One of the most characteristic aspects of clinical psychology is, as we have seen, psychological exploration, and within it one of the first tasks that was assigned to computing was the management of personality questionnaires, the first field to which computing was applied in psychology and that has reached great development (Rome,

Swenson, Mataya, McCarthy, Pearson, Keating, & Hathaway, 1962; Marks & Seeman, 1963; Lachar, 1973; Seisdedos & Roig-Fusté, 1986; Roig-Fusté, 1993; Roig-Fusté, 2017). An example of managing a personality questionnaire in Python can be found here:

`https://github.com/NerdiOrg/Python-IPIP-BFFM`

Regarding a questionnaire from the International Personality Item Pool organization (`https://ipip.ori.org/`), which although it is not presented in a graphic environment and is cumbersome to manage by asking for a response for each item followed by a verification of said response, it may be interesting to know and serve as an example.

In our work for many years (Seisdedos and Roig-Fusté, 1986) in the management of personality questionnaires with the help of computers, we considered the following aspects:

Data entry.
Administration of questionnaires directly by computer.
From an answer sheet filled out by the subject.
Correction
Preparation of results.
Report with scores and graphs.
Different types of explanatory textual reports.

Administration of the Questionnaire

Administering questionnaires via a computer is not a new topic (Rome et al., 1962; Seisdedos and Roig-Fusté, 1986) and has its advantages and disadvantages. Among the advantages are a reduction of errors and the ability to directly process the client's answers, avoiding having to use an optical reader or manually record answers. As a disadvantage, you will need to have a computer terminal for each subject who is answering the test. Nowadays this is not much of an inconvenience because almost everyone has a computer, tablet, or smartphone that can connect to a web page where they can answer a questionnaire. The logical question is whether computer administration is equivalent to a classic pencil and paper version. Although there may be small variations in the results, in general the two are considered equivalent.

As an example, to show possibilities and see the programming of a task of this type, let's suppose a 10-question anxiety test, which the subject must answer with `true` or `false`.

The administration of the test should begin, as always, by recording the subject's data: identifier (usually the name), age, sex, level of education, etc. The next screen, which we will start with here, should present the test instructions and allow the subject all the time they want to read them. We will then present the questions, one by one, offering the possibility of answering, in this case `true` or `false`, to continue.

Before we start writing the program, let's think of some questions for our anxiety questionnaire:

1.	I feel tense without knowing why.
2.	I have had panic attacks.
3.	I'm not worried about anything. (R)
4.	I often have the feeling that something unpleasant is about to happen imminently.
5.	My sleep is peaceful. (R)
6.	I'm usually nervous.
7.	I often feel my heart palpitating
8.	I feel insecure when I must go to a place I don't know.
9.	Things that come up unexpectedly make me feel uneasy.
10.	Sometimes I feel a strong oppression in my chest.

The code (R) in questions 3 and 5 indicates that these questions score the opposite of all the others, so while almost all of them score in the True option, questions 3 and 5 will score in the False option.

See Program 5-4.

Program 5-4.

```
# Questionario.0.4.py / Dr. Roig
# Program questionnaire / Enter personal data 10.09.2023

import PySimpleGUI as sg
import pyttsx3

def say(txt):
    veu = pyttsx3.init()
```

```
    veu.setProperty("rate", 110)

    veu.say(txt)
    veu.runAndWait()

# Instructions
layout = [[sg.Text('Below you will find a series of statements,', font=("Helvetica", 20))],

          [sg.Text('which should indicate whether they fit what happens to you.', font=("Helvetica", 20))],
          [sg.Text('If the statement is true or mostly true for you,', font=("Helvetica", 20))],
          [sg.Text('answer by clicking the true button, if it is false or mostly', font=("Helvetica", 20))],
          [sg.Text('false, click on the false button.', size=(50, 2), font=("Helvetica", 20))],
          [sg.Button('Next')]]

# Submit instructions
window = sg.Window('Administer questionnaire / Instructions',
layout)

# 4 - Event Loop
while True:
    event, values = window.read()
    if event in (None, 'Next'):
        break
window.close()

# questionnaire
questions = ["I often feel tense without knowing why.",
             "I've had panic attacks.",
             "I'm not worried about anything.",
             "I often have the feeling that something unpleasant is going to happen imminently.",
```

```
                 "My sleep is peaceful.",
                 "I'm usually nervous.",
                 "I often feel my heart palpitating",
                 "I feel insecure when I have to go to a place I don't
                 know.",
                 "Things that come up unexpectedly scare me."
                 "Sometimes I feel a strong oppression in my chest."]

answers = [ '?', '?', '?', '?', '?', '?', '?', '?', '?', '?']
question = questions[0]

# Administer the questionnaire ------------------------------------
# Submit questions
content = [[sg.Text("", font=("Helvetica", 30))],
           [sg.Button('Listen')],
           [sg.Text("", font=("Helvetica", 30))],
           [sg.Text(question, key = 'result', font=("Helvetica",
           25))],
           [sg.Text("", font=("Helvetica", 50))],
           [sg.Button('True'), sg.Button('False')]]

window01 = sg.Window('Administer questionnaire / questions',
content,size=(1350,350))

control = 0
while True:

    if control > 8:
        break

    # collect response
    event, values = window01.read()
    print(event, values)

    if event in (None, 'Hear'):
        say(question)
```

```

    if event in (None, 'True'):
        answers[control] = 'V'
        control = control + 1

    if event in (None, 'False'):
        answers[control] = 'F'
        control = control + 1

    question = questions[control]
    window01['result'].update(question)

# Close admin window
window01.close()

# Thank you window
# Administration completed / thank you for collaboration
final = [[sg.Text('Test finished.', font=("Helvetica", 30))],
         [sg.Text('Thank you for your collaboration.',
font=("Helvetica", 30))],
         [sg.Text('', font=("Helvetica", 25))],
         [sg.Button('Exit')]]

# Create thank you window
window02 = sg.Window('Administer questionnaire / Test Completed',
final)

# Loop waiting for events
while True:
    event, values = window02.read()
    if event in (None, 'Exit'):
        break

# Close thank you window
window02.close()
```

The program starts as always with the file identification and name data, in lines 1 and 2.

Lines 4 and 5 import the libraries necessary for the program to function, the first for the graphical environment, and the second for the voice synthesis of the questions. In a computerized questionnaire, it is interesting to foresee the possibility of presenting the questions orally for subjects with reading problems.

Lines 7 to 12 define a function that will be necessary to synthesize the voice in the case that the subject, in addition to reading the question, wants to hear it. This option is very interesting for subjects with poor reading ability or vision problems. This option has been on the mind of psychologists from the beginning because some questionnaires were provided on cassette tapes or CDs. What we are now proposing is to fully integrated the capability into the administration program, which is much more comfortable to use. As we have already said when talking about transforming text to voice, if the accent provided by the available libraries does not seem the most appropriate or is not very human, it would be possible to do it in another way: recording each of the questions in an MP3 file, which could be called `item001.mp3`, `item002.mp3`, ..., and opening the file corresponding to the item when the examinee asks to hear the question (Figure 5-4).

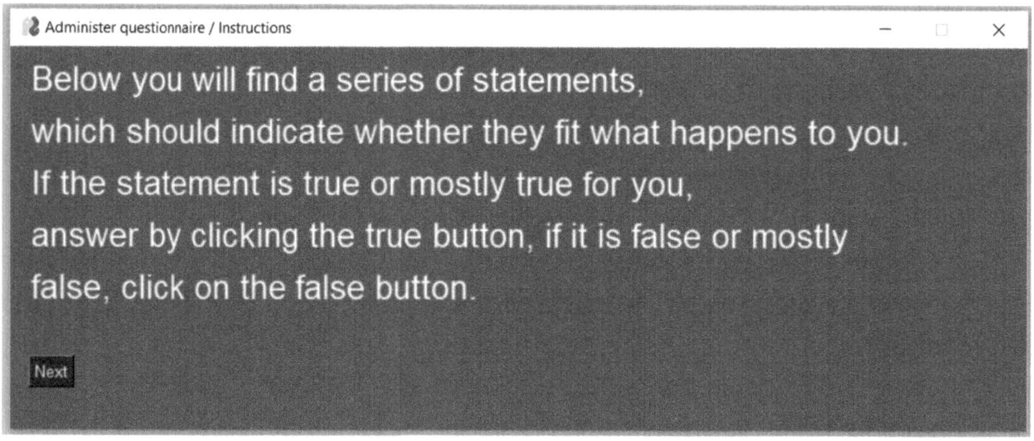

Figure 5-4. *Instructions*

Lines 14 to 20 present the instructions screen and contain the mechanism to start the test. The test will not start until the subject clicks the continue button, so it is up to the subject to decide how long they need to read and understand the instructions. A button could be added to this screen to enable the instructions to be spoken.

Lines 32 to 42 contain the 10-statement questionnaire that we have improvised to present this example. The questions can be as numerous as you like, but they must be organized on a list so that they can be presented one after the other in an orderly fashion.

Line 44 starts a list with answers from 1 to 10. If there were more questions in the questionnaire, this list would be longer, as long as the questionnaire itself.

Line 45 extracts the first question from the questions list to present it on the administration screen, as shown in Figure 5-5.

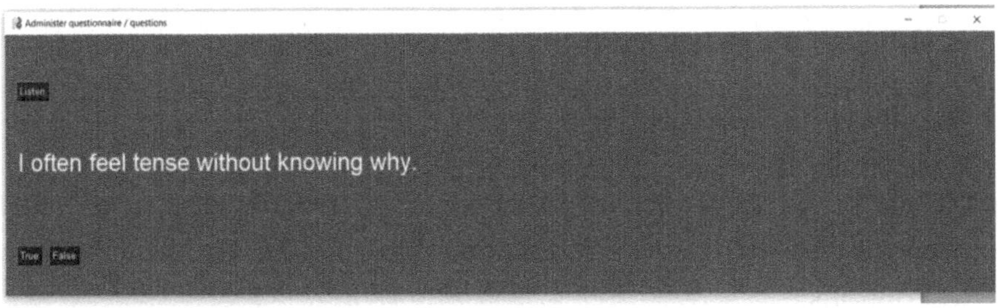

Figure 5-5. *First question*

Putting the number in the question is optional; it is generally not included in computer applications of this type, since it could be distracting.

Lines 47 to 54 contain the layout of the questionnaire administration screen. This layout has materialized thanks to line 56. This line contains the window ID (window01), the title (Manage questionnaire/questions), the screen layout (content), and the screen size (size = 1350, 350). All these parameters can vary in their values to adapt to the needs of the questionnaire. Pay attention to the length of the questions so that the screen is sized to contain them in their entirety, with the font size you have chosen.

Line 58 starts at zero, a control variable that will contain the number of questions being worked on and will allow the administration to end once the last question is reached.

Lines 59 to 80 contain the strategy for moving from one question to another and collecting the answers. This is done using a `while` loop with the `'while True:'` command; this is an infinite loop that we must break with a `break` command when we pass the last question.

Line 83 closes the administration window when it is no longer needed.

The rest of the program presents the thank you and test completed screen, as shown in Figure 5-6, with a button to exit the program.

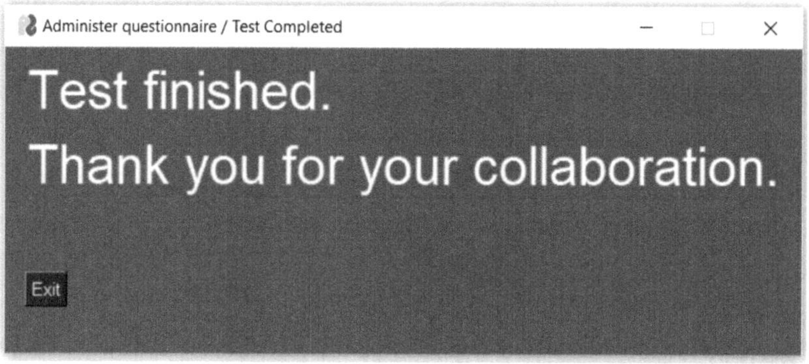

Figure 5-6. *Test completion screen*

If the questionnaire questions had five answers instead of just two, as in this case, in the screen design (lines 49 to 54) we should have (line 54) five buttons labeled with each of the answer options.

Record Answers to a Questionnaire

We may have one or more test sheets, conveniently filled out by a subject, and we want to enter the data into the computer to obtain the results. In this case, we can use an optical mark reader or a desktop scanner, or we can type the answers directly into the computer. The optical reader is expensive and not very feasible for processing only a few cases. Using a desktop scanner is possible; however, programming software that transforms the image obtained into answers is complex. We will therefore opt for the last possibility of typing the answers directly if we have not administered the questionnaire directly by computer.

We have already seen the possibility of working in a text-only console environment and in a graphical environment with the Python turtle library. Let's look at some more options (see Program 5-5).

Program 5-5.

```
# Enter answers
import PySimpleGUI as sg

l1 = sg.Text("Write the answers in blocks of 5, using '1' for",
```

```
key='-OUT-', font=('Arial Bold', 20), expand_x=True,
justification='left')
l2 = sg.Text("true, '2' for false and '3' for absent.", key='-OUT-',
font=('Arial Bold', 20), expand_x=True, justification='left')
l3 = sg.Text("Block 1, items 1 to  5 ", font=('Arial Bold', 15))
l4 = sg.Text("Block 2, items 6 to 10", font=('Arial Bold', 15))
t1 = sg.Input('', key='Input1', font=('Arial Bold', 20),
size=(5,200))
t2 = sg.Input('', key='Input2', font=('Arial Bold', 20),
size=(5,200))
b1 = sg.Button('Ok', key='-OK-', font=('Arial Bold', 20))

layout = [[l1], [l2], [l3, t1], [l4, t2], [b1]]

window = sg.Window('Response input demo', layout, size=(600, 240))

while True:
    event, values = window.read()
    if event == 'Input1':
        window['Input1'].update(values['Input1'][:-1])
        window['Input2'].update(values['Input2'][:-1])
    if event == '-OK-':
        break

block1 = values['Input1']
block2 = values['Input2']
blocks = block1 + block2

answers = ""

for i in range(len(blocks)):
    if blocks[i] == '1':
        answers = answers + 'V'
    elif blocks[i] == '2':
        answers = answers + 'F'
```

```
35        else:
36            answers = answers + '?'
37
38    print(answers)
39
40    window.close()
```

In lines 5 to 11 we define the content of the window, which is specified in line 13 and materialized in line 15. The answers are entered in blocks; the fewer items each block has, the less chance there is of making mistakes. In any case, these can be corrected whenever you want on the same screen before clicking the Ok button (Figure 5-7). You can place as many blocks as you want on the screen, one next to the other or below, and make them of 5, 10, 25, or 50 elements.

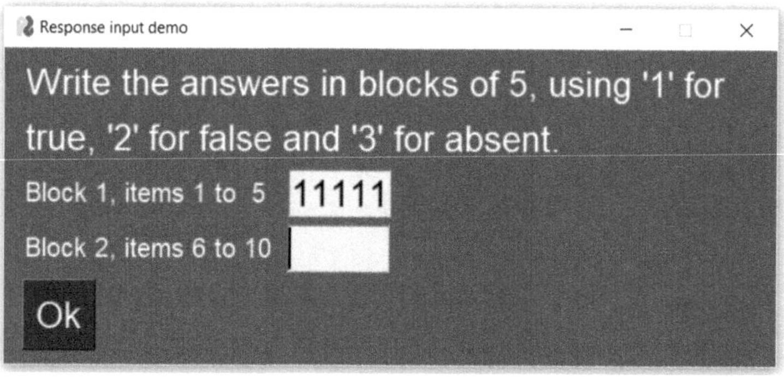

Figure 5-7. *Answers are entered in blocks*

To enter information, contiguous keys are often used. The objective is to obtain a chain of "T" and "F" to process the results, such as the following in the case of our questionnaire:

```
'VVFFVFFVFF'
```

When you click the Ok key, the program will add the blocks into a single variable and transform 1 into V, 2 into F, and 3 or any other key pressed into a missing data, which is specified with a question mark: ?.

This screen, in addition to allowing responses to be entered, could be used to record the subject's identification data: age, sex, etc.

This is not usually the way to enter data for a questionnaire that we use in our programs, but it is a valid, simple, and easy way to program. In our daily professional work, we enter item by item, counting with the backspace key to go back and correct, as shown in Figure 5-8.

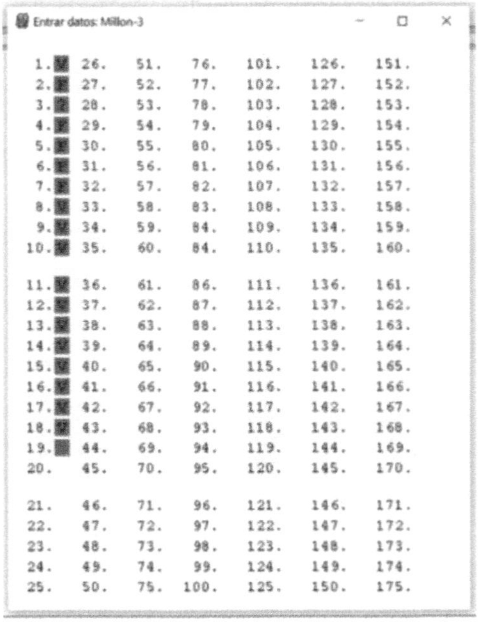

Figure 5-8. *Entering questionnaire data with the Pygame library*

In this case, the Pygame library is used, and all the elements of the screen are drawn when they are needed. There are still other possibilities of programming questionnaire data entries such as the one presented in Figure 5-9 and Figure 5-10, made with the guizero library.

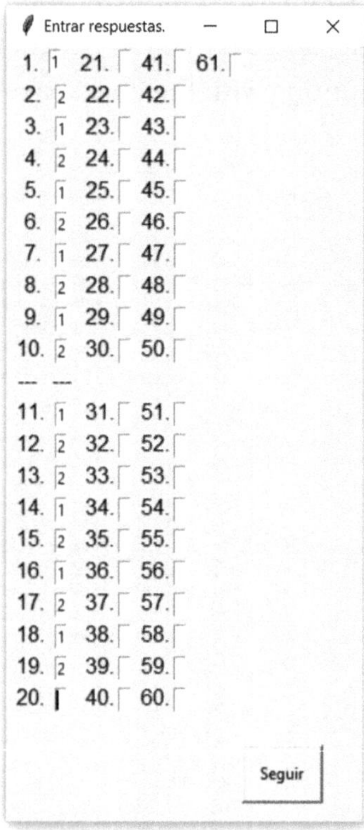

Figure 5-9. Data entry with the guizero library

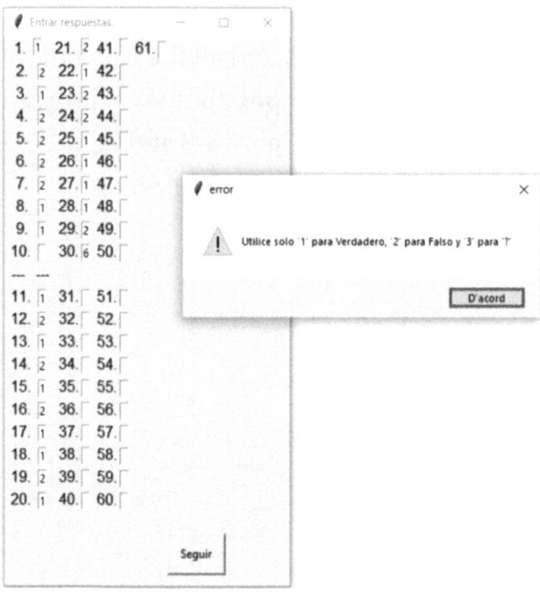

Figure 5-10. Error message when an unacceptable answer is entered

In this case, 61 items are offered, but as many items as fit on the screen can be included. The 1 key is used for true, 2 for false, and 3 when there is no response.

Naturally, the input of each text box must be protected so that it does not allow any other key to be entered other than those mentioned and so that it returns a single character. This also means that by pressing one of the keys mentioned, the text box is filled, and the cursor is placed in the next box to produce a new answer with a single keystroke. In this case, the correction of any possible error is easy since the user can replace the answer that exists in any box with the correct answer.

Should the user press a key other than 1, 2, or 3, in a true/false questionnaire, they will receive a warning and will not be allowed to proceed until they acknowledge the prompt and then enter a valid value.

It is possible to give only two options, removing option '3' which corresponds to the question mark. This is not advisable in a data entry form, because it is possible that someone has left a question blank or with a double answer (true and false) and the examiner has not noticed. It is also possible to allow five answers and one question mark, or any number desired.

Recording responses with Pygame or guizero in these ways is somewhat more complex to program and would contain hundreds of lines of code, so we do not consider it useful to show the program here. You can attempt to program something similar when you have more knowledge of Python, by searching for information about the use of the libraries we have mentioned.

Get Test Results

This section of the program is about correcting the different scales and finding the corresponding typical scores for each of them. We start with a prefilled response variable, in line 4, to test the program; in the final program, this variable would come from the previous section, either from the administration of the test or from the recording of responses from the sheet filled out by the subject.

In line 11, the direct scores of the test scales are initialized to zero. In lines 14 to 16, the scale of invalid scores is corrected, that is, the number of question marks in the response string.

Lines 19 and 20 contain the correction key for the anxiety scale. Lines 22 to 25 check the key for true (T) matches with the subject's answers, adding one point to the scale for each match. The same is done on lines 27 to 29 for false (F) answers.

Lines 33 and 34 contain the scale statistics for calculating typical scores. See Program 5-6.

Program 5-6.

```
1    # Correct questionnaire
2
3    # variable with the answers
4    resQuest = "TTF?FFTFFT"
5
6    # We initialize the direct scores of the questionnaire, as only
7    # we have planned a general anxiety score initialized with
8    # two notes, the first, pdQuest[0] will be the number of answers not
9    # valid and the second the anxiety score.
10
11   pdQuest = [0, 0]
12
13   # we check the number of invalid responses
14   for i in range(len(resQuest)):
15       if resQuest[i] == "?":
16           pdQuest[0] = pdQuest[0] + 1
17
18   # correct the anxiety scale
19   s01T = (1, 2, 4, 6, 7, 8, 9, 10)
20   s01F = (3, 5)
21
22   for i in range(len(s01T)):
23       if resQuest[s01T[i]-1] == "T":
24           pdQuest[1] = pdQuest[1] + 1
25
26   for i in range(len(s01F)):
27       if resQuest[s01F[i]-1] == "F":
28           pdQuest[1] = pdQuest[1] + 1
29
30   # Transform direct score into typical score
31   # Statistical data of the scales
```

```
32  estQuest = [['?', 0.01, 3.51],
33  ['A', 0.50, 2.82]]
34  # initialize typical scores
35  ptQuest = [0, 0]
36
37  for i in range(len(pdQuest)):
38      ptQuest[i] = round(50 + (10 * (pdQuest[i]- estQuest[i][1]) /
    estQuest[i][2]),3)
39
40  print(pdQuest)
41  print(ptQuest)
```

Line 36 resets the typical scale scores to zero. Lines 38 and 39 perform the calculation according to the following formula:

$$T = 50 + \frac{10\left(x_i - M\right)}{sd}$$

This obtains a typical score with a mean of 50 and a standard deviation of 10, where x_i is the subject's score, M is the mean of the contrast group and sd, the standard deviation, of the same group.

The assignment of standard scores could also be done by consulting a grading table. This system is more advisable in current tests that have scales with normalized T scores in which the editor of the test makes the adjustments that suit them, generally without specifying them clearly and without even publishing the statistical data of the scales. If it is not done in this way, significant variations of several points can be found with reference to the editor's data.

Lines 41 and 42 have been added just to check the results.

Running this program, with the default responses on line 4, we get the following results:

```
[1, 6]
[52,821, 69,504]
```

The direct score of the invalid response scale is 1, and the direct score of the anxiety scale is 6. This corresponds to typical scores of 52.821 and 69.504, respectively. These results can be rounded to 53 and 70 in the same program. The results can be presented in a graphical form, as we will see later.

If the questionnaire has more scales, more values will have to be added to `pdQuest` and `ptQuest`, along with more correction keys and more statistical data, enabling their use, through a loop, for all the scales.

Presentation of Results

To provide an example of a report, we will leave aside the questionnaire we have considered so far, which has only one variable and would not allow us to create an adequate graph, and take a questionnaire better known for its graph and interpretation: the original MMPI (Hathaway and McKinley, 1940).

To present the results, a PDF document can be created that, once saved on the hard drive, can be printed or sent by email, depending on the needs. This document can integrate graphics and text so that the results can be presented in the most convenient way. The graphics can be imported from a library or drawn directly on paper. I have chosen the latter option, which, although more laborious, offers cleaner graphics that are adapted to our needs.

To design the PDF file, as always, we will use a library, in our case reportlab. This is imported in the initial lines, lines 4 to 11, along with other libraries necessary for the program to function correctly.

In lines 13 to 16, values for variables such as `nom`, `edat`, `sex`, `resp`, and `ptMMPI` are predetermined, just to test the program; these values, in a definitive program, would be obtained from the sections we have previously explained so that in a definitive program these lines would be eliminated.

Lines 19 and 20 contain the details of the professional responsible for the examination, which will be printed at the beginning of each page of the report.

Lines 23 to 29 capture the system date and format it in the usual way in our country.

Line 32 enters the dimensions of the sheet that we will use in the report, in our case Din A4.

Lines 39 and 40 specify fonts that will be available and that we can use in the script. Line 43 selects a font for the script that follows.

Lines 54 to 181 draw the test graph. This includes drawing the frame and placing the reference labels, printing the subject's typical scores, and drawing the graph line. This is done by determining each scale where it is located on the graph according to its typical score and then drawing the corresponding line between two consecutive scales using the `c.line()` command. For example, on line 130:

```
c.line(60, a, 83, b)
```

where a and b are the heights calculated from two consecutive scales (L and F), 60 and 83 are the values where these scales are located across the graph. These last two values are fixed and different for each of the scales in the graph. See Program 5-7.

Program 5-7.

```
# ProgInformeMMPI001.py / Dr. Roig / 09/13/2023
# Original MMPI graph and interpretation

from datetime import date
from datetime import datetime
import time
from reportlab.lib.pagesizes import A4
from reportlab.pdfgen import canvas
from reportlab.pdfbase import pdfmetrics
from reportlab.pdfbase.pdfmetrics import registerFontFamily
from reportlab.pdfbase.ttfonts import TTFont

nom = "Example Subject"
age = "44"
sex = "M" # M - Male, F - Female
resp = "Dr. Roig"
ptMMPI = [0, 55, 68, 49, 66, 54, 55, 73, 41, 53, 58, 74, 57, 63]

user1 = "Dr. Roig. Clinical Psychology."
user2 = "c/. L'Equador, 21. 2°. 1ª. / 08029 - BARCELONA / 93 451 24
82."

# get system date
ara = datetime.now()
date = '{}/{}/{}'.format(ara.day, ara.month, ara.year)
a = len(date)
date1 = date[:a-4]
date2 = date[a-2:a]
```

```
date = date1 + date2

# dimensions of the full
w, h = A4
c = canvas.Canvas("PsicMMPIreport.pdf", pagesize=A4)

x = 120
y = h - 45

# Registered font family
pdfmetrics.registerFont(TTFont('Vera', 'Vera.ttf'))
pdfmetrics.registerFont(TTFont('Courier', 'courier.ttf'))

# Set font for entire pdf.
c.setFont('Vera', 11)
# -Page 1----------------------------------------
c.drawString(20, h-20, user1)
c.drawString(20, h-35, user2)
c.setFont('Vera', 25)
c.drawString(460, 790, "MMPI")
# Font courier ......................
c.setFont( 'Courier', 12)
c.drawString(30, 770, "Name: ")
c.drawString(90, 770, nom)
c.drawString(350, 770, date)

c.drawString(30, 755, "Age: ")
c.drawString(70, 755, age)
c.drawString(130, 755, "Sex: ")

if sex == 'M':
    c.drawString(170, 755, "Male.")

if sex == 'F':
    c.drawString(170, 755, "Female.")
```

```

# Gràfica ..........................................
#Mark
c.setLineWidth(1.5)
c.rect(50, 440, 330, 250)

# horizontal underline
c.setLineWidth(3)
c.line(53, 438, 383, 438)

# vertical underline
#c.line(383, 693, 383, 448)
c.line(382, 687, 382, 437)
c.setLineWidth(0.5)

c.setFont('Courier', 9)

c.drawString(50, h-415, "LFK 1 2 3 4 5 6 7 8 9 0")
c.drawString(55, 415, str(ptMMPI[1]))
c.drawString(77, 415, str(ptMMPI[2]))
c.drawString(99, 415, str(ptMMPI[3]))

c.drawString(151, 416, str(ptMMPI[4]))
c.drawString(173, 416, str(ptMMPI[5]))
c.drawString(195, 416, str(ptMMPI[6]))
c.drawString(217, 416, str(ptMMPI[7]))
c.drawString(239, 416, str(ptMMPI[8]))
c.drawString(260, 416, str(ptMMPI[9]))
c.drawString(282, 416, str(ptMMPI[10]))
c.drawString(304, 416, str(ptMMPI[11]))
c.drawString(326, 416, str(ptMMPI[12]))
c.drawString(348, 416, str(ptMMPI[13]))

# a l'esquerra value scale
c.drawString(32, h-400, " 0")
c.drawString(32, h-380, "10")
```

```
c.drawString(32, h-360, "20")
c.drawString(32, h-340, "30")
c.drawString(32, h-320, "40")
c.drawString(32, h-300, "50")
c.drawString(32, h-280, "60")
c.drawString(32, h-260, "70")
c.drawString(32, h-240, "80")
c.drawString(32, h-220, "90")
c.drawString(27, h-200, "100")
c.drawString(27, h-180, "110")
c.drawString(27, h-160, "120")

# vertical lines
# separators
c.line(135, 685, 135, 445)

# levels, 50 pt
c.line(54, 545, 380, 545)

# levels, 70 pt
c.line(54, 584, 380, 584)

# draw result lines
c.setLineWidth(3)
# stroke color: 0, 0, 0 = black; 1, 1, 1 = white; 1, 0, 0 = red
c.setStrokeColorRGB(1, 0, 0) # Stroke color

# Valid
# L, F
a = 445 + ptMMPI[1] * 2.01
b = 445 + ptMMPI[2] * 2.01
c.line(60, a, 83, b)

# F, K
a = 445 + ptMMPI[2] * 2.01
```

```
b = 445 + ptMMPI[3] * 2.01
c.line(83, a, 105, b)

# 1 , 2
a = 445 + ptMMPI[4] * 2.01
b = 445 + ptMMPI[5] * 2.01
c.line(156, a, 179, b)


# 23
a = 445 + ptMMPI[5] * 2.01
b = 445 + ptMMPI[6] * 2.01
c.line(179, a, 202, b)

# 3, 4
a = 445 + ptMMPI[6] * 2.01
b = 445 + ptMMPI[7] * 2.01
c.line(202, a, 225, b)

# 4, 5
a = 445 + ptMMPI[7] * 2.01
b = 445 + ptMMPI[8] * 2.01
c.line(225, a, 244, b)

# 5, 6
a = 445 + ptMMPI[8] * 2.01
b = 445 + ptMMPI[9] * 2.01
c.line(244, a, 267, b)

# 6, 7
a = 445 + ptMMPI[9] * 2.01
b = 445 + ptMMPI[10] * 2.01
c.line(267, a, 290, b)

# 7, 8
```

```
a = 445 + ptMMPI[10] * 2.01
b = 445 + ptMMPI[11] * 2.01
c.line(290, a, 311, b)

# 8, 9
a = 445 + ptMMPI[11] * 2.01
b = 445 + ptMMPI[12] * 2.01
c.line(311, a, 334, b)

# 9, 10
a = 445 + ptMMPI[12] * 2.01
b = 445 + ptMMPI[13] * 2.01
c.line(334, a, 354, b)

# page change -Page 2--------------------------------------------
c.showPage()
c.setFont('Vera', 11)
c.drawString(20, h-20, user1)
c.drawString(20, h-35, user2)

# Font courier ......................
c.setFont( 'Courier', 11)

c.drawString(30, h-60, nom)
c.drawString(450, h-60, date)

c.setFont('Courier', 12)
c.drawString(30, 750, "This interpretive report is suitable for professional use only,")
c.drawString(30, 735, "by a qualified psychologist. It has been drawn, automatically,")
c.drawString(30, 720, "taking into account only the test results, so it is")
c.drawString(30, 705, "professional responsibility to integrate these results into the")
```

```
c.drawString(30, 690, "context and circumstances of the person being
examined.")


# Print text report................................
placeLine = 660
c.drawString(30, placeLine, "The most notable features of this
profile are:")
placeLine = placeLine - 15

# L between 45 and 55
if ptMMPI[1] > 44 and ptMMPI[1] < 56:
    c.drawString(30, placeLine, "Tends to give socially accepted
    responses regarding self-control")
    placeLine = placeLine - 15
    c.drawString(30, placeLine, "and moral values.")
    placeLine = placeLine - 15

# F between 60 and 70
if ptMMPI[2] > 59 and ptMMPI[1] < 71:
    c.drawString(30, placeLine, "This profile should be interpreted
    with caution, since the subject")
    placeLine = placeLine - 15
    c.drawString(30, placeLine, "admitsa significant amount of
    experiences, feelings, or symptoms")
    placeLine = placeLine - 15
    c.drawString(30, placeLine, "unusual, which suggests that he may
    have psychiatric problems")
    placeLine = placeLine - 15
    c.drawString(30, placeLine, "important.")
    placeLine = placeLine - 15

# K
```

```
# Hs between 60 and 70
if ptMMPI[4] > 59 and ptMMPI[4] < 71:
    c.drawString(30, placeLine, "He reports a slightly higher than average number of physical complaints,")
    placeLine = placeLine - 15
    c.drawString(30, placeLine, "which reflects a certain concern for bodily functions and the")
    placeLine = placeLine - 15
    c.drawString(30, placeLine, "general health.")
    placeLine = placeLine - 15

# D between 45 and 55
if ptMMPI[5] > 44 and ptMMPI[5] < 56:
    c.drawString(30, placeLine, "He sees life with a mix of optimism and pessimism.")
    placeLine = placeLine - 15

# Hy between 45 and 55
if ptMMPI[6] > 44 and ptMMPI[6] < 56:
    pass

# Pd between 70 and 79
if ptMMPI[7] > 69 and ptMMPI[7] < 80:
    c.drawString(30, placeLine, "Somewhat rebellious and nonconformist. Avoids close personal ties and")
    placeLine = placeLine - 15
    c.drawString(30, placeLine, "He is probably very dissatisfied with his family and social life.")
    placeLine = placeLine - 15

# Mf under 45 - male
if ptMMPI[8] < 45 and sex == "M":
    c.drawString(30, placeLine, "Places a heavy emphasis on male interests.")
    placeLine = placeLine - 15
```

```

# Pa between 45 and 55
if ptMMPI[9] > 44 and ptMMPI[9] < 56:
    c.drawString(30, placeLine, "Respect the opinions of others
without excessive sensitivity.")
    placeLine = placeLine - 15

# Pt between 56 and 65
if ptMMPI[10] > 55 and ptMMPI[10] < 66:
    c.drawString(30, placeLine, "He is conscientious, orderly, and
self-critical.")
    placeLine = placeLine - 15

# Sc between 70 and 70
if ptMMPI[11] > 69 and ptMMPI[11] < 80:
    c.drawString(30, placeLine, "Probably somewhat eccentric,
solitary and withdrawn. He suffers from")
    placeLine = placeLine - 15
    c.drawString(30, placeLine, "many internal conflicts.")
    placeLine = placeLine - 15

# Between 56 and 65
if ptMMPI[12] > 55 and ptMMPI[12] < 66:
    c.drawString(30, placeLine, "Rather energetic and enthusiastic,
he cultivates a wide variety of.")
    placeLine = placeLine - 15
    c.drawString(30, placeLine, "interests.")
    placeLine = placeLine - 15




# If between 56 and 65
if ptMMPI[13] > 55 and ptMMPI[13] < 66:
    c.drawString(30, placeLine, "He remains reserved in situations
and environments that are not")
```

```
291         placeLine = placeLine - 15
292         c.drawString(30, placeLine, "appropriate for him.")
293         placeLine = placeLine - 15
204
295     c.showPage()
        c.save()
```

Preparation of the Written Report

Lines 183 to 187 change pages, select the font type and size for the new page, and write the identification data of the professional responsible for the report in the header of the page. Lines 189 to 201 print the fixed text of the document that reports on how the texts written have been generated and the precautions to be taken when using the content of the report. It should be noted that the wording of the report refers to standard interpretations of the test and does not consider the subject's situation. In addition, it is also possible that the test does not correctly assess some of the features considered in the case of the subject of the report, either due to under- or over-assessment.

From line 203 onward, the textual report is written from texts that are chosen based on the values reached by the variables or scales being considered. These conditions can be simple or complex; that is, they can consider the score of a single scale or several of them. Here we have given as an example only some paragraphs from an old program of ours for interpreting the original MMPI (Seisdedos and Roig-Fusté, 1986). The paragraphs used contain only simple conditions, but complex conditions can be included that involve the scores of several scales. Decision trees as extensive and complex as desired can reach a given textual conclusion.

Note that the text is written in lines of suitable width and that each line, when printed, decreases the variable `situarLinea` to a value of 15. By modifying this value, the written lines can be brought closer or closer together. If this were not done, the entire content of the report would be written on the same line and would not be readable.

Lines 289 and 290 close the report and save it.

The report obtained by running this program is saved in a PDF file at the end of the program, with the name given to the canvas on which to work (line 33), in our case `informePsicMMPI.pdf`. This name could include the name of the subject to avoid overwriting each report with the next report; in this case, the name on line 33 would have to be replaced by a variable that would be the sum of the report name and the subject name. Figures 5-11 and 5-12 shown an example of the output, with a graph drawn by the computer and a textual explanation for the results of the specific subject.

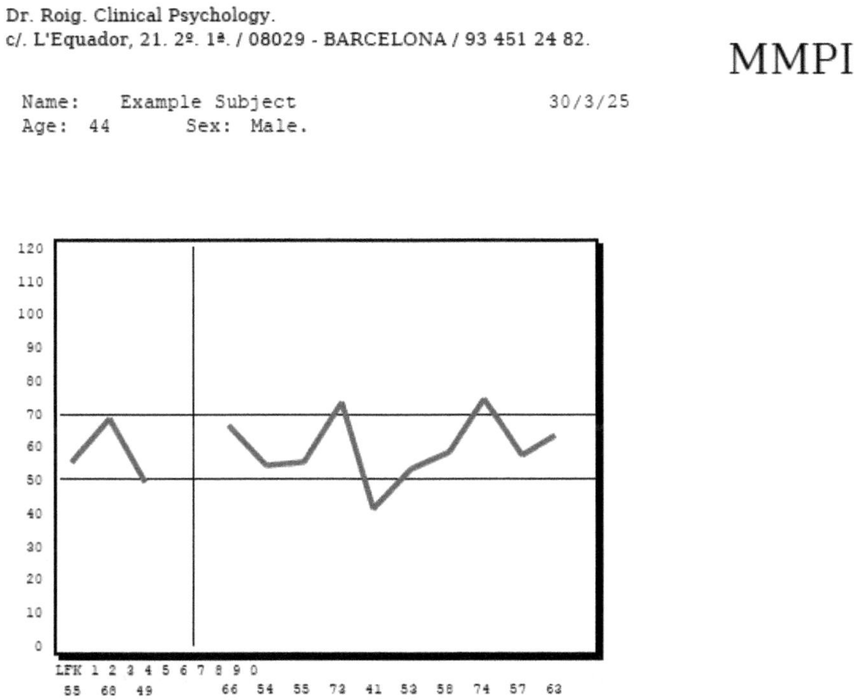

***Figure 5-11.** Graph drawn by the computer*

Dr. Roig. Clinical Psychology.
c/. L'Equador, 21. 2º. 1ª. / 08029 - BARCELONA / 93 451 24 82.

```
Example Subject                                                30/3/25

This interpretive report is suitable for professional use only,
by a qualified psychologist. It has been drawn, automatically,
taking into account only the test results, so it is
professional responsibility to integrate these results into the
context and circumstances of the person being examined.

The most notable features of this profile are:
Tends to give socially accepted responses regarding self-control
and moral values.
This profile should be interpreted with caution, since the subject
admitsa significant amount of experiences, feelings, or symptoms
unusual, which suggests that he may have psychiatric problems
important.
He reports a slightly higher than average number of physical complaints,
which reflects a certain concern for bodily functions and the
general health.
He sees life with a mix of optimism and pessimism.
Somewhat rebellious and nonconformist. Avoids close personal ties and
He is probably very dissatisfied with his family and social life.
Places a heavy emphasis on male interests.
Respect the opinions of others without excessive sensitivity.
He is conscientious, orderly, and self-critical.
Probably somewhat eccentric, solitary and withdrawn. He suffers from
many internal conflicts.
Rather energetic and enthusiastic, he cultivates a wide variety of.
interests.
He remains reserved in situations and environments that are not
appropriate for him.
```

Figure 5-12. *Textual explanation*

More information about the preparation and use of computerized reports can be found in Lachar (1973), Bucher (1987) and Roig-Fusté (2020).

A Card Sorting Test

In this section we will see the possibilities of Python in a card sorting test like the Wisconsin Card Sorting Test (Grant and Berg),[1] inspired by previous studies of sorting tasks by Gelb and Goldstein, carried out in the 1940s on brain-injured patients. There have been multiple adaptations of the Wisconsin test and many computerized versions; many of them can be found on the Internet. It is a difficult test to administer manually due to the vague instructions provided, which are necessary to assess the subject's

[1] Grant, DA, Berg, EA (No date). The Wisconsin Card Scoring Test (Sic). Directions for administration and scoring. Department of Psychology. University of Wisconsin.

adaptive capacity since these can generate questions and complaints from the subject being examined. The evaluation of perseverative responses is also confusing and ambiguous (Axelrod, Greve, & Goldman, 1994; Berry, 1996; Flashman, Mandir, Horner, & Freides, 1991; Howlett & Moseley, 2024). In the many versions I have seen on the Internet, most likely designed by programmers who have no knowledge of psychology, much less neuropsychology, and who lack a deep understanding of the test, most of the instructions are wrong, which drastically modifies the difficulty of the test and generally makes it useless for assessing the subject's adaptive capacity. For our version, we have considered some of the modifications proposed by Teuber, Battersby, and Bender (1951), although we have followed the guidelines of the original authors regarding the number of stimuli, the order in which they are presented, the correction rules, and the criteria for ending or interrupting the test.

To administer the test, it is necessary to have 64 drawings in BMP file format, which contain stimuli of four different colors (red, blue, green, and yellow), four different shapes (triangle, star, cross, and circle), and four elements that are numbered from 1 to 4. These drawings can be found on the Internet or can be easily drawn with any drawing program such as Gimp or Inkscape. To use our program, it is essential that the cards have the name specified in the `cards` matrix on line 112 of the program so that it can load and use them as well as correctly correct the test. The name contains two letters and a number. The first letter indicates the shape of the figures on the card: T for triangle, E for star, Z for cross, and C for circle. The second letter indicates the colors: R for red, V for green, m for yellow, and A for blue. Finally, the number indicates the number of elements that the card contains.

Figure 5-13 presents the instructions.

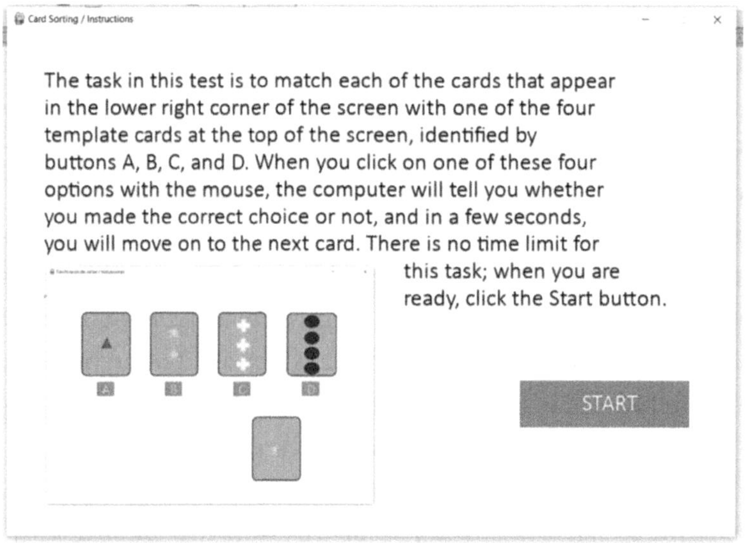

***Figure 5-13.** Instructions*

Once the test has started, the subject click the button located under a card. When the answer is correct, the program indicates it with a green message (Figure 5-14).

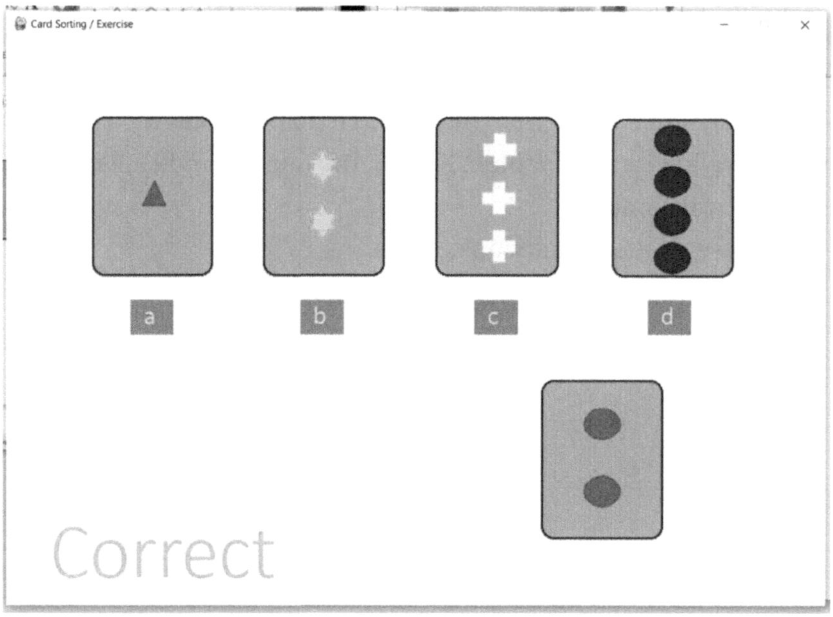

***Figure 5-14.** Correct answer*

When it is not correct, a red message appears (Figure 5-15).

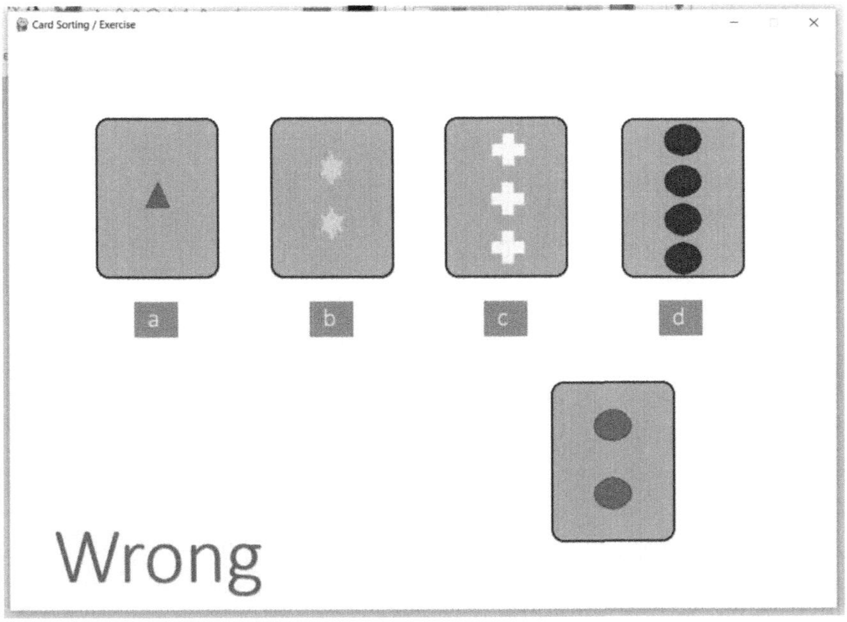

Figure 5-15. *Wrong answer*

At the end of the test, the program displays the screen shown in Figure 5-16.

Figure 5-16. *The test has ended*

For the sake of brevity, we include only the administration of the test in Program 5-8. The results of the test can be seen in the report example on the following pages; we have seen this type of management in the previous program `ProgInformeMMPI001.py`.

Program 5-8.

```
# TCCW v 0.2.5/ TCCW025.py
# Dr. Josep M. Roig / 02.02.25


import sys
import pygame
import time
import sqlite3
from datetime import date
from datetime import datetime
from reportlab.lib.pagesizes import A4
from reportlab.pdfgen import canvas
from reportlab.pdfbase import pdfmetrics
from reportlab.pdfbase.pdfmetrics import registerFontFamily
from reportlab.pdfbase.ttfonts import TTFont
from reportlab.pdfbase.pdfmetrics import registerFontFamily

from reportlab.pdfbase.ttfonts import TTFont
pdfmetrics.registerFont(TTFont('Vera', 'Vera.ttf'))
pdfmetrics.registerFont(TTFont('VeraBd', 'VeraBd.ttf'))
pdfmetrics.registerFont(TTFont('VeraIt', 'VeraIt.ttf'))
pdfmetrics.registerFont(TTFont('VeraBI', 'VeraBI.ttf'))

# captar la data del sistema
ara = datetime.now()
data = '{}/{}/{}'.format(ara.day, ara.month, ara.year)
a = len(data)
data1 = data[:a-4]
data2 = data[a-2:a]
data = data1 + data2
```

```

usuario1 = "Dr. Roig. Psicología Clínica."
usuario2 = "c/. L'Equador, 21. 2º. 1ª. / 08029 - BARCELONA / 93 451 24 82."

# iniciar variables de mostra ####### -BORRAR- ###############################
nom = 'Example Subject'
edat = '53'
sex = 'M' # M - Masculino, F - Femenino
formacio ='2'
res = 'Dr. Roig' # Responsable / contrato, identificar desde el programe i
impedir que es modifiqui
diagnostic = ""
obs = '' # observacions, max 500 caracters
id = 936
#####################################################################

pygame.init()
# Define colors
WHITE = (255, 255, 255)
RED = (255, 0, 0)


# Pantalla d'instruccions -------------------------------------------
screen = pygame.display.set_mode((950, 650))
pygame.display.set_caption('Card Sorting / Instructions')
textFont = pygame.font.SysFont("Calibri", 30)


running = True
while running:
    screen.fill((255,255,255))
```

```
    text = textFont.render("The task in this test is to match each of
    the cards
that appear", True, (0, 0, 0))
    screen.blit(text,(50,50))

    text = textFont.render("in the lower right corner of the screen
    with one of
the four", True, (0, 0, 0))
    screen.blit(text,(50, 85))

    text = textFont.render("template cards at the top of the screen,
    identified
by ", True, (0, 0, 0))
    screen.blit(text,(50, 120))

    text = textFont.render("buttons A, B, C, and D. When you click
    on one of
these four ", True, (0, 0, 0))
    screen.blit(text,(50, 155))

    text = textFont.render("options with the mouse, the computer will
    tell you
whether", True, (0, 0, 0))
    screen.blit(text,(50, 190))

    text = textFont.render("you made the correct choice or not, and
    in a few
seconds,", True, (0, 0, 0))
    screen.blit(text,(50, 225))

    text = textFont.render("you will move on to the next card. There
    is no time
limit for", True, (0, 0, 0))
    screen.blit(text,(50, 260))

```

```
    text = textFont.render("this task; when you are", True,
     (0, 0, 0))
    screen.blit(text,(520, 295))

    text = textFont.render("ready, click the Start button.", True,
    (0, 0, 0))
    screen.blit(text,(520, 330))

    player_image = pygame.image.load('C:\\Clac\\Cartas\\' +
    'pantallaEx.bmp')
    screen.blit(player_image, (50, 300))

    rectangle = pygame.draw.rect(screen, (70, 180, 20),
    (670,450,220,60), 0)
    text = textFont.render("START", True, (255, 255, 255))
    screen.blit(text,(750,465))
    pygame.display.flip()

    for event in pygame.event.get():
        if event.type == pygame.QUIT: sys.exit()

        if event.type == pygame.MOUSEBUTTONDOWN:
            #if pygame.mouse.get_pressed()[0]: # Left click
            x, y = pygame.mouse.get_pos() # Get click position

            if rectangle.collidepoint(x, y):
                running = False


# Exercici -----------------------------------------------------
---------
screen = pygame.display.set_mode((950, 650))
pygame.display.set_caption('Card Sorting / Exercise')
# Fill the screen with a color
screen.fill(WHITE)
```

```
pygame.display.flip()

Cartas = ["bln.BMP", "CR2.BMP", "Em1.BMP", "ZV4.BMP", "TA2.BMP",
          "CR3.BMP", "EA1.BMP", "TV3.BMP", "ZA2.BMP", "ER1.BMP",
          "Cm2.BMP", "TA1.BMP", "ZR4.BMP", "EV3.BMP", "CA4.BMP",
          "Tm3.BMP", "ZA1.BMP", "ER2.BMP", "Tm4.BMP", "ZV1.BMP",
          "CA2.BMP", "ZR3.BMP", "TV2.BMP", "EA4.BMP", "ZR2.BMP",
          "CV4.BMP", "ER3.BMP", "TV1.BMP", "Zm3.BMP", "ER4.BMP",
          "CA3.BMP", "TR4.BMP", "CV2.BMP", "EA3.BMP", "TR2.BMP",
          "Cm3.BMP", "TA4.BMP", "CV1.BMP", "Em3.BMP", "CV2.BMP",
          "Tm1.BMP", "ZA4.BMP", "CV3.BMP", "EA2.BMP", "Zm4.BMP",
          "CR1.BMP", "TA3.BMP", "EV4.BMP", "Zm1.BMP", "CR4.BMP",
          "Tm2.BMP", "CR1.BMP", "Em4.BMP", "TR3.BMP", "EV2.BMP",
          "Cm1.BMP", "ZA3.BMP", "TV4.BMP", "Em2.BMP", "CA1.BMP",
          "ZV3.BMP", "Cm4.BMP", "TR1.BMP", "Zm2.BMP", "EV1.BMP",
          "CR2.BMP", "Em1.BMP", "ZV4.BMP", "TA2.BMP", "CR3.BMP", # ---------
          "EA1.BMP", "TV3.BMP", "ZA2.BMP", "ER1.BMP", "Cm2.BMP",
          "TA1.BMP", "ZR4.BMP", "EV3.BMP", "CA4.BMP", "Tm3.BMP",
          "ZA1.BMP", "ER2.BMP", "Tm4.BMP", "ZV1.BMP", "CA2.BMP",
          "ZR3.BMP", "TV2.BMP", "EA4.BMP", "ZR2.BMP", "CV4.BMP",
          "ER3.BMP", "TV1.BMP", "Zm3.BMP", "ER4.BMP", "CA3.BMP",
          "TR4.BMP", "CV2.BMP", "EA3.BMP", "TR2.BMP", "Cm3.BMP",
          "TA4.BMP", "CV1.BMP", "Em3.BMP", "CV2.BMP", "Tm1.BMP",
          "ZA4.BMP", "CV3.BMP", "EA2.BMP", "Zm4.BMP", "CR1.BMP",
          "TA3.BMP", "EV4.BMP", "Zm1.BMP", "CR4.BMP", "Tm2.BMP",
          "CR1.BMP", "Em4.BMP", "TR3.BMP", "EV2.BMP", "Cm1.BMP",
          "ZA3.BMP", "TV4.BMP", "Em2.BMP", "CA1.BMP", "ZV3.BMP",
          "Cm4.BMP", "TR1.BMP", "Zm2.BMP", "EV1.BMP", "EV1.BMP"]


#resp = [] # Respostes
resp = [  '0-',  ' 1-',  ' 2-',  ' 3-',  ' 4-',  ' 5-',  ' 6-',  ' 7-',  ' 8-',
' 9-',
```

```
            '10-', '11-', '12-', '13-', '14-', '15-', '16-', '17-', '18-', '19-',
            '20-', '21-', '22-', '23-', '24-', '25-', '26-', '27-', '28-', '29-',
            '30-', '31-', '32-', '33-', '34-', '35-', '36-', '37-', '38-', '39-',
            '40-', '41-', '42-', '43-', '44-', '45-', '46-', '47-', '48-', '49-',
            '50-', '51-', '52-', '53-', '54-', '55-', '56-', '57-', '58-', '59-',
            '60-', '61-', '62-', '63-', '64-', '65-', '66-', '67-', '68-', '69-',
            '70-', '71-', '72-', '73-', '74-', '75-', '76-', '77-', '78-', '79-',
            '80-', '81-', '82-', '83-', '84-', '85-', '86-', '87-', '88-', '89-',
            '90-', '91-', '92-', '93-', '94-', '95-', '96-', '97-', '98-', '99-',
           '100-','101-','102-','103-','104-','105-','106-','107-','108-','109-',
           '110-','111-','112-','113-','114-','115-','116-','117-','118-','119-',
           '120-','121-','122-','123-','124-','125-','126-','127-','128-','129-']

score = [[ 0, 0, 0, 0, 0, 0, 0], # errors
         [ 0, 0, 0, 0, 0, 0, 0], # successes
         [ 0, 0, 0, 0, 0, 0, 0], # perseverative errors
         [ 0, 0, 0, 0, 0, 0, 0], # non-perseverative errors
         [ 0, 0, 0, 0, 0, 0, 0]] # unique


columna = 0 # value of the column where the values of the score
          matrix will be
recorded

TIEMPO_RETARDO = 2
cat = ['C', 'F', 'N', 'C', 'F', 'N', 'X'] # Categories
itemsCambio = []
iConsecut = 10 # Consecutive correct answers (in the standard test
            there are 10)
<....................
numeroCategoria = 1
numCat = 0 # completed categories
categoriaActual = cat[numCat] # Current category
categoriaAnterior = "X"
aciertosConsecutivos = 0
```

```
errores = 0
erroresPersevera = 0
valoracio = ''
puntua = ''
I = 1 # number of the card presented
NumCartaMax = 0 # number of the last letter presented
correct = False


running = True
while running:
    textFont = pygame.font.SysFont("Calibri", 30)
    # comprobar condiciones de interrupción -------------

    if I > 63 and numCat == 0: # 63 y cat 0
        running = False

    if I > 127 or numCat > 5: #128 o cat > 6
        running = False


    # present stimulus screen -------------------
    screen.fill((255,255,255))

    player_image01 = pygame.image.load('C:\\Clac\\Cartas\\' + 'TR1.BMP')
    screen.blit(player_image01, (100, 90))

    player_image02 = pygame.image.load('C:\\Clac\\Cartas\\' + 'EV2.BMP')
    screen.blit(player_image02, (300, 90))

    player_image03 = pygame.image.load('C:\\Clac\\Cartas\\' + 'Zm3.BMP')
    screen.blit(player_image03, (500, 90))

    player_image04 = pygame.image.load('C:\\Clac\\Cartas\\' + 'CA4.BMP')
    screen.blit(player_image04, (700, 90))
```

```

        # Draw buttons
        labelA = pygame.draw.rect(screen, (70, 180, 20), (145,300,50,40), 0)
        textA = textFont.render("a", True, (255, 255, 0))
        screen.blit(textA,(160,305))
        labelB = pygame.draw.rect(screen, (70, 180, 20), (345,300,50,40), 0)
        textB = textFont.render("b", True, (255, 255, 0))
        screen.blit(textB,(360,305))
        labelC = pygame.draw.rect(screen, (70, 180, 20), (545,300,50,40), 0)
        textC = textFont.render("c", True, (255, 255, 0))
        screen.blit(textC,(560,305))
        labelD = pygame.draw.rect(screen, (70, 180, 20), (745,300,50,40), 0)
        textD = textFont.render("d", True, (255, 255, 0))
        screen.blit(textD,(760,305))

        # Present stimulus card ················
        Carta = 'C:\\Clac\\Cartas\\' + Cartas[I]
        player_image00 = pygame.image.load(Carta)
        screen.blit(player_image00, (620, 390))

        pygame.display.flip()

        # Collect response ······················
        pulsado = ''
        EsperaResposta = True
        while EsperaResposta:
            for event in pygame.event.get():
                if event.type == pygame.QUIT: # Sortir
                    pygame.quit()
                    sys.exit()


                if event.type == pygame.MOUSEBUTTONDOWN:
                    x, y = pygame.mouse.get_pos() # Get click position

```

```
                if labelA.collidepoint(x, y): # Answer A
    ............................
                    pulsado = 'A'

                    # Score and evaluate response
                    valoracio = valoracio + str(I) +", a- "
                    aux = 'R' in Cartas[I]
                    if aux == True:
                        puntua = puntua + 'C'
                        aux = False
                    aux = 'T' in Cartas[I]
                    if aux == True:
                        puntua = puntua + 'F'
                        aux = False
                    aux = '1' in Cartas[I]
                    if aux == True:
                        puntua = puntua + 'N'
                        aux = False

                    if categoriaActual in puntua:
                        correct = True
                        puntua = puntua + ', 1'
                    else:
                        puntua = puntua + ', 0'

                    valoracio = valoracio + puntua
                    resp[I] = valoracio

                    # Count consecutive hits
                    if correct == True:
                        aciertosConsecutivos = aciertosConsecutivos + 1
                        score[1][numCat] = score[1][numCat] + 1  # acumulación de aciertos
```

```

            # Inform the subject of the result
            textFont = pygame.font.SysFont("Calibri", 90)
            text = textFont.render("Correct", True, (52,
                235, 204))
            screen.blit(text,(50,550))
            pygame.display.flip()
            time.sleep(TIEMPO_RETARDO)
          else:
            # If the answer is not correct, the
            consecutive correct
answers are set to zero,
            # an error is noted and it is assessed
            whether the error
is perseverative or unique.
            aciertosConsecutivos = 0
            score[0][numCat] = score[0][numCat] + 1  #
            Total error
accumulation

            # Check if it is a perseverative error  -----
            -----------
------
            print('Categoria anterior y carta: ',
            categoriaAnterior,
resp[I])
            if categoriaAnterior in resp[I]:
                score[2][numCat] = score[2][numCat] + 1
            else:
                score[3][numCat] = score[3][numCat] + 1

            # Check if it is a unic error
            if 'C' in resp[I] or 'F' in resp[I] or 'N' in
resp[I]:
                pass
```

```
                    else:
                        score[4][numCat] = score[4][numCat] + 1

                    # Inform the subject of the error ---
                    textFont = pygame.font.SysFont("Calibri", 90)
                    text = textFont.render("Wrong", True, (247, 7, 35))
                    screen.blit(text,(50,550))
                    pygame.display.flip()
                    time.sleep(TIEMPO_RETARDO)

                if aciertosConsecutivos == iConsecut:
                    # Save the previous category before moving to the next one
                    categoriaAnterior = cat[numCat]
                    itemsCambio.append(I)
                    numCat = numCat + 1
                    categoriaActual = cat[numCat]
                    aciertosConsecutivos = 0

                valoracio =''
                puntua = ''
                I = I + 1

                EsperaResposta = False
                correct = False

            if labelB.collidepoint(x, y): # B..............................
                pulsado = 'B'

                # record and evaluate the response
                valoracio = valoracio + str(I) +", b- "
                aux = 'V' in Cartas[I]
                if aux == True:
```

```
            puntua = puntua + 'C'
            aux = False
        aux = 'E' in Cartas[I]
        if aux == True:
            puntua = puntua + 'F'
            aux = False
        aux = '2' in Cartas[I]
        if aux == True:
            puntua = puntua + 'N'
            aux = False

        if categoriaActual in puntua:
            correct = True
            puntua = puntua + ', 1'
        else:
            puntua = puntua + ', 0'

        valoracio = valoracio + puntua
        resp[I] = valoracio

        if correct == True:
            aciertosConsecutivos = aciertosConsecutivos + 1
            score[1][numCat] = score[1][numCat] + 1
            textFont = pygame.font.SysFont("Calibri", 90)
            text = textFont.render("Correct", True, (52,
                    235, 204))
            screen.blit(text,(50, 550))
            pygame.display.flip()
            time.sleep(TIEMPO_RETARDO)
        else:
            aciertosConsecutivos = 0
            score[0][numCat] = score[0][numCat] + 1
            errores = errores + 1

            # Is it a perseverative response?
```

```
                if categoriaAnterior in resp[I]:
                    score[2][numCat] = score[2][numCat] + 1
                else:
                    score[3][numCat] = score[3][numCat] + 1

                # Is it unique?
                if 'C' in resp[I] or 'F' in resp[I] or 'N' in resp[I]:
                    pass
                else:
                    score[4][numCat] = score[4][numCat] + 1

                # Inform the subject ---
                textFont = pygame.font.SysFont("Calibri", 90)
                text = textFont.render("Wrong", True,
                       (247, 7, 35))
                screen.blit(text,(50,550))
                pygame.display.flip()
                time.sleep(TIEMPO_RETARDO)

            if aciertosConsecutivos == iConsecut:
                categoriaAnterior = cat[numCat]
                itemsCambio.append(I)
                numCat = numCat + 1
                categoriaActual = cat[numCat]
                aciertosConsecutivos = 0

            valoracio =''
            puntua = ''
            I = I + 1
            EsperaResposta = False
            correct = False


        if labelC.collidepoint(x, y):# C ............................
```

```
pulsado = 'C'

valoracio = valoracio + str(I) +", c- "
aux = 'm' in Cartas[I]
if aux == True:
    puntua = puntua + 'C'
    aux = False
aux = 'Z' in Cartas[I]
if aux == True:
    puntua = puntua + 'F'
    aux = False
aux = '3' in Cartas[I]
if aux == True:
    puntua = puntua + 'N'
    aux = False

if categoriaActual in puntua:
    correct = True
    puntua = puntua + ', 1'
else:
    puntua = puntua + ', 0'

valoracio = valoracio + puntua
resp[I] = valoracio

if correct == True:
    aciertosConsecutivos = aciertosConsecutivos + 1
    score[1][numCat] = score[1][numCat] + 1
    textFont = pygame.font.SysFont("Calibri", 90)
    text = textFont.render("Correct", True, (52,
          235, 204))
    screen.blit(text,(50,550))
    pygame.display.flip()
    time.sleep(TIEMPO_RETARDO)
else:
```

```
                errores = errores + 1
                score[0][numCat] = score[0][numCat] + 1
                aciertosConsecutivos = 0

                # Is it perseverative?
                print('Categoria anterior y carta: ', categoriaAnterior,
    resp[I])
                if categoriaAnterior in resp[I]:
                    score[2][numCat] = score[2][numCat] + 1
                else:
                    score[3][numCat] = score[3][numCat] + 1

                # Is it unique?
                if 'C' in resp[I] or 'F' in resp[I] or 'N' in resp[I]:
                    pass
                else:
                    score[4][numCat] = score[4][numCat] + 1

                # inform the subject ---
                textFont = pygame.font.SysFont("Calibri", 90)
                text = textFont.render("Wrong", True, (247, 7, 35))
                screen.blit(text,(50,550))
                pygame.display.flip()
                time.sleep(TIEMPO_RETARDO)

            if aciertosConsecutivos == iConsecut:
                categoriaAnterior = cat[numCat]
                itemsCambio.append(I)
                numCat = numCat + 1
                categoriaActual = cat[numCat]
                aciertosConsecutivos = 0
            valoracio =''
```

```
                puntua = ''
                I = I + 1

                EsperaResposta = False
                correct = False


            if labelD.collidepoint(x, y): # D

                pulsado = 'D'
                # score and evaluate response
                valoracio = valoracio + str(I) +", d- "
                aux = 'A' in Cartas[I]
                if aux == True:
                    puntua = puntua + 'C'
                    aux = False
                aux = 'C' in Cartas[I]
                if aux == True:
                    puntua = puntua + 'F'
                    aux = False
                aux = '4' in Cartas[I]
                if aux == True:
                    puntua = puntua + 'N'
                    aux = False

                if categoriaActual in puntua:
                    correct = True
                    puntua = puntua + ', 1'
                else:
                    puntua = puntua + ', 0'

                valoracio = valoracio + puntua
                resp[I] = valoracio

                if correct == True:
```

```
    aciertosConsecutivos = aciertosConsecutivos + 1
    score[1][numCat] = score[1][numCat] + 1
    textFont = pygame.font.SysFont("Calibri", 90)
    text = textFont.render("Correct", True, (52, 235, 204))
    screen.blit(text,(50,550))
    pygame.display.flip()
    time.sleep(TIEMPO_RETARDO)
else:
    errores = errores + 1
    score[0][numCat] = score[0][numCat] + 1
    aciertosConsecutivos = 0

    # Is it perseverative?
    print('Categoria anterior y carta: ', categoriaAnterior,
resp[I])
    if categoriaAnterior in resp[I]:
        score[2][numCat] = score[2][numCat] + 1
    else:
        score[3][numCat] = score[3][numCat] + 1

    # Is it unique?
    if 'C' in resp[I] or 'F' in resp[I] or 'N' in resp[I]:
        pass
    else:
        score[4][numCat] = score[4][numCat] + 1

    print('Resp. id ', resp[I], 'Punt. perseveratiu',
score[2][numCat])

    # inform the subject ---
    textFont = pygame.font.SysFont("Calibri", 90)
```

```
                        text = textFont.render("Wrong", True, (247, 7, 35))
                        screen.blit(text,(50,550))
                        pygame.display.flip()
                        time.sleep(TIEMPO_RETARDO)


                    if aciertosConsecutivos == iConsecut:
                        categoriaAnterior = cat[numCat]
                        itemsCambio.append(I)
                        numCat = numCat + 1
                        categoriaActual = cat[numCat]
                        aciertosConsecutivos = 0

                    valoracio =''
                    puntua = ''
                    I = I + 1

                    EsperaResposta = False
                    correct = False

#    if numCat == 6: # cuando numCat alcanza el valor 6 se interrumpe la prueba
#        running = False



NumCartaMax = I # total number of stimuli presented

# anular el primer error perseverativo y pasarlo a error no perseverativo
for ii in range(1, 6):
    print('correcio perseveratiu', ii, score[2][ii])
    if score[2][ii] > 0:
        score[2][ii] = score[2][ii] - 1
```

```
            score[3][ii] = score[3][ii] + 1


# Save results to a file --------------------------------
with open('DatgCC.dat', 'a') as f:
    #   resultat = [nom, edat, sex, formació, data, resp, diagnostic, observacions]
    f.write(nom)
    f.write("\n")
    f.write(edat)
    f.write("\n")
    f.write(sex)
    f.write("\n")
    f.write(data)
    f.write("\n")
    f.write(res)
    f.write("\n")
    f.write(diagnostic)
    f.write("\n")


    for i in range(1, 129):
        f.write(resp[i])
        f.write("\n")

    f.write("Categorias completadas: ")
    f.write(str(numCat))
    f.write("\n")
    f.write("Errores: ")
    f.write(str(errores))
    f.write("\n")
    f.write("Errores perseverativos: ")
    f.write(str(erroresPersevera))
    f.write("\n")
    f.write("% Errores perseverativos: ")
```

```
    f.write("\n")
    f.write("Índice función ejecutiva: ")
    f.write("\n")

    f.write("-----------------------------------------------------")
    f.write("\n")



# Final thanks screen ----------------------------
screen = pygame.display.set_mode((1000, 650))
pygame.display.set_caption('Card sorting / Test completed.')
textFont = pygame.font.SysFont("Calibri", 70)
screen.fill((255,255,255))

running = True
while running:

    text = textFont.render("Test completed.", True, (0, 0, 0))
    screen.blit(text,(50, 100))

    text = textFont.render("Thank you very much for", True, (0, 0, 0))
    screen.blit(text,(50, 200))
    text = textFont.render("your collaboration.", True, (0, 0, 0))
    screen.blit(text,(50, 270))

    rectangle = pygame.draw.rect(screen, (70, 180, 20),
    (670,500,220,70), 0)
    text = textFont.render("EXIT", True, (255, 255, 255))
    screen.blit(text,(720,500))
    pygame.display.flip()

    for event in pygame.event.get():
        if event.type == pygame.QUIT: sys.exit()

```

```
            if event.type == pygame.MOUSEBUTTONDOWN:
                x, y = pygame.mouse.get_pos() # Get click position

                if rectangle.collidepoint(x, y):
                    running = False


# Save information in a database -----------------------------------
con = sqlite3.connect("RClasificacioTarjetes.db")
cur = con.cursor()

r000 = resp[0]
r001 = resp[1]
r002 = resp[2]
r003 = resp[3]
r004 = resp[4]
r005 = resp[5]
r006 = resp[6]
r007 = resp[7]
r008 = resp[8]
r009 = resp[9]
r010 = resp[10]
r011 = resp[11]
r012 = resp[12]
r013 = resp[13]
r014 = resp[14]
r015 = resp[15]
r016 = resp[16]
r017 = resp[17]
r018 = resp[18]
r019 = resp[19]
r020 = resp[20]
r021 = resp[21]
r022 = resp[22]
r023 = resp[23]
```

```
r024 = resp[24]
r025 = resp[25]
r026 = resp[26]
r027 = resp[27]
r028 = resp[28]
r029 = resp[29]
r030 = resp[30]
r031 = resp[31]
r032 = resp[32]
r033 = resp[33]
r034 = resp[34]
r035 = resp[35]
r036 = resp[36]
r037 = resp[37]
r038 = resp[38]
r039 = resp[39]
r040 = resp[40]
r041 = resp[41]
r042 = resp[42]
r043 = resp[43]
r044 = resp[44]
r045 = resp[45]
r046 = resp[46]
r047 = resp[47]
r048 = resp[48]
r049 = resp[49]
r050 = resp[50]
r051 = resp[51]
r052 = resp[52]
r053 = resp[53]
r054 = resp[54]
r055 = resp[55]
r056 = resp[56]
r057 = resp[57]
r058 = resp[58]
```

```
r059 = resp[59]
r060 = resp[60]
r061 = resp[61]
r062 = resp[62]
r063 = resp[63]
r064 = resp[64]
r065 = resp[65]
r066 = resp[66]
r067 = resp[67]
r068 = resp[68]
r069 = resp[69]
r070 = resp[70]
r071 = resp[71]
r072 = resp[72]
r073 = resp[73]
r074 = resp[74]
r075 = resp[75]
r076 = resp[76]
r077 = resp[77]
r078 = resp[78]
r079 = resp[79]
r080 = resp[80]
r081 = resp[81]
r082 = resp[82]
r083 = resp[83]
r084 = resp[84]
r085 = resp[85]
r086 = resp[86]
r087 = resp[87]
r088 = resp[88]
r089 = resp[89]
r090 = resp[90]
r091 = resp[91]
r092 = resp[92]
r093 = resp[93]
```

```
r094 = resp[94]
r095 = resp[95]
r096 = resp[96]
r097 = resp[97]
r098 = resp[98]
r099 = resp[99]
r100 = resp[100]
r101 = resp[101]
r102 = resp[102]
r103 = resp[103]
r104 = resp[104]
r105 = resp[105]
r106 = resp[106]
r107 = resp[107]
r108 = resp[108]
r109 = resp[109]
r110 = resp[110]
r111 = resp[111]
r112 = resp[112]
r113 = resp[113]
r114 = resp[114]
r115 = resp[115]
r116 = resp[116]
r117 = resp[117]
r118 = resp[118]
r119 = resp[119]
r120 = resp[120]
r121 = resp[121]
r122 = resp[122]
r123 = resp[123]
r124 = resp[124]
r125 = resp[125]
r126 = resp[126]
r127 = resp[127]
r128 = resp[128]
```

```


dat = (nom, edat, sex, formacio, data, diagnostic, res, obs,
       r000, r001, r002, r003, r004, r005, r006, r007, r008, r009,
       r010, r011, r012, r013, r014, r015, r016, r017, r018, r019,
       r020, r021, r022, r023, r024, r025, r026, r027, r028, r029,
       r030, r031, r032, r033, r034, r035, r036, r037, r038, r039,
       r040, r041, r042, r043, r044, r045, r046, r047, r048, r049,
       r050, r051, r052, r053, r054, r055, r056, r057, r058, r059,
       r060, r061, r062, r063, r064, r065, r066, r067, r068, r069,
       r070, r071, r072, r073, r074, r075, r076, r077, r078, r079,
       r080, r081, r082, r083, r084, r085, r086, r087, r088, r089,
       r090, r091, r092, r093, r094, r095, r096, r097, r098, r099,
       r100, r101, r102, r103, r104, r105, r106, r107, r108, r109,
       r110, r111, r112, r113, r114, r115, r116, r117, r118, r119,
       r120, r121, r122, r123, r124, r125, r126, r127, r128)


cur.execute('INSERT INTO Sujetos VALUES(?,?,?,?,?,?,?,?,\
            ?,?,?,?,?,?,?,?,?,?,?,?,?,?,?,?,?,?,?,?,?,?,?,?,?,?,?,?,?,?,\
            ?,?,?,?,?,?,?,?,?,?,?,?,?,?,?,?,?,?,?,?,?,?,?,?,?,?,?,?,?,?,\
            ?,?,?,?,?,?,?,?,?,?,?,?,?,?,?,?,?,?,?,?,?,?,?,?,?,?,?,?,?,?,\
            ?,?,?,?,?,?,?,?,?,?,?,?,?,?,?,?,?,?,?,?,?,?,?,?,?,?,?,?,?,?,\
             ?,?,?,?,?,?,?,?,?)', dat)

con.commit()
con.close



# Print report ============================================


# Exit the program  -------------------------------------------------
pygame.quit()
```

```
811   sys.exit()
812
813
      if __name__ == '__main__':
          print("The program is running as the main program.")
```

Lines 1 and 2 contain the program's identification. Lines 5 to 14 import the libraries that will be necessary for the program to work. Lines 16 to 20 initialize the subject identification variables. Lines 23 to 29 introduce the date directly from the computer. Lines 31 to 32 identify the program's user, and these variables will be printed in the report. Line 34 initializes the Pygame library. Lines 36 to 39 define the colors that Pygame will use.

Lines 41 to 93 make up the first instruction screen that allows the subject to read the instructions and start the test by clicking the start button.

The test itself starts on line 97, with the definition of the screen (lines 97 to 101) and the definition of the variables (lines 103 to 167).

On line 170 the loop that will present the stimuli begins. This loop will end after presenting 64 cards if the subject has not completed any category, when the subject has completed 6 categories, or when reaching card 128, the last of the cards in the set.

The subject's response is recorded on lines 218 to 222. If this response is an exit response such as clicking the close window icon at the top right, the program ends (lines 223 to 225). If the response is to click one of the buttons, the program continues with the evaluation of the response. The response is evaluated separately according to the button clicked by the subject. The response `a` is evaluated from lines 232 to 307. First, the match between the stimulus card and the card chosen by the subject is checked; then the response is rated as correct or incorrect, and the subject is informed of the correct result. If it is incorrect, it is analyzed for whether the response has been assigned considering the previous category or whether it is unique, that is, does not match any classification criteria. The subject is then informed of the incorrect result. The variables are set to their initial value, a new stimulus is moved on to, and a new turn of the loop is allowed.

For answers b, c, and d, the same procedures are performed.

On line 538, the results are written to a file, and on line 612 the results report is written, as shown in Figures 5-17 and 5-18.

Dr. Roig. Psicologia Clinica.
c/. L'Equador, 21. 2º. 1ª. / 08029 - BARCELONA / 93 451 24 82.

Clasificación de tarjetas.

Name: Example Subject 30/3/25 Exp.: 936
Age: 53 Sex: Male. Requested by: Dr. Roig

● Answers:

1, d- F, 0	33, d- C, 0	65, a- C, 0	97, d- C, 0
2, b- F, 0	34, a- CF, 1	66, c- C, 0	98, a- CF, 1
3, b- C, 1	35, c- CN, 0	67, b- C, 0	99, c- CN, 0
4, a- F, 0	36, d- CN, 0	68, d- C, 0	100, d- CN, 0
5, a- C, 1	37, b- C, 0	69, a- C, 0	101, b- C, 0
6, d- C, 1	38, c- CN, 0	70, d- C, 0	102, c- CN, 0
7, b- C, 1	39, b- CN, 0	71, b- C, 0	103, b- CN, 0
8, c- F, 0	40, c- C, 0	72, d- C, 0	104, c- C, 0
9, b- F, 0	41, d- CN, 0	73, a- CN, 0	105, d- CN, 0
10, c- C, 1	42, b- C, 0	74, c- C, 0	106, b- C, 0
11, d- C, 1	43, d- C, 0	75, d- C, 0	107, d- C, 0
12, a- C, 1	44, c- CF, 1	76, a- C, 0	108, c- CF, 1
13, b- CF, 1	45, a- CN, 0	77, b- CF, 1	109, a- CN, 0
14, d- CFN, 1	46, d- C, 0	78, d- CFN, 1	110, d- C, 0
15, c- CN, 1	47, b- CF, 1	79, c- CN, 0	111, b- CF, 1
16, d- C, 1	48, c- CF, 1	80, d- C, 0	112, c- CF, 1
17, a- C, 1	49, a- C, 0	81, a- C, 0	113, a- C, 0
18, c- C, 1	50, c- C, 0	82, c- C, 0	114, c- C, 0
19, b- C, 1 C	51, a- CN, 0	83, b- C, 0	115, a- CN, 0
20, d- CF, 1	52, c- C, 0	84, d- CF, 1	116, c- C, 0
21, a- C, 0	53, a- CF, 1	85, a- C, 0	117, a- CF, 1
22, b- CN, 0	54, b- CFN, 1	86, b- CN, 0	118, b- CFN, 1
23, d- CN, 0	55, c- C, 0	87, d- CN, 0	119, c- C, 0
24, a- C, 0	56, d- C, 0	88, a- C, 0	120, d- C, 0
25, b- C, 0	57, b- C, 0	89, b- C, 0	121, b- C, 0
26, a- C, 0	58, c- C, 0	90, a- C, 0	122, c- C, 0
27, b- C, 0	59, d- CF, 1	91, b- C, 0	123, d- CF, 1
28, c- CFN, 1	60, b- C, 0	92, c- CFN, 1	124, b- C, 0
29, a- C, 0	61, c- C, 0	93, a- C, 0	125, c- C, 0
30, d- CF, 1	62, a- CFN, 1	94, d- CF, 1	126, a- CFN, 1
31, a- CF, 1	63, c- CF, 1	95, a- CF, 1	127, c- CF, 1
32, b- CN, 0	64, b- CF, 1	96, b- CN, 0	128, b- CF, 1

● Results:

Completed categories: 1

Punctuation	1	2	3	4	5	6	Total
Total errors	5	79	0	0	0	0	84
Correct	14	30	0	0	0	0	44
Perseverative errors	--	78	0	0	0	0	78
non-perseverative E.	5	1	0	0	0	0	6
Unique	0	0	0	0	0	0	0

Figure 5-17. *Sample report, page 1*

Dr. Roig. Psicologia Clinica.
c/. L'Equador, 21. 2º. 1ª. / 08029 - BARCELONA / 93 451 24 82.

Example Subject 30/3/25 Exp.: 936 Hoja 2.

This interpretive report is suitable for professional use only, by a qualified psychologist. It has been automatically prepared based only on the test results; therefore, it is the professional's responsibility to integrate these results into the context and circumstances of the person being examined.

This subject's results are far below what could be expected given his age and training.
He has only completed one category, which reveals problems with cognitive flexibility, poor analytical skills, and possibly rigid behavior and poor adaptation to changing life circumstances. He demonstrates a lack of analytical skills, attention problems, and poor working memory.
The results are consistent with a prefrontal brain injury, since he has been able to complete a classification category, but subsequently remained unchanged in the same criterion, despite repeated incorrect responses. Consider the subject's observation data while performing the test, and the subsequent interview about their behavior and the criteria they followed in performing the task, to delve deeper into the meaning of the results and discern possible causes and diagnoses.

Figure 5-18. *Sample report, page 2*

The report can be expanded as much as desired by adding conditions and interpretive texts of results.

Summary

In this chapter, you saw the administration of some classic tests, which can be administered by means of a computer, and the management of personality questionnaires. In the next chapter, you will see how to deal with statistical calculations.

CHAPTER 6

Applications of Statistics and Data Mining

In this chapter, we will analyze the statistical calculation possibilities that Python offers, and we will see how to perform some of these calculations with powerful free libraries.

Statistics are essential to bring order and information to the vast amounts of data produced daily in our society, but statistics also lie at the core of artificial intelligence, machine learning, and data science. Statistics deals with collecting, analyzing, and understanding data and aims to develop models that can make decisions in the presence of uncertainty (Ghosh, 2022; Haslwanter, 2016; Nawaz, 2020; Saunders, 2018).

It is traditional and much more convenient, since the democratization of personal computers at the end of the 20th century, to perform statistical calculations in a computerized manner, especially if it involves processing very large samples. This is done by those who can or those who know how to use one of the existing statistical programs, to go further in less time and with less effort. This has undoubted advantages but also some disadvantages, such as the excessive application of statistical methods where they are not appropriate or the incorrect application of them. In addition, the reduced need to understand the underlying calculations can sometimes lead to a poor understanding of the methods being applied. It is also true that some of the most common statistical calculations can be performed with tools available to everyone such as spreadsheets (Quirk, 2016), but programming languages such as Python or R, with specific applications for psychology (Mair, 2018), are more powerful and flexible. Receiving training in one of them opens many possibilities.

There are also good statistical programs that allow all kinds of calculations. There are commercial ones (SPSS, STATA, BMPD, KNIME...), which tend to be expensive, but there are also free ones that perform the same functions at no cost (OpenStats, PPSP), as well as specialized languages for statistics that are very powerful, such as the aforementioned

J. M. Roig-Fusté, *Python for Psychology, Social Sciences, and Education*,
https://doi.org/10.1007/979-8-8688-2355-8_6

R, which is also free. However, programming statistical applications in a language that is known adds flexibility to the application and allows the program to be adapted to one's own needs. In any case, the purpose of this chapter is to show the power of Python in the field of statistical calculations.

Simple Statistics in Python

Python offers its own functions for descriptive and inferential statistics, which are directly used to calculate various values or carry out certain procedures. Let's first look at some functions of the statistics module for descriptive statistics:

`statistics.mean()`: Arithmetic means ("average") of data.

`statistics.fmean()`: Fast floating-point arithmetic mean.

`statistics.geometric_mean()`: Geometric mean of the data.

`statistics.harmonic_mean()`: Harmonic mean of data.

`statistics.median()`: Median (middle value) of the data.

`statistics.median_low()`: Low median of data.

`statistics.median_high()`: Median high data.

`statistics.median_grouped()`: Median, or 50th percentile, of the grouped data.

`statistics.mode()`: Single mode (most common value) of discrete data.

`statistics.multimode()`: List of modes (most common values) of discrete or nominal data.

`statistics.quantiles()`: Divides the data into intervals with equal probability.

`statistics.pstdev()`: Population standard deviation.

`statistics.pvariance()`: Population variance.

`statistics.stdev()`: Sample standard deviation.

`statistics.variance()`: Sample variance.

For example, to calculate the mean of a variable in a sample, we must apply the following formula:

$$M = \frac{\Sigma x_i}{N - 1}$$

x_i represents all the known values of the variable and N the number of values. It is therefore necessary to add up all the scores in the sample [$\sum x_i$] and divide this value by the number of cases minus one, a correction that is applied because it is a sample; if we had all the values in the population, we would have to divide by N.

To find the standard deviation, we must apply the following formula:

$$\vartheta = \sqrt{\frac{\Sigma x^2 - \frac{(\Sigma x)^2}{N}}{N - 1}}$$

In this case, we should also calculate the sum of squares of all the values of the variable studied: [$\sum x_i^2$]. To apply these formulas in any computer language, we should write a loop to obtain in advance the sum of all the values of the variable and the squares of these values before performing the corresponding calculations; in Python it is enough to write this:

```
M = statistics.mean('variable name')
```

And this:

```
sd = statistics.stdev('variable name)
```

The values of the variable must first be entered into the computer or read from a file, and the statistics module must be imported. This is certainly easy and also represents a considerable saving in programming time.

Python has a built-in statistics module, with the following functions:

Name	Activity
`mean()`	Calculate the arithmetic mean.
`median()`	Calculate the mean value or median.
`mode()`	Calculate the mode or most frequent value.

(continued)

Name	Activity
`st.mode()`	Provides the most frequent value in the sample. An error occurs if more than one mode is found.
`quantiles()`	Divide the data into intervals with equal probability.
`pvariance()`	Calculates the population variance or square root of the standard deviation.
`stdev()`	Calculate the standard deviation of a sample.
`variance()`	Calculates the variance of a sample.

Here's an example of a small statistical program:

```
# Statistical data processing
# Descriptive statistics
# 13.05.2021

import statistics

data = [7, 1, 33, 21, 34, 34, 35, 36, 23, 22, 12, 66, 33, 34, 31, 32, 33]

print("Mean: ", statistics.mean(data))
print("Floating point mean: ", statistics.fmean(data))
print("Geometric mean: ", statistics.geometric_mean(data))
print("Harmonic mean: ", statistics.harmonic_mean(data))
print("Median: ", statistics.median(data))
print("Low median: ", statistics.median_low(data))
print("Median high: ", statistics.median_high(data))
print("50th percentile: ", statistics.median_grouped(data))
print("Mode: ", statistics.mode(data))
print("Multimode: ", statistics.multimode(data))
print( "Quartiles: ", statistics.quantiles( data ))

print("Population standard deviation: ", statistics.pstdev(data))
print("Variance: ", statistics.pvariance(data))
print("Sample standard deviation ", statistics.stdev(data))
print("Sample variance: ", statistics.variance(data))
```

Exit:

```
Average: 28.647058823529413
average: 28.647058823529413
Geometric mean: 22.591462278359497
Harmonic mean: 10.137781387132097
Median: 33
Low median: 33
Medium high: 33
50th percentile: 32.666666666666664
Fashion: 33
Multimodal : [33, 34]
Quartiles : [21.5, 33.0, 34.0]
Population standard deviation: 13.91969056650068
Variance: 193.75778546712803
Sample standard deviation 14.34808862039901
Sample variance: 205.86764705882354
```

It is common for the output to have the high number of decimals that we see. To avoid this, we can use the `round()` function, which allows us to choose the number of decimals that we want to see. Three decimals are a common presentation in statistics. For example, for the average of the previous program, in line 8 we could write the following:

```
print("Mean: ", round(statistics.mean(data), 3))
```

This would result in the following:

```
Average: 28,647
```

The same can be done in all the calculations in this program if we want to have values with only three decimal places.

Decimals can also be formatted in another way, requesting the number of decimals we want with the % sign, so if we change line 9 of the program to the following:

```
print("Mean: %0.3f" %statistics.mean(data))
```

we will obtain this average again with three decimal places.

This program has been created using Python's own statistics library, but in many cases, we will need other libraries for our work that will make our task easier and expand the calculation possibilities.

Let's look at another example; see Program 6-1.

Program 6-1.

```
1  # Reasoning test statistics: 27.04.2022
2
3  import numpy as np
4  import statistics
5  import matplotlib.pyplot as plt
6  from scipy.stats import norm
7
8  reasoning = [23, 28, 28, 31, 29, 26, 17, 29, 28, 20,
9  22, 29, 29, 20, 22, 23, 23, 25, 37, 31,
10 30, 27, 21, 31, 32, 21, 27, 27, 27, 30,
11 22, 27, 22, 21, 19, 34, 27, 32, 27, 25,
12 30, 23, 30, 19, 22, 30, 25, 29, 31, 22,
13 15, 29, 25, 27, 28, 22, 23, 24, 22, 18,
14 28, 26, 30, 30, 24, 28, 29, 28, 27, 32,
15 31, 29, 26, 29, 22, 28, 29, 28, 29, 28,
16 30, 28, 15, 25, 32, 31, 35, 24, 29, 19,
17 24, 28, 26, 18, 20, 24, 27, 22, 22, 25]
18
19 mean = round(statistics.mean(reasoning), 3)
20 sd = round(statistics.stdev(reasoning), 3)
21
22
23 plt.hist(reasoning)
24 plt.title('Reasoning frequency distribution')
25 plt.xlabel('Scores')
26 plt.ylabel('Frequencies')
27 plt.show()
```

This program collects the scores from a reasoning test in the list on lines 8 to 17 and requests the mean and standard deviation of the sample on lines 19 and 20.

If we run this program, we get the following results:

```
Media: 26.08
Standard deviation: 4.359
```

On lines 25 to 29 we draw the frequency histogram (Figure 6-1).

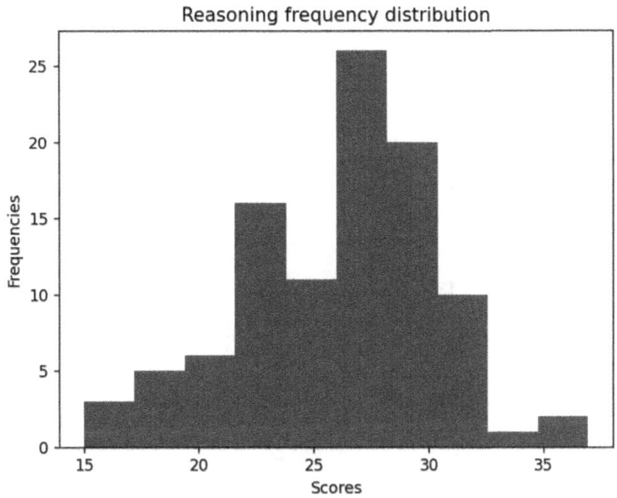

***Figure 6-1.** Reasoning frequency distribution*

In the program we have presented, the data to be analyzed, as an example, is included in the program itself as a list. When the amount of data is very large, it will not be practical to copy this information into the program, due to the time required to complete this task, the ease of making mistakes, and because when we want to use the program with another set of data, we will have to rewrite the program. Generally, the data is found in separate files that the program reads when it starts, to carry out its analysis work. For this data processing, the Pandas library (Chen, 2017) will be very useful. It must be installed before it can be used, which can be done with the pip program, as we have already explained.

Before moving on to Pandas, a few words about how to store data for processing. The data must be organized as a matrix and in a way that the program understands. As an example, we will use our own file called `Aptitudes` that comes from the results of an aptitude test called SIEP that we published a few years ago (Roig-Fusté, 2007). Pandas can understand different types of files, but we will use a plain-text file, that is, one that contains only text, without formatting characters.

This is a file of 400 cases, of which only the first cases are presented in the form of a table in which each column is a variable, and each row is a subject. Here are the first lines of the file:

	Sex	**age**	**ra**	**cv**	**cn**
001	1	25	23	34	18
002	1	23	28	33	31
003	1	24	28	33	27
004	1	22	31	39	25
005	1	22	29	34	34
006	2	21	26	27	18
007	1	23	17	32	29
008	1	26	29	20	32
009	2	20	28	30	19
010	2	20	21	30	21
.	.	....	....	....	....
....	.	....	....	....	....
400	2	39	29	20	20

The rows that represent subjects are numbered, but this number is not part of the data in the file. The first row defines the variables in the file: the first variable, column 1, is sex: 1 for males and 2 for females. The second variable is age in years; the third is the direct score for Abstract Reasoning from our SIEP battery; the fourth variable is the score for the Verbal Comprehension test; and the last variable is the score for the Numerical Ability test, both from the same SIEP battery.

With the Pandas library and its DataFrames function, it is possible to read data files like ours and manipulate these data to study them or perform calculations. Pandas reads Excel files with the `read_excel()` method by installing the `xlrd` module. Plain-text files or CSV files can be read with the `read_csv()` method; SQL database files can be read with the `read_sql()` method, which requires the import of a database module such as sqlite3.

Another Python statistical library is SciPy, which contains many functions.

Other statistical calculations that can be performed are correlations or multivariate analysis. In the case of Pearson correlation and in manual calculations we use the following formula:

$$r_{xy} = \frac{xy - \frac{\Sigma x \Sigma y}{N}}{\sqrt{\left(x - \frac{x^2}{N}\right)\left(y - \frac{y^2}{N}\right)}}$$

As we can see in the formula, the data we need to calculate a correlation is as follows: the x and y values for each subject, the squares of these values, and the product of x and y for each subject. Let's look at a simple case of the scores of 12 subjects on an aptitude test; RA refers to the score in abstract reasoning and V to the score in verbal reasoning.

Subject	RA	RA2	V	V 2	RA x V
1	23	529	34	1156	782
2	28	784	33	1089	924
3	28	784	33	1089	924
4	31	961	39	1521	1209
5	29	841	34	1156	986
6	26	676	27	729	702
7	17	289	32	1024	544
8	29	841	20	400	580
9	28	784	30	900	840
10	21	441	30	900	630
11	30	900	17	289	510
12	29	841	24	576	696
Σ	319	8671	353	10829	9327

Applying the previous formula, we obtain the correlation between the Abstract Reasoning test and the Verbal Ability test:

$$r_{xy} = \frac{9327 - \frac{319 \cdot 353}{12}}{\sqrt{\left(8671 - \frac{319^2}{12}\right)\left(10829 - \frac{353^2}{12}\right)}} = -0{,}195$$

Let's see how we can do the same task in Python:

```
import numpy as np
import matplotlib as plt

x_R = np.array ([23, 28, 28, 31, 29, 26, 17, 29, 28, 21, 30, 29])
y_V = np.array ([34, 33, 33, 39, 34, 27, 32, 20, 30, 30, 17, 24])

rxy = np.corrcoef ( x_R , y_V )
print( rxy )
```

The output of this program is as follows:

```
[[ 1. -0.19528919]
[-0.19528919 1.]]
```

The output of this program is expressed in a square matrix, in which the first row corresponds to the variable abstract reasoning and the second to verbal reasoning. The same occurs with the columns, so the table tells us in the first row that the correlation between abstract reasoning and abstract reasoning is 1, while the correlation between abstract reasoning and verbal reasoning is -0.195. The same is true for the second row in which the correlation between verbal reasoning and abstract reasoning is -0.195 and between verbal reasoning and verbal reasoning is 1. The correlation of these two factors in our sample is negative and low, which is acceptable for two variables that are considered different aptitudes. Naturally the example has very few cases; therefore, the results cannot be considered representative of anything, but the variables, in this case, x_R and y_V, can be downloaded from a file and can contain thousands of cases in order to perform calculations that provide more representative results.

Multivariate Statistics and Factor Analysis

Python allows for more complex statistical calculations such as factor analysis. Factor analysis is a mathematical procedure based on some of Sperman's ideas, which was developed during the first half of the 20th century; it is currently widely used in biological, psychological, social, and educational research. More information on this method can be found in Adcock (1954), Child (1990), Fruchter (1954), Gorsuch (2015), and Kline (1994).

The objective of factor analysis is to reduce the number of observed variables by discovering underlying unobservable variables. It consists of two steps:

- Factor extraction. Principal component analysis and common factor analysis.
- Rotation. This involves finding uncorrelated factors to improve interpretation. It can be orthogonal or oblique and can be carried out using various methods: Varimax, Quartimax, and Promax.

The factor loading is a matrix that shows the relationship of each variable with the underlying factor. It is the correlation coefficient between the variable and the factors found that show the variance explained by the observed variables.

Eigenvalues represent the variance explained by each factor out of the total variance. They are used to determine the most likely number of underlying factors, which will be those with values greater than 1.

Communalities are the sum of the squared loads for each variable and represent the common variance; they are between 0 and 1, and values closer to 1 correspond to greater variance.

In Python, for factor analysis, we will use the `factor_analizer` library. Complete information about this library can be found here:

`https://factor-analyzer.readthedocs.io/en/latest/index.html`

Let's look at an example program; see Program 6-2.

Program 6-2.

```
import pandas as pd
from factor_analyzer import FactorAnalyzer

# read data file
```

```
data = pd.read_csv ('siep.csv')

# print file read
print(data)

# choose columns for calculation
util = list ( range(2, 5))
matrix_t = data.iloc [ :, util ]

# print job matrix
print( matrix_t )
print()
print()


# perform factor analysis
result = FactorAnalyzer ( rotation = ' promax ')
result.fit ( matrix_t )

print("eigenvalues: ")
print(result.get_eigenvalues())
print()

print('Rotated matrix:')
print(result.loadings_)
print()
print('Communities:')
print( result.get_communalities ())
```

Results:

```
Sex Ed RA RV RN
0 V 25 23 34 18
1 V 23 28 33 31
2 V 24 28 33 27
3 V 22 31 39 25
```

```
4 V 22 29 34 34
.. .. .. .. .. ..
395 M 22 36 19 18
396 M 35 25 25 18
397 V 34 0 19 24
398 M 29 28 36 23
399 M 37 21 32 23

[400 rows x 5 columns]
     RA RV RN
0 23 34 18
1 28 33 31
2 28 33 27
3 31 39 25
4 29 34 34
.. .. .. ..
395 36 19 18
396 25 25 18
397 0 19 24
398 28 36 23
399 21 32 23

[400 rows x 3 columns]

Unrotated matrix:
[[ 0.60772631 -0.1507877 0.10370807]
[0.5213583 0.22485944 0.04620518]
[0.65180279 -0.03926752 -0.13365327]]

eigenvalues:
(array ([1.66891504, 0.72377477, 0.60731019]),
 array ([0.96630283, 0.02425688, -0.10050528]))

Rotated matrix (varimax):
[[0.53249411 0.26308484 0.2237408]
[0.22083629 0.49306112 0.18064667]
[0.38450277 0.32711231 0.43520934]]
```

```
Rotated matrix (promax):
[[0.57713528 0.0312436 0.04017175]
[0.02361174 0.53309989 0.02360955]
[0.13547041 0.06447531 0.49654773]]

Communalities:
[0.33567506 0.28531042 0.26906895]
```

This program allows you to perform an exploratory factor analysis; let's see how.

Lines 1 and 2 import the libraries needed by the program. Line 5 reads our data file called `siep.csv`, which comes from the application of our own aptitude test with three factors of abstract, verbal, and numerical reasoning (RA, RV, RN), and which contains 400 cases (Roig-Fusté, 2007). To make sure that the program has read the file correctly and that it contains the data we want, we print a sample on line 8.

The file `siep.csv` read contains five columns. The first two, sex and age, are not valid for factor analysis, so in lines 11 and 12 we create a clean matrix, without these columns, for our work. Next, in line 15, the header of said matrix is printed, now with only three columns, to check that we are working with the correct data.

The actual factor analysis is performed on lines 21 and 22, indicating the type of rotation desired. The eigenvalues are printed on line 25. The rotated matrix is then printed on line 29 and the communalities on line 32.

The rotated matrix of the results allows us to see three factors, the first related to abstract reasoning, the second to verbal ability, and the third to numerical ability, as expected given the content of the exercises proposed in each section of the test.

Other Useful Python Libraries for Statistics

Python includes packages and libraries that can be easily used for statistical tasks. These are the most interesting ones:

1. NumPy for mathematical functions
2. Pandas for data processing
3. Statistics: Python built-in module for statistical functions
4. Matplotlib for visualization and plotting of graphs
5. SciPy.stats module for basic and advanced statistical functions

6. Statsmodels for statistical models
7. PyMC for Bayesian modeling and inference

Some calculations can be performed using several of these libraries, in which case the user must choose which one to apply.

Statistics are also used in so-called data mining or big data. It allows large amounts of data to be processed using proprietary methods to study a phenomenon or draw conclusions from the data that are available, which cannot be obtained in any other way. It aims to extract knowledge from accumulated data files, which are generally very large.

Summary

In this chapter, you learned how to analyze the statistical calculation possibilities that Python offers and how to perform some of these calculations with powerful free libraries. In the next chapter, you will learn about the value of Python in education.

CHAPTER 7

Python in Education

In this chapter, we will see some examples of how computing can enhance learning and help develop some skills.

That computing could be applied on a massive scale to education and would bring about a great change in it is an idea that has been around for a long time; for example, Kemeny (1972) dedicated a chapter of his book to education more than 50 years ago. At that time, the author considered that the computer was too expensive a substitute for a book and too poor a substitute for a teacher. In the years since then, things have changed a lot; computing can no longer be described as expensive, and its benefits have become much richer.

The expansion of computers and Internet connections has reached high percentages among teachers and students in our environment, at all levels of education; this makes it a necessary tool, as well as interesting and valuable, to enhance learning and face new challenges. Many students use the computer to write, read, consult information, save data, and play. Teachers can use the computer to manage their work, write, read, and naturally teach through multiple strategies. For the uses mentioned, there are specific applications that can be used immediately without a great learning effort; however, we cannot speak of a true educational revolution without introducing programming into teaching from a very early age (Tollervey, 2015; Williamson, 2018). Programming opens a new horizon since it allows the creation of applications tailored to each subject and each situation and helps students structure their thinking and develop their logical capacity. Programming can be introduced into teaching through simple ideas, such as turtle graphics, Logo language, or Scratch language (Marji, 2014) and computer games, an activity that usually arouses a high motivation in the student that helps to consolidate learning. Programming games is undoubtedly a demanding task, requiring both creativity and computer and programming knowledge, as well as perseverance and patience. Many specific books refer to game programming in Python for children or adolescents (Briggs, 2012; B. McManus, 2018; Payne, 2015; Payne, 2019; Richardson,

J. M. Roig-Fusté, *Python for Psychology, Social Sciences, and Education*,
https://doi.org/10.1007/979-8-8688-2355-8_7

2015; Sweigart, 2017), which can be used to introduce students to this activity. Students can use this programming knowledge for other activities in the future and later in the working world.

The first area in which Python is used, within education, is to teach programming, where the aim is to start with a more accessible and clear language. It allows students to become familiar with the dynamics of programming computers and to move on to more complex and therefore more powerful languages. This role of introductory language had initially been performed by BASIC (Kemeny and Kurtz, 1964) in the 1970s, and later, in the 1980s, the role was assigned to Pascal (Wirth, 1970). Later, with the appearance of graphical environments, such as Windows, Delphi (which was Pascal in a visual environment), or Visual Basic (whose nuclear structure was BASIC), it took over. Currently, both languages, Visual Basic and Delphi, have been practically abandoned, and other more modern languages, such as Python, Java, or JavaScript, have replaced them.

It is currently believed that it is better to introduce children to computing and therefore programming as early as possible (Somma, 2020), because the activity of programming develops problem-solving skills, which are necessary for a changing world like ours and for the future. It also promotes the tenacity and perseverance of the student. Some countries have made efforts to make programming a reality from elementary school, and some authors strongly recommend it (Somma, 2020; Tollervey, 2015). We know that children are creative and imaginative, they are not afraid of new technologies, and they learn better by doing, which allows them to take full advantage of this new resource. Computing also ensures equal opportunities if it is made available to all children equally through school and is not an elitist resource that favors, like many others, only the luckiest.

Python is currently considered to be one of the best options, if not the best, to enter the world of computing and programming because it is free and simple to use. It also comes with extensive documentation and power provided by the large number of libraries that can be used by this language. Finally, once you learn it, you can continue working with it, in any type of project, however complex it may be, in professional fields.

Teachers can combine computer-assisted teaching with their own knowledge to create applications in different fields from mathematics (Farrell, 2019; Saha, 2015) to car driving or airplane flight simulators. Educational material can be made interactive to provide instant feedback to students and reinforce knowledge.

Another field that requires programming and computer resources is called e-learning (electronic learning), or education and training via the Internet. Python is a language that allows interaction with the Internet and is also used in web page design.

The use of computer games can also be effective for teaching, developing, or re-educating certain skills, or for reinforcing certain knowledge; this is the field known as serious games and has been used for education (Cai, van Joolingen, & Veermans, 2021; Ma, Oikonomou, & Jain, 2011; Michael & Chen, 2006), rehabilitation (Morales, 2019), and mental health and psychotherapy (Brooks, Brahnam, & Jain, 2014; Ma, Jain, & Anderson, 2014; Matthews, & Coyle, 2010). Games have the advantage that they are usually more motivating for students than any other type of activity or work.

Teaching programming to young people can be undertaken at all levels. At the earliest levels, students often program simple computer games themselves, which are more motivating for them and can be done in teams, while also developing their ability to cooperate (Payne, 2015, 2019; Sweigart, 2017; Weinachter; 2016). At higher levels, applications related to the subjects that the student is studying in the corresponding course can be tested, although the programming of more advanced games should not be ruled out, which represent suitable challenges to make the individual progress in their knowledge and achievements (Kinsley and McGugan, 2015).

Overall, Python's impact on education is already significant and has changed the way programming is taught and computer science concepts are approached. The following are some of the key aspects of this impact:

1. **Ease of learning:** Python stands out for its simple and readable syntax, making it an ideal language for programming beginners. This ease of learning has allowed students of all ages and educational levels to engage in programming effectively and without feeling overwhelmed by the activity.

2. **Focus on problem solving:** Python focuses on problem solving and programming logic, rather than technical aspects and syntactical complexities. This allows students to concentrate on developing algorithms and solutions, which foster computational thinking and the ability to tackle real-world problems.

3. **Versatility:** Python is a versatile language, used in a wide range of applications, from web development and scientific computing to artificial intelligence and data analysis. This versatility allows students to explore different areas of interest and see practical applications of programming in various fields.

4. **Community and resources:** The Python community is large and active, meaning that students have access to a wealth of online resources, tutorials, help forums, and open-source libraries. This facilitates independent learning and problem-solving as students' progress through their programming journey.

5. **Job readiness:** As programming becomes an essential skill in many professional fields, learning Python in school gives students a competitive edge in the job market. Python skills are in demand in a variety of job fields, including technology, finance, scientific research, and almost every other field of work.

6. **Practical projects:** Python allows educators and students to create practical projects and real-world applications relatively quickly. This improves knowledge retention as students can see tangible results of their work, which in turn fosters motivation and continued interest in programming.

7. **Focus on creativity:** Python allows students to express their creativity through programming. They can develop games, mobile apps, automation tools, etc., which makes the learning process more exciting and personalized.

8. **Inclusivity:** Python's accessibility and open community have helped make programming more inclusive. It has promoted diversity in the tech industry by giving a wide range of people the opportunity to learn to code and contribute.

So, we can now say that computer science in general, and Python in particular, has had a transformative impact on education by making programming more accessible, engaging, and relevant to students of all ages. Its focus on problem solving, versatility, and active community has helped cultivate vital digital skills for the 21st century and has prepared students for a variety of educational and professional opportunities. This means that we can judge the effectiveness of a school by the way it teaches and applies to programming.

The following are simple examples of Python programs that could be used to teach basic programming concepts:

- **Simple calculator:** A program that allows the user to perform basic mathematical operations.

```
num1 = float (input("Enter the first number: "))
num2 = float (input("Enter the second number: "))

sum = num1 + num2
subtraction = num1 - num2
multiplication = num1 * num2
division = num1 / num2

print("Sum:", sum)
print("Subtraction:", subtraction)
print("Multiplication:", multiplication )
print("Division:", division )
```

- **Guess the number:** A simple game where the program chooses a random number and the player tries to guess it.

```
import random

secret_number = random.randint (1, 100)
attempts = 0

while True:
    guess = int (input("Try to guess the number: "))
    attempts += 1

    if attempt < secret_number:
        print("Too low.")
    elif attempt > secret_number:
        print("Too high.")
    else:
        print( f"Correct ! You guessed it in {tries} tries!")
        break
```

- **Temperature converter:** A program that converts a temperature in degrees Celsius to Fahrenheit.

```
celsius = float (input("Enter the temperature in degrees Celsius: "))
fahrenheit = (celsius * 9/5) + 32
print("The temperature in degrees Fahrenheit is:", fahrenheit)
```

- **Multiplication table generator:** A program that generates the multiplication table for a given number.

```
number = int (input("Enter a number to generate its multiplication table: "))

for i in range (1, 11):
result = number * i
print(f"{number} x {i} = {result}")
```

These are just simple examples to illustrate how basic programming concepts can be used in Python. As students gain more knowledge and become more familiar with computer science, they will be able to create more complex programs and useful applications in various fields.

Learning Educational Content

All educational subjects can benefit from computer applications that interact with the student, providing them with knowledge and hours of individual practice. To do this, an initial time must be dedicated to creating the programs, but once these are working and it has been proven that they are effective, they can be used as many times as desired and with as many students as necessary; thousands or millions of them can benefit from the work done.

Programs designed for education do not have to be complex in design, even though today's computers offer undeniable advantages in image or video presentation, voice stimuli, or even virtual reality, which can improve student motivation. All of these aspects are available in Python, requiring certain knowledge that can be acquired in practice, starting with simple developments that can be expanded and improved with use.

Here we provide an example of a simple Python program that can help users learn English vocabulary. In this case, the program presents the user with an English word and asks them to enter its Spanish translation. It then checks whether the answer is correct and provides feedback.

```
1   # English-Spanish vocabulary dictionary
2   vocabulary = {
3       "apple": "apple",
4   "cat": "cat",
5   "dog": "dog",
6       " sun ": "sun",
7   " tree ": "tree"
8   # Add more words and translations here
9   }
10
11  def learn_vocabulary (vocabulary):
12      print("Welcome to the vocabulary learning program!")
13
14      for english_word , spanish_translation in vocabulary.items ():
15  answer = input( f"What is the translation of '{ english_word }' into
    Spanish?"). lower ()
16
17          if answer == english_translation:
18              print("Correct! Excellent work!")
19          else:
20              print( f"Incorrect . The correct translation is '{
21  spanish_translation }'.")
22
23      print("You have completed vocabulary learning!")
24
    learn_vocabulary (vocabulary)
```

In this example, the program presents English words from the dictionary contained in the vocabulary variable on line 2, which can be as extensive as desired, and asks the user to enter the Spanish translation. It then checks whether the answer is correct and provides feedback.

Please remember that this is a simple example and that more advanced features can be added, such as graphical presentation of the program, presenting the word in written and verbal form, awarding points for correct answers, saving user progress, including options for repeating incorrect words, or even connecting to a larger database of words and definitions, all of which make more sense in a program containing 1,000 or 2,000 words, for example.

Finally, let's look at two examples of programs for performing simple tasks that can be used in primary education or re-education. We will present an educational game for reproducing sequences that require skill, memory, and sound discrimination. It is a version of the memory game called Simon, which was very successful in the 1980s and has also been used in psychomotor stimulation of young children and neuropsychological rehabilitation of brain-injured subjects. Later, we will see a topographic memory task.

An Example: Simon

The Simon memory game consists of a screen with four buttons that simulate colored lights. These buttons light up in a predetermined random pattern, in an increasingly long sequence of lights that are activated associated with a particular sound for each one. Once the computer has presented the complete sequence, the subject must repeat it by pressing the buttons in the correct order. Each time the player is able to repeat the complete sequence successfully, the next sequence adds one more element, until the subject fails to reproduce it. See Program 7-1.

Program 7-1.

```
# Versión del juego 'Simon', 1.11.2023 / Symon04.py

import random, sys, time, pygame
from pygame.locals import *

# constantes -------------------------------------------
CPS = 35 # configuración de cuadros por segundo
ANCHOPANTALLA = 1060
ALTOPANTALLA = 550
VELOCIDADPARPADEO = 500 # valor en milisegundos
```

```
RETARDO = 200 # valor en milisegundos
DIMENSIONBOTON = 160  #200

ESPACIOENTREBOTON = 30
TIEMPOESPERA = 8 # segundos antes de que termine la prueba si no se
presiona ningún botón.

# Constantes de colores
WHITE        = (255, 255, 255)
BLACK        = (  0,   0,   0)
BRIGHTRED    = (255,   0,   0)
RED          = (155,   0,   0)
BRIGHTGREEN  = (  0, 255,   0)
GREEN        = (  0, 155,   0)
BRIGHTBLUE   = (  0,   0, 255)
BLUE         = (  0,   0, 155)
BRIGHTYELLOW = (255, 255,   0)
YELLOW       = (155, 155,   0)
DARKGRAY     = ( 40,  40,  40)

MARGENX = int((ANCHOPANTALLA - (2 * DIMENSIONBOTON) -
ESPACIOENTREBOTON)
/ 2)
MARGENY = int((ALTOPANTALLA - (2 * DIMENSIONBOTON) -
ESPACIOENTREBOTON) /
2)

# Rectangulos de los cuatro botones
YELLOWRECT = pygame.Rect(MARGENX, MARGENY, DIMENSIONBOTON,
DIMENSIONBOTON)
BLUERECT   = pygame.Rect(MARGENX + DIMENSIONBOTON +
ESPACIOENTREBOTON,
MARGENY, DIMENSIONBOTON, DIMENSIONBOTON)
REDRECT    = pygame.Rect(MARGENX, MARGENY + DIMENSIONBOTON +
ESPACIOENTREBOTON, DIMENSIONBOTON, DIMENSIONBOTON)
```

```
GREENRECT  = pygame.Rect(MARGENX + DIMENSIONBOTON +
ESPACIOENTREBOTON,
MARGENY + DIMENSIONBOTON + ESPACIOENTREBOTON, DIMENSIONBOTON,
DIMENSIONBOTON)

def checkForQuit():
    for event in pygame.event.get(QUIT): # Salir del programa
    al cerrar
la ventana
        pygame.quit()
        sys.exit()

    for event in pygame.event.get(KEYUP): # captar pulsaciones
    de tecla
        if event.key == K_ESCAPE:
            pygame.quit()
            sys.exit()

def parpadeo(color, velocidadAnimacion = 50):
    if color == YELLOW:
        sound = NOTA1
        flashColor = BRIGHTYELLOW
        rectangle = YELLOWRECT
    elif color == BLUE:
        sound = NOTA2
        flashColor = BRIGHTBLUE
        rectangle = BLUERECT
    elif color == RED:
        sound = NOTA3
        flashColor = BRIGHTRED
        rectangle = REDRECT
    elif color == GREEN:
        sound = NOTA4
        flashColor = BRIGHTGREEN
        rectangle = GREENRECT

```

```
    origSurf = DISPLAYSURF.copy()
    flashSurf = pygame.Surface((DIMENSIONBOTON, DIMENSIONBOTON))
    flashSurf = flashSurf.convert_alpha()
    r, g, b = flashColor
    sound.play()
    for start, end, step in ((0, 255, 1), (255, 0, -1)): #
    animation loop
        for alpha in range(start, end, velocidadAnimacion * step):
            checkForQuit()
            DISPLAYSURF.blit(origSurf, (0, 0))
            flashSurf.fill((r, g, b, alpha))
            DISPLAYSURF.blit(flashSurf, rectangle.topleft)
            pygame.display.update()
            CPSCLOCK.tick(CPS)
    DISPLAYSURF.blit(origSurf, (0, 0))

def drawButtons():
    pygame.draw.rect(DISPLAYSURF, YELLOW, YELLOWRECT)
    pygame.draw.rect(DISPLAYSURF, BLUE,   BLUERECT)
    pygame.draw.rect(DISPLAYSURF, RED,    REDRECT)
    pygame.draw.rect(DISPLAYSURF, GREEN,  GREENRECT)

def testOver(color=WHITE, velocidadAnimacion=50):
    # reproduce todas las notas a la vez y luego muestra el fondo
    origSurf = DISPLAYSURF.copy()
    flashSurf = pygame.Surface(DISPLAYSURF.get_size())
    flashSurf = flashSurf.convert_alpha()
    NOTA1.play() # reproduce los cuatro NOTA aproximadamente al mismo
    tiempo.
    NOTA2.play()
    NOTA3.play()
    NOTA4.play()
    r, g, b = color
    for i in range(4): # hacer 4 veces flash
        for start, end, step in ((0, 255, 1), (255, 0, -1)):
```

```
            # La primera iteración de este bucle establece el siguiente bucle for
            # para pasar de 0 a 255, el segundo de 255 a 0.
            for alpha in range(start, end, velocidadAnimacion * step):
                # bucle de animación
                # alfa significa transparencia. 255 es opaco, 0 es
                invisible
                checkForQuit()
                flashSurf.fill((r, g, b, alpha))
                DISPLAYSURF.blit(origSurf, (0, 0))
                DISPLAYSURF.blit(flashSurf, (0, 0))
                drawButtons()
                pygame.display.update()
                CPSCLOCK.tick(CPS)

def getButtonClicked(x, y):
    if YELLOWRECT.collidepoint((x, y)):
        return YELLOW
    elif BLUERECT.collidepoint((x, y)):
        return BLUE
    elif REDRECT.collidepoint((x, y)):
        return RED
    elif GREENRECT.collidepoint((x, y)):
        return GREEN


# programa ---------------------------------------------
global CPSCLOCK, DISPLAYSURF, FONT, NOTA1, NOTA2, NOTA3, NOTA4

pygame.init()
CPSCLOCK = pygame.time.Clock()
DISPLAYSURF = pygame.display.set_mode((ANCHOPANTALLA, ALTOPANTALLA))
pygame.display.set_caption('Simon.')

```

```
FONT = pygame.font.Font(None, 30)

infoSurf = FONT.render('Play the sequence by left button clicking of the
mouse on the appropriate square.', 1, BLACK)
infoRect = infoSurf.get_rect()
infoRect.topleft = (20, ALTOPANTALLA - 45)
# cargar los archivos de sonido
NOTA1 = pygame.mixer.Sound('NOTA1.wav')
NOTA2 = pygame.mixer.Sound('NOTA2.wav')
NOTA3 = pygame.mixer.Sound('NOTA3.wav')
NOTA4 = pygame.mixer.Sound('NOTA4.wav')

# Inicia variables para una nueva ejecución
patronColores = [] # almacena los patrones de color
currentStep = 0    # el color que el jugador debe pulsar a continuación
lastClickTime = 0  # tiempo del último botón pulsado por el jugador
Puntos = 0

# Cuando es falso, el ordenador emite los patrones. Cuando es cierto,
# espera la respuesta del jugador.
waitingForInput = False

while True: # bucle principal de la tarea
    clickedButton = None # botón pulsado: YELLOW, RED, GREEN, o BLUE
    DISPLAYSURF.fill(WHITE)
    drawButtons()

    PuntosSurf = FONT.render('Points: ' + str(Puntos), 1, BLACK)
    PuntosRect = PuntosSurf.get_rect()
    PuntosRect.topleft = (860, 10)
    DISPLAYSURF.blit(PuntosSurf, PuntosRect)

    DISPLAYSURF.blit(infoSurf, infoRect)

```

```
    checkForQuit()
    for event in pygame.event.get(): # bucle de manejo de eventos
        if event.type == MOUSEBUTTONUP:
            mousex, mousey = event.pos
            clickedButton = getButtonClicked(mousex, mousey)

    if not waitingForInput:
        # Ejecuta la secuencia
        pygame.display.update()
        pygame.time.wait(900)
        patronColores.append(random.choice((YELLOW, BLUE, RED,
        GREEN)))
        print(patronColores)  #  <=========
        for button in patronColores:
            parpadeo(button)
            pygame.time.wait(RETARDO)
        waitingForInput = True
    else:
        # espera que el jugador de la respuesta
        if clickedButton and clickedButton ==
        patronColores[currentStep]:
            # botón correcto pulsado
            parpadeo(clickedButton)
            currentStep += 1
            lastClickTime = time.time()

            if currentStep == len(patronColores):
                # pulsado el último boton del patrón
                Puntos += 1
                waitingForInput = False
                currentStep = 0 # reiniciar al primer paso

        elif (clickedButton and clickedButton !=
patronColores[currentStep]) or (currentStep != 0 and time.time() -
```

```
TIEMPOESPERA > lastClickTime):
            # pulsación incorrecta o tiempo  de espera superado
            testOver()

            # Restablecer las variables para una nueva ejecución
            patronColores = []
            currentStep = 0
            waitingForInput = False
            Puntos = 0
            pygame.time.wait(1000)

    pygame.display.update()
    CPSCLOCK.tick(CPS)
```

Figure 7-1 shows the game start screen.

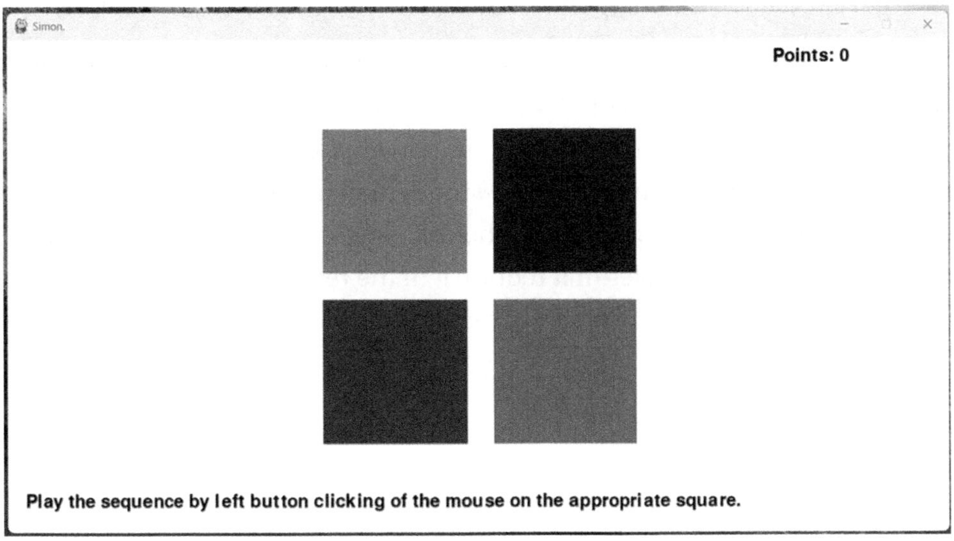

Figure 7-1. *Presentation of the Simon program home screen*

This initial screen is where the player sees the pattern offered by the computer and the one that must be entered in response with the mouse.

After the identification line, lines 3 and 4 import the libraries necessary for the program to run: `random` and `sys`.

Lines 6 through 28 specify the values of the constants that we will need in various parts of the program.

Lines 31 and 32 define the screen margins based on their dimensions.

Lines 34 through 38 define the dimensions of the various colored buttons that will be displayed on the screen.

Lines 40 through 49 control the output of the program.

Lines 51 to 82 provide the flashing sensation of buttons that are illuminated.

The `drawButtons()` function, on lines 84 through 88, draws the buttons on the screen.

The program consists of the following functions:

- `checkForQuit` exits the program if the window is closed or the Esc key is pressed.
- `blinking` animates the squares in the light on/off effect.
- `testOver` checks if the test has finished.
- `getButtonClicked` supports a mouse click response on each square.

The program itself starts on line 124, starting Pygame, variables, and loading sound files. The main loop starts on line 152, where the screen is prepared, the sequence of colors and sounds is presented, and the program is checked for an exit command. The subject's response is also submitted by pressing the left mouse button until the end of the sequence. The response's accuracy is checked, and if so, it goes to the next cycle of the loop, initializing the variables that require it. If the response is not correct, the test is interrupted, and the exercise starts again from the beginning.

Summary

In this chapter, you saw examples of how computing can enhance learning and help you develop some skills. In the next chapter, we will talk about cognitive retraining.

CHAPTER 8

Cognitive Retraining

In this chapter, we will see some cognitive rehabilitation tasks related to attention and memory.

In the late 1970s, video games began to be used as a way of complementing therapeutic action in subjects with brain damage (Lynch, 2002; Bradley, Welch and Skilbeck, 1993). The appearance of personal computers facilitated both the appearance of new specific tasks that could be developed with the help of a computer, as well as the continued use of video games for motivational purposes and to implement basic skills in the field of perception, reaction speed, decision making and cognitive development of people who had seen their brain skills drastically diminished due to an accident or illness.

The software used in cognitive rehabilitation basically comes from video games, educational programs or programs designed by re-educators (Lynch, 2002) and although their cost and ease of application are, in general, very favorable, and they are considered a valuable complement to re-education, their effectiveness is still highly debated today given that often the subject can handle the task on the computer well but this ability is not generalized to everyday life tasks.

The activities presented by the computer require the subject or patient to manipulate standard input devices (keyboard, mouse or joystick) to control movements, position and speed of the elements on the screen, which implies fast reaction time, sustained attention, divided attention, visual tracking, acquisition of objectives and anticipation of the effect of the responses, all of which are skills that need to be developed and perfected in subjects with cerebral disabilities, so subjecting them to these activities can be interesting, especially if we take into account that the computer environment maintains the subject's motivation.

Some of the games that were initially used in re-education, rehabilitation can now be obtained for free from archive sites such as `https://www.myabandonware.com/` or `https://oldgamesdownload.com/`.

J. M. Roig-Fusté, *Python for Psychology, Social Sciences, and Education*,
https://doi.org/10.1007/979-8-8688-2355-8_8

Here we will only present some simple games that require quick reaction time, sustained and divided attention, and hand-eye coordination. Currently, more complex activities can be programmed that involve virtual reality, a topic that we will briefly discuss later.

An Example: Cancellation of Points

An easy activity to program is to cancel points that appear on the screen, at a certain rate, with a mouse click. To write this simple program, we will use the guizero library that we have already used previously to make a graphical menu; so in line 4 of the following program, we import all the components that we need from guizero (App, Text, Waffle, and PushButton). Next, we import other libraries that may be necessary for the program, lines 5–7. See Program 8-1.

The program itself starts on line 47 and runs through line 67. It should be noted that this is an event-driven program, i.e., a program that will display a screen and wait for the operator to interact with it. This means counters or conditions cannot be placed in the body of the program, which would block it, and that these structures, if necessary, must be placed in programmed functions with different purposes. In this case, the functions are `add_point`, `delete_point`, `counter`, and `close`, defined on lines 14, 22, 33, and 41.

Program 8-1.

```
1   # Delete points. deletePoints.py
2   # Dr. Roig / 10.28.24 / Version 0.1
3
4   from guizero import App, Text, Waffle, PushButton
5   from random import randint
6   import sys
7   import time
8
9   # Variables --------------------------------
10
11  global score
12  score = 0
13
14
```

```
# functions--------------------------------
def add_point ():
    x, y = randint (0,9), randint (0,9)
    while board [x,y].dotty == True:
        x, y = randint (0,9), randint (0,9)
    board[x, y].dotty = True
    board.set_pixel (x,y,"red")
    board.after (1000, add_point) # add a point every second

def delete_point (x, y):
    # declare the variable puntua as global
    global score

    if board[ x,y ].dotty == True:
        board[ x,y ] .dotty = False
        board.set_pixel (x,y,"white")
        score = score + 1
        score_sample.value = 'Score ' + str(score)
        score_sample.size = 20

def counter():
    text.value = int(text.value) + 1
    if int(text.value) > 30:
        board.hide()
        text.hide()
        text.hide()
        # text = Text(app, text = " Exercise completed.")

def close():
# Ask the user if they really want to close the window
    if app.yesno ("Close", "Do you want to quit?"):
        app.destroy()

# program -------------------------------------
app = App("Delete the points", height =450, width =540)

```

```
51  instructions = Text(app, text =" Click with the mouse on the")
52  instructions.size = 25
53  instructions = Text(app, text ="points to delete.")
54  instructions.size = 25
55
    board = Waffle(app, width=10, height=10, command= delete_point )
56  board.after (1000, add_point) # add a point for each circle cancelled
57  score_sample = Text(app, text ="Score: " + str (score))
58  score_sample.size = 20
59
60  text = Text(app, text ="Time")
61  text = Text(app, text ="1")
62
63  text.repeat (1000, counter) # Call counter () every second
64
65  button = PushButton (app, text = ' Exit ', command= close )
66  app.display()
67
68  sys.exit()
```

The program starts on line 47, displaying a grid of 100 white squares, which is set on line 54 by indicating the height and width of the grid. When indicating these values, it is necessary to consider that the grid does not exceed the limits of the screen.

The white squares randomly turn into red dots at a rate of one every second, as shown in Figure 8-1.

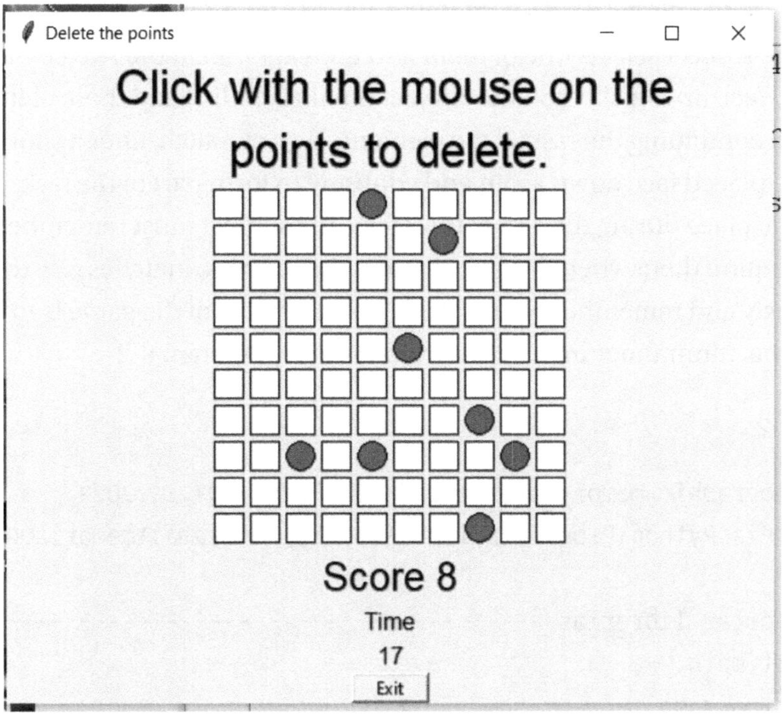

Figure 8-1. *Game screen*

These red dots disappear if the subject clicks the left mouse button with the pointer on them, and one dot is counted for each click made. In line 35, a specific time in seconds can be programmed for the exercise in the counter function, and the dots can appear quickly by changing the value in line 62, which is set to one second, indicated in milliseconds (1000).

The program awards one point for each circle cancelled and counts the time it should be running, in this case half a minute. When awarding the speed of appearance of the points and the duration of the task, the subject's condition must be considered, as well as their capacity and the fatigue that the task may cause. It is not advisable for this type of exercise to last very long due to its monotony and induce fatigue.

Topographic Memory

The following example is based on the classic topographic memory game that can be used with small children or in re-education tasks for brain-injured people who need to exercise their attention and memory. The task consists of pairs of elements that are distributed in a disordered manner. At the beginning they are hidden, like face-down cards, and the subject selects one of them and then another. If the two elements that are momentarily face up match, then the subject obtains credits, and these elements do not count toward continuing the task. If the elements do not match, after a short space of time they are placed face down again and continue to form part of the task. The elements do not change place during the game; therefore, the subject must remember their location to require them when the first element they choose matches one that they have seen previously and remembers its location. The objective of the game is to discover all the pairs in the minimum number of movements. See Program 8-2.

Program 8-2.

```
# Topographic memory exercise / Dr. Roig - 07.11.2022
# H:\PiacPython\ProgramesLlibre\memory(Memorama)\memoria007.py

# importar librerias ---------------------------------------
import math
import pygame
from pygame import mixer
from pygame.locals import *
import random
import sys
from sys import exit
import time

# Constantes
altura_areaInf = 60  # Bottom button, to start game
medida_dibujo = 150  # Image measurement in pixels

# Colour
BLANCO = (255, 255, 255)
NEGRO = (  0,   0,   0)
AZUL =  ( 30, 136, 229)

# Control variables
tiempo = 0
```

```
tiempoInicial = 0
intentos = 0

# Start pygame
pygame.init()
pygame.font.init()
pygame.mixer.init()


# Reverse of the drawings
REVERSO = pygame.image.load("revers.png")
TIEMPO_EXPOSICION_IMAGENES = 3  # en segundos


class dibujo:
    def __init__(self, arxiu_imagen):
        self.mostrar = True
        self.descubierto = False
        self.arxiu_imagen = arxiu_imagen
        self.imagen = pygame.image.load(arxiu_imagen)
        print(self.imagen)


# Drawing matrix ....................................
matriz_dib = [
    [dibujo("broccoli.png"), dibujo("broccoli.png"),
     dibujo("cabbage.png"), dibujo("cabbage.png"),
     dibujo("limon.png"), dibujo("limon.png")],
    [dibujo("carrots.png"), dibujo("carrots.png"),
     dibujo("lettuce.png"), dibujo("lettuce.png"),
     dibujo("fresa.png"), dibujo("fresa.png")],
    [dibujo("mushrooms.png"), dibujo("mushrooms.png"),
     dibujo("onion.png"), dibujo("onion.png"),
     dibujo("manzana.png"), dibujo("manzana.png")],
```

```
    [dibujo("pepper.png"), dibujo("pepper.png"),
     dibujo("tomato.png"), dibujo("tomato.png"),
     dibujo("platano.png"), dibujo("platano.png")],
]


# Calculate the screen size based on the size of the squares
anchura_pantalla = (len(matriz_dib[0]) * medida_dibujo) + 40
altura_pantalla = ((len(matriz_dib) * medida_dibujo) + altura_
areaInf)
anchura_areaInf = anchura_pantalla

# Button font
tamanyo_fuente = 45
fuente = pygame.font.SysFont("verdana", tamanyo_fuente)
xFuente = 200
yFuente = 600

# The rectangular button at the bottom of the screen
areaInf = pygame.Rect(0, altura_pantalla - altura_areaInf,
                      anchura_areaInf, altura_pantalla)

# Flag to know if the card should be hidden within N seconds
ultimos_segundos = None
jugar = True
juego_iniciado = False

# x1 and y1 for the first card
x1 = None
y1 = None
# x2 and y2 for the second card
x2 = None
y2 = None


```

```
# Funciones -----------------------------------------------------
--------------------
def checkForQuit():
    for event in pygame.event.get(QUIT): # Salir del programa
    al cerrar
la ventana
        pygame.quit()
        sys.exit()

    for event in pygame.event.get(KEYUP): # captar pulsaciones
    de tecla
        if event.key == K_ESCAPE:
            pygame.quit()
            sys.exit()


# Ocultar todos los dibujos de la matgriz / matriz_dib
def ocultar_matriz_dib():
    for fila in matriz_dib:
        for dibujo in fila:
            dibujo.mostrar = False
            dibujo.descubierto = False


def aleatorizar_matriz_dib():
    # Elegir X e Y aleatorios, intercambiar
    cantidad_filas = len(matriz_dib)
    cantidad_columnas = len(matriz_dib[0])
    for y in range(cantidad_filas):
        for x in range(cantidad_columnas):
            x_aleatorio = random.randint(0, cantidad_columnas - 1)
            y_aleatorio = random.randint(0, cantidad_filas - 1)
            dibujo_temporal = matriz_dib[y][x]
            matriz_dib[y][x] = matriz_dib[y_aleatorio][x_aleatorio]
            matriz_dib[y_aleatorio][x_aleatorio] = dibujo_temporal
```

```


def comprobar_si_gana():
    if gana():
        reiniciar_juego()


# Returns False if at least one drawing is NOT discovered or True if
all are discovered
def gana():
    for fila in matriz_dib:
        for dibujo in fila:
            if not dibujo.descubierto:
                return False
    return True


def iniciar_juego():
    global juego_iniciado
    # Aleatorizar 2 veces
    for i in range(2):
        aleatorizar_matriz_dib()
    ocultar_matriz_dib()
    juego_iniciado = True


def reiniciar_juego():
    global juego_iniciado
    juego_iniciado = False


# start task -----------------------------------------------------------
# Instructions
screen = pygame.display.set_mode((960, 540), RESIZABLE, 32)
screen.fill(BLANCO)
```

```

pygame.display.set_caption('Memory exercise / instructions')
letra = pygame.font.SysFont('verdana', 25)

txt01 = letra.render('On the next screen, you will find 24 cards with
question', 0, (0,0,0))
txt02 = letra.render('marks, hiding 12 pairs of pictures. You
must find
each pair', 0, (0,0,0))
txt03 = letra.render('in as few attempts as possible. Left-click on a
card and then', 0, (0,0,0))
txt04 = letra.render('on any other. If the picture on the cards
matches, they will', 0, (0,0,0))
txt05 = letra.render('remain on the screen, and you can continue
playing to find', 0, (0,0,0))
txt06 = letra.render("new pairs. If they don't match, they will
disappear immediately.", 0, (0,0,0))
txt07 = letra.render('Make sure you memorize the picture and its
position on the', 0, (0,0,0))
txt08 = letra.render('screen to find the pairs more quickly.', 0,
(0,0,0))
txt09 = letra.render('', 0, (0,0,0))
txt10 = letra.render('', 0, (0,0,0))
txt11 = letra.render('', 0, (0,0,0))
txt12 = letra.render("When you're ready, press the spacebar.", 0,
(0,0,0))

screen.blit(txt01, (40, 50))
screen.blit(txt02, (40, 80))
screen.blit(txt03, (40, 110))
screen.blit(txt04, (40, 140))
screen.blit(txt05, (40, 170))
screen.blit(txt06, (40, 200))
screen.blit(txt07, (40, 230))
screen.blit(txt08, (40, 260))
```

```
screen.blit(txt09, (40, 290))
screen.blit(txt10, (40, 320))

screen.blit(txt12, (40, 380))

pygame.display.update()

key_pressed = False
while not key_pressed: # Esperar que el sujeto haya leido las
instrucciones.
    for event in pygame.event.get():
        if event.type == pygame.KEYDOWN:
            key_pressed = True

iniciar_juego()

# draw screen
pantalla = pygame.display.set_mode((anchura_pantalla, altura_
pantalla))
pygame.display.set_caption('Memory Exercise')

# Task loop.
while True:
    # Collect events
    for event in pygame.event.get():
        # exit event
        if event.type == pygame.QUIT:
            pygame.quit()
            sys.exit()
        # Click event, user plays
        elif event.type == pygame.MOUSEBUTTONDOWN and jugar:

            # Click on the button, the game starts if it is
            not started
yet.
```

```
            xAbsoluto, yAbsoluto = event.pos
            if areaInf.collidepoint(event.pos):
                if not juego_iniciado:
                    iniciar_juego()

            else:
                # If the game is not started, the click is ignored
                if not juego_iniciado:
                    continue

                x = math.floor(xAbsoluto / medida_dibujo)
                y = math.floor(yAbsoluto / medida_dibujo)
                # If the card is already uncovered, it does nothing.
                dibujo = matriz_dib[y][x]
                if dibujo.mostrar or dibujo.descubierto:
                    continue

                if x1 is None and y1 is None:
                    x1 = x
                    y1 = y
                    matriz_dib[y1][x1].mostrar = True
                    intentos = intentos + 1
                    pIntentos = "Trials: " + str(intentos)
                    pantalla.blit(fuente.render(str(intentos), True,
                    BLANCO), (xFuente, yFuente))
                    pygame.display.update()

                else:
                    # If are looking for a partner, compare
                    x2 = x
                    y2 = y
                    matriz_dib[y2][x2].mostrar = True
                    dibujo1 = matriz_dib[y1][x1]
                    dibujo2 = matriz_dib[y2][x2]
```

```
                    # If they match, they are uncovered.
                    if dibujo1.arxiu_imagen == dibujo2.arxiu_imagen:
                        matriz_dib[y1][x1].descubierto = True
                        matriz_dib[y2][x2].descubierto = True
                        x1 = None
                        x2 = None
                        y1 = None
                        y2 = None

                    else:
                        # If they do not match, they hide in
                        2 seconds
                        ultimos_segundos = int(time.time())
                        # It can't continue the game until the
                        time is up.
                        jugar = False
                comprobar_si_gana()

    ahora = int(time.time())

    if ultimos_segundos is not None and ahora - ultimos_segundos >=
TIEMPO_EXPOSICION_IMAGENES:
        matriz_dib[y1][x1].mostrar = False
        matriz_dib[y2][x2].mostrar = False
        x1 = None
        y1 = None
        x2 = None
        y2 = None
        ultimos_segundos = None

        jugar = True

    pantalla.fill(BLANCO)
    # Flags to place the various images
```

```
    x = 0
    y = 0
    # Tour matriz_dib
    for fila in matriz_dib:
        x = 40  # starts placing drawings 40 pixels from the left
        margin
        for dibujo in fila:

            if dibujo.descubierto or dibujo.mostrar:
                pantalla.blit(dibujo.imagen, (x, y))
            else:
                pantalla.blit(REVERSO, (x, y))
            x += medida_dibujo
        y += medida_dibujo

    # Draw the button at the bottom of the screen
    if juego_iniciado:
        pygame.draw.rect(pantalla, BLANCO, areaInf)
        pantalla.blit(fuente.render(
            "Trials: ", str(intentos), True, BLANCO), (xFuente,
             yFuente))
        pygame.display.update()
    else:
        pygame.draw.rect(pantalla, AZUL, areaInf)
        pantalla.blit(fuente.render(
            "Restart game", True, BLANCO), (xFuente, yFuente))

    pygame.display.update()


pygame.QUIT
sys.exit()
```

The program initially offers some instructions (Figure 8-2).

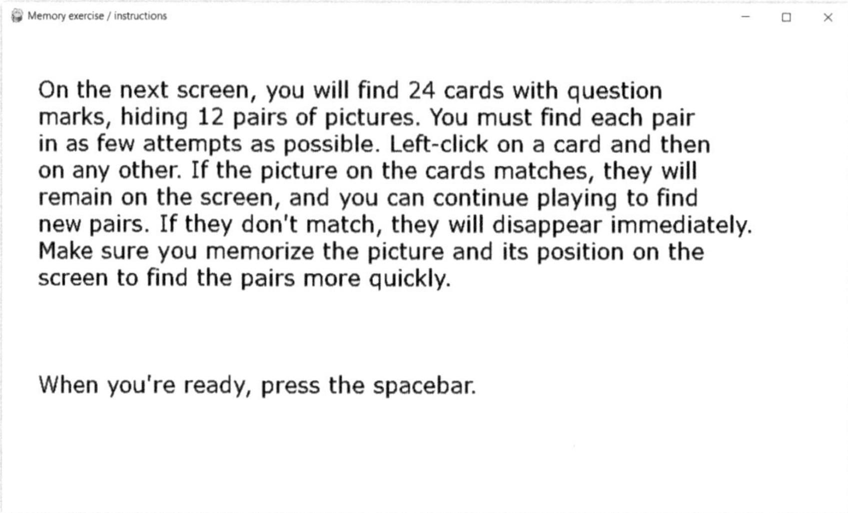

Figure 8-2. *Instructions*

When the subject has read the instructions and agrees to continue, the program presents the 24 cards face down (Figure 8-3) and waits for the subject's first click. After this, the image of the chosen card is displayed, and the second click is awaited. After this, the subject checks to see if the images are the same. In this case (Figure 8-4), the images remain on the screen. If they are not the same, the images are hidden again after three seconds to give the subject time to memorize their position to make the right moves in the future.

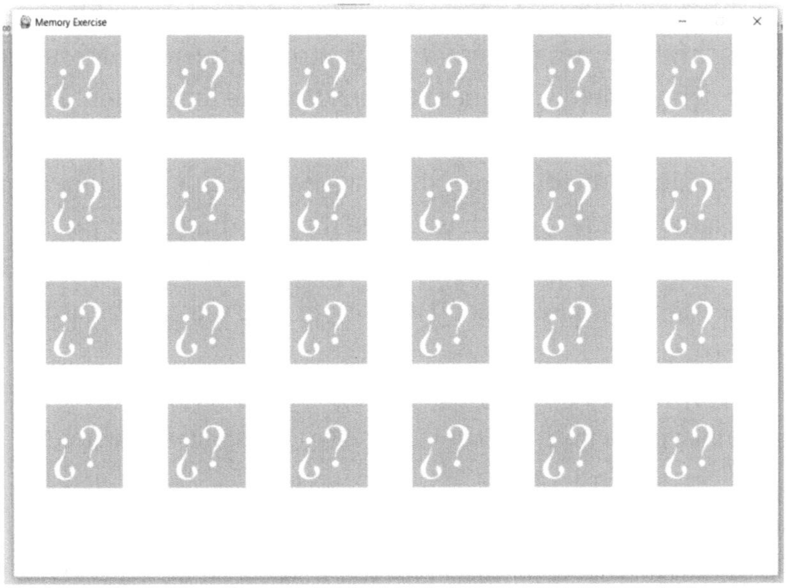

Figure 8-3. *Waiting for subject first click*

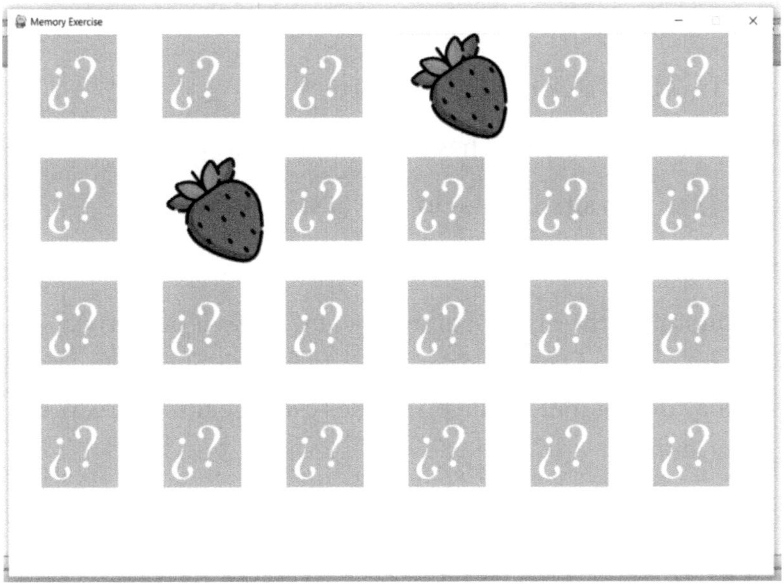

Figure 8-4. *The images are the same*

The task ends when all the pairs have been discovered.

In lines 5 to 12, the libraries necessary for their operation are imported. Constants and variables are defined below. In lines 30 to 32, Pygame has started. The image on the back of the cards and the exposure time of the images are defined and loaded.

The matrix containing the drawings, `drawing_matrix`, is a two-dimensional matrix with six columns and four rows, which is loaded into the drawing class.

Next, the screen size is calculated to accommodate all the drawings, and the font to be used in the Pygame window is set. The bottom area that will be used to provide information is also created.

The game starts on line 160, creating the window and displaying the instructions. This screen remains visible until the subject presses the spacebar, when the task itself begins.

The game has the following features:

- `checkForQuit`: Check if the subject has located all the pairs.
- `randomize_matrix_drawings`: Mix the drawings before starting the activity.
- `hide_draw_array`: Hide the drawings.
- `check_if_win`: Check if the pair is correct.
- `Win`: It reports that the task has been successfully completed.
- `start game`: Sets all variables to zero to start the task.
- `restart game`: Restarts.

The game randomizes the array of drawings and keeps it hidden, lets the use choose the drawings two by two, and checks if the drawings match in the function. If they match, the user wins. If they do not match, the user hides them again. When all the drawings are revealed, the game ends.

Another Way to Schedule a Topographic Memory Task

As we have already mentioned, any task can be scheduled in many ways. To illustrate this, we will schedule the previous task again in a more compact way, with the help of the Tkinter library. See Program 8-3.

Program 8-3.

```
from tkinter import *
from tkinter import messagebox
import random
import sys

intentos = 0

class Carta:
    def __init__(self):
        self.valor = 0
        self.posicion = 0
        self.oculto = True
        self.figura = PhotoImage(file = "reverso.png")

class Pantalla:
    global intentos
    def __init__(self):
        self.ventana = Tk()
        self.ventana.title('Topographic memory exercise')
        self.ventana.geometry('500x500')
        self.botones = []
        self.cartas = []
        self.temporal = Carta()
        self.a = 0
        self.par = 0
        self.seguir = True
        self.reverso = PhotoImage(file = "reverso.png")
        self.crearTablero()
        self.mezclar()
        self.ventana.mainloop()

    def crearTablero(self):
        contador = 0
        for i in range(4):
```

```
            j = 0
            for j in range(4):
                btn = Button(self.ventana, command = lambda a =
                contador:self.revisar(a),
                             height = 80, width = 80, image =
                             self.reverso)
                btn.place(x = (j + 1)*80, y = (i + 1)*80)
                self.botones.append(btn)
                contador += 1

    def mezclar(self):
        i = 1
        while(i<=8):
            carta1 = Carta()
            carta1.valor = i
            carta1.figura = PhotoImage(file = str(i) + ".png")
            carta2 = Carta()
            carta2.valor = i
            carta2.figura = PhotoImage(file = str(i) + ".png")
            self.cartas.append(carta1)
            self.cartas.append(carta2)
            i += 1
        cartasTemporal = []
        while len(self.cartas) > 0:
            posicion = random.randrange(0, len(self.cartas))
            cartasTemporal.append(self.cartas.pop(posicion))
        self.cartas = cartasTemporal

    def revisar(self, a):
        global intentos
        if self.seguir == True and self.cartas[a].oculto == True:
            self.botones[a].config(image = self.cartas[a].figura)
            if self.par == 0:
                self.temporal = self.cartas[a]
                self.cartas[a].oculto = False
```

```
                self.temporal.posicion = a
                self.par = 1
            elif self.par == 1:
                self.par = 0
                if self.temporal.valor == self.cartas[a].valor:
                    self.cartas[a].oculto = False
                    bandera = True
                    for elemento in self.cartas:
                        if elemento.oculto  == True:
                            bandera = False
                            break
                    if bandera == True:
                        messagebox.showinfo("Fin", "Tarea finalizada")
                else:
                    self.a = a
                    self.seguir = False
                    self.ventana.after(1100, self.cubrir)

                intentos = intentos + 1
                print(intentos)

    def cubrir(self):
        self.cartas[self.temporal.posicion].oculto = True
        self.botones[self.temporal.posicion].config(image =
self.reverso)
        self.botones[self.a].config(image = self.reverso)
        self.seguir = True


app = Pantalla()
sys.exit()
```

The first four lines import the libraries needed for the program; line 6 defines the variable's attempts as a global variable. The program consists of two classes: the first `Card` and the second `Screen`.

The `Card` class defines the characteristics of the images that will be presented in the exercise, such as `value`, which specifies whether it is even or not; `position`, which places it on the screen; `hidden` with values of `True` or `False`, depending on whether the image is hidden or not; and `figure`, which contains the filename of the image.

The `Screen` class is used to create the work screen and the variables to manage the exercise: a button array, a card array, a temporary variable to save the first card chosen, the variable `a` with the position of the second card chosen, the variable `par` to know if it is the first or the second card, and the variable `ready` in True allows the game to continue. The variable `back` saves the image of the back of the cards.

The `Screen` class also has various methods for creating the cards on the screen, shuffling the cards before starting the task, and checking whether the cards are the same or different, as well as checking whether the task has finished with all the cards face up.

The program starts with the screen shown in Figure 8-5.

***Figure 8-5.** Program start*

At the end of the task, when all the elements are uncovered, the screen in Figure 8-6 appears.

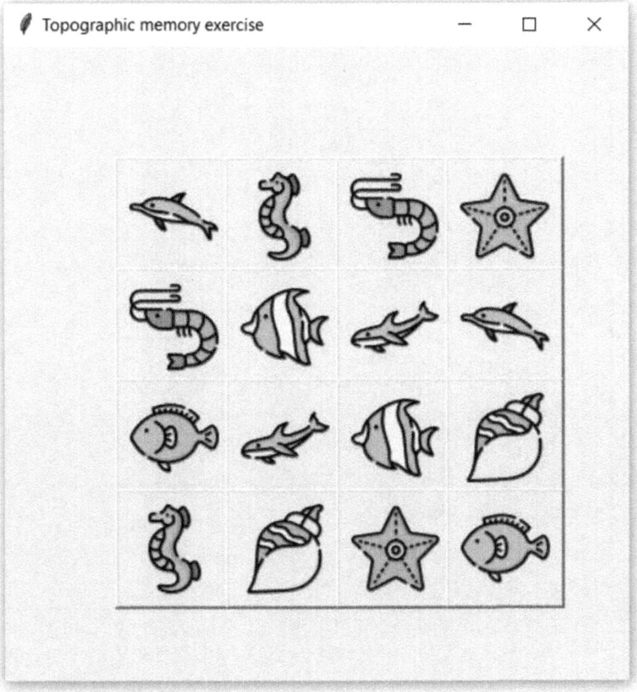

Figure 8-6. *End of the task*

Computer programming allows for personalized education, not only because it can implement tailor-made plans for each student but also because it facilitates a deep understanding of each student's progress, since all interactions that the subject has with the computer can be recorded. Developing educational programs is time-consuming and expensive, but once developed, they can be applied to millions of people, which represents great efficiency. In addition, new developments in virtual reality, which can also be easily programmed in Python (Eichenberg, 2012; Manolas, Xanthidou and Xanthidis, 2022), will improve the learning process.

Summary

In this chapter, you saw some cognitive rehabilitation tasks related to attention and memory, which the computer handles with great efficiency. In the next chapter, you will see how Python can also be used in social research.

CHAPTER 9

Social Research

In this chapter, we will see some examples of tasks applicable to social research, developed with Python.

Social research is a broad field that covers opinion studies (Fink, 1995; Peterson, 2000), personal relationships, leadership, simulations (Gilbert and Troitzsch, 2005), social networks (Brooker, 2020; Foster, Ghani, Jarmin, Kreuter and Lane, 2017), etc., plus all the theoretical developments that attempt to explain relational dynamics. Python can be useful in many of these fields, but here we will mention only two examples: survey management and sociometric testing.

Survey Management with Python

Surveys are a common form of data collection in social research. This method is like the psychological questionnaires we've already discussed and can be administered in different ways: through an interview, on paper, or online.

Survey management with Python can cover a variety of areas, from creating and publishing surveys online to data collection and analysis. Tools like Flask and Django, as well as libraries like the ArcGIS API for Python, can be used to create web survey applications, while libraries like Pandas facilitate the analysis of data collected, whether online or in any other form.

Python allows for the processing of both open-ended and closed-ended surveys, where responses are made by choosing one of the predetermined options on a five- or seven-point Likert scale. Open-ended surveys are more difficult to analyze and will be managed using natural language analysis techniques, which we'll discuss later.

It's advisable to start by drafting a set of questions related to the topic we want to research, and from which we'll build our survey. Once the survey is written, it's wise to evaluate the questions through a pilot study with a small number of subjects, before creating the final survey.

J. M. Roig-Fusté, *Python for Psychology, Social Sciences, and Education*,
https://doi.org/10.1007/979-8-8688-2355-8_9

Once the data has been collected, it must be cleaned. This means removing surveys that were not answered correctly and are not advisable to process, as well as those with missing data. The Pandas library can be used for this task.

The internal consistency of the questions can then be analyzed using an index such as Cronbach's alpha; the Pandas library can also be used for this purpose.

Descriptive statistics can be analyzed with NumPy and inferential statistics with Pandas Scikit-Learn or SciPy.

Analysis of open-ended surveys can be carried out with SpaCy, which allows you to identify the words and themes that appear in the responses.

Sociometric Tests

Sociometric testing is a simple technique that can be applied to small groups of people who have known each other for a long time or who spend time together in a specific setting, such as a school classroom. Initially, information must be collected from each person in the group, through an interview or a questionnaire, about their likes and dislikes toward the rest of the people in the group. The design of this technique began with the work of the Romanian psychiatrist Jacob Lévy Moreno (1934), who emigrated to the United States in 1925, where he investigated social interactions in a prison environment, representing them on a map he called a sociogram (Marineau, 1989).

Here we will limit ourselves to developing a small example. For further information on sociometry, see Bukowski and Cillessen (1998), Gronlund (1959), Jennings (1959), Moreno (1956), Northway (1957, 1967), and Roistacher (1974).

Sociometric test management in Python allows you to quickly and easily analyze attraction and rejection relationships within a group of subjects. This technique also allows you to visualize a group's social structure through a sociogram. In Python, social network analysis libraries are used to more easily construct and visualize these sociograms.

The process of using the sociometric test in Python requires the following steps:

1. **Data collection:**

   Data should be collected on each group member's preferences for other members of the same group. This can be done through a questionnaire or survey, in which participants select which people they like to work or associate with and which they don't.

2. **Creation of a sociometric matrix:**

   The election data is organized in a matrix, where each row and column represents a group member. A cell in the matrix indicates whether a member has chosen another (attraction) or not (rejection).

3. **Matrix analysis:**

   Python can be used to analyze the sociometric matrix and calculate indices such as the number of times a member is chosen, the number of times they choose others, and the degree of group cohesion.

4. **Visualization of the sociogram:**

   The networkx and matplotlib libraries can be used to graphically represent the data in a sociogram, showing the attraction and rejection relationships between group members.

Program 9-1 shows the code for an example sociometric test.

Program 9-1.

```
# Sociogram management 2025.07.01

import tkinter as tk
import matplotlib.pyplot as plt
import networkx as nx


class SociogramApp:
    def __init__(self, root):
        self.root = root
        self.root.title("Sociogram")
        self.subject_entries = []
        self.choices = []
        self.subject_names = []
        self.choice_vars = []

```

```
        self.setup_initial_ui()

    def setup_initial_ui(self):
        self.clear_window()
        tk.Label(self.root, text="Enter number of subjects (5 to 10):").pack()
        self.num_subjects_entry = tk.Entry(self.root)
        self.num_subjects_entry.pack()
        tk.Button(self.root, text="Submit", command=self.get_subject_count).pack()

    def get_subject_count(self):
        try:
            count = int(self.num_subjects_entry.get())
            if 5 <= count <= 10:
                self.subject_count = count
                self.setup_subject_input()
            else:
                messagebox.showerror("Error", "Please enter a number between 8 and 10.")
        except ValueError:
            messagebox.showerror("Error", "Invalid number.")

    def setup_subject_input(self):
        self.clear_window()
        tk.Label(self.root, text="Enter names of the subjects:").pack()
        self.subject_entries = []
        for _ in range(self.subject_count):
            entry = tk.Entry(self.root)
            entry.pack()
            self.subject_entries.append(entry)
        tk.Button(self.root, text="Next", command=self.get_subject_names).pack()

```

```python
    def get_subject_names(self):
        self.subject_names = [entry.get().strip() for entry in self.subject_entries]
        if "" in self.subject_names or len(set(self.subject_names)) != self.subject_count:
            messagebox.showerror("Error", "All names must be unique and non-empty.")
            return
        self.setup_choice_input()

    def setup_choice_input(self):
        self.clear_window()
        tk.Label(self.root, text="Select one choice for each subject:").pack()
        self.choice_vars = []
        for name in self.subject_names:
            frame = tk.Frame(self.root)
            frame.pack()
            tk.Label(frame, text=f"{name} chooses:").pack(side=tk.LEFT)
            var = tk.StringVar()
            var.set(self.subject_names[0])
            dropdown = tk.OptionMenu(frame, var, *[n for n in self.subject_names if n != name])
            dropdown.pack(side=tk.LEFT)
            self.choice_vars.append((name, var))
        tk.Button(self.root, text="Generate Sociogram", command=self.generate_sociogram).pack()

    def generate_sociogram(self):
        choices = {name: var.get() for name, var in self.choice_vars}
        G = nx.DiGraph()
        G.add_nodes_from(self.subject_names)
        for src, dst in choices.items():
```

```
            G.add_edge(src, dst)

        plt.figure(figsize=(8, 6))
        pos = nx.spring_layout(G)
        nx.draw(G, pos, with_labels=True,
node_color='lightblue', edge_color='gray',
node_size=2000, font_size=10, arrows=True)
        plt.title("Sociogram")
        plt.show()


    def clear_window(self):
        for widget in self.root.winfo_children():
            widget.destroy()


if __name__ == "__main__":
    root = tk.Tk()
    app = SociogramApp(root)
    root.mainloop()
```

In this program, the Tkinter library allows the graphical presentation of the program; networkx is used to create and manipulate the graph; and matplotlib allows the visualization of the result, showing the nodes (subjects) and the edges (relationships).

This simplified example illustrates how Python libraries can be used to represent and analyze data from a sociometric test. In practice, the code can be adapted to include different data types, more complex analyses, and more detailed visualizations.

Figure 9-1 illustrates the sociogram.

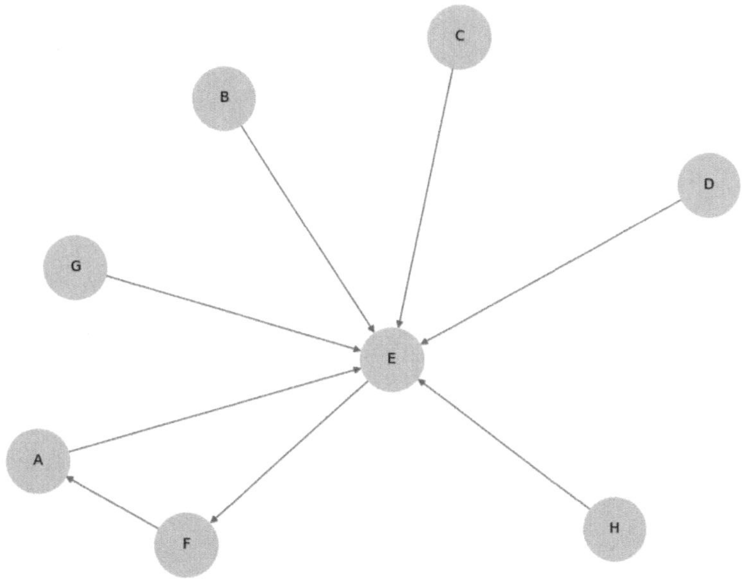

Figure 9-1. *Sociogram*

The graph represents a group of six members, each represented by a circle, with the choices each makes. In this case, only one choice per subject has been considered; more weighted choices can be considered depending on whether it is the first, second, etc.

Summary

In this chapter, you saw examples of tasks applicable to social research, developed with Python. In the next chapter, you will see applications for artificial intelligence.

CHAPTER 10

Artificial Intelligence and Machine Learning/Deep Learning

In this chapter, we will see some examples of artificial intelligence that can be useful in human sciences, developed with the help of Python.

The programs we've presented so far do things that are intended to be useful and correct. In a certain sense, we can say they're intelligent, but they're not intelligent on their own; instead, it is because their creator has built rational mechanisms into them. However, once written, they act on their own without any intervention from the programmer, so we could say the programmer has endowed them with intelligence, and this intelligence, abstracted from the programmer, could be called artificial intelligence. The next step is to consider whether the program simply reproduces what the programmer has prepared, which would not be a sign of great intelligence or whether it's capable of learning on its own and going beyond the programmer's own abilities. Some believe that only the first option is possible, thereby denying the possibility of the existence of an independent artificial intelligence. However, others believe the second option will be reached, in which intelligent programs, once created, will no longer depend on a programmer and will act on their own, creating an intelligence more remarkable than human intelligence, which will allow them to create other, more advanced programs and continue to evolve. It's hard to say what things will be like in 20 or 30 years, but certainly, at some point or another, the second option is very likely to emerge.

The first intelligent applications emerged in fields such as expert systems, to help professionals make decisions, and computer simulations of reality (Downey, 2023), to study and develop theories or to train subjects to perform tasks such as driving a car or flying a plane. Artificial intelligence is a fairly young science that began with the ideas of

J. M. Roig-Fusté, *Python for Psychology, Social Sciences, and Education*,
https://doi.org/10.1007/979-8-8688-2355-8_10

Alan Turing and takes its name from a conference organized by John McCarthy in 1956 at Dartmouth's College of New Hampshire, a conference that was at the time of little use (Coperland, 1993).

Perspectives on Artificial Intelligence

Despite the incredible advances it has already achieved to date, AI continues to make mistakes, "hallucinate" (invent data or references that don't exist), and generate code with significant operational vulnerabilities if its training hasn't been sufficiently extensive or the instructions it is provided are inaccurate or incomplete. Therefore, currently, blind trust in AI entails significant risks, especially if adequate verification and validation processes for its operation and the results it provides aren't established.

An expert system can be a program for interpreting a psychological test such as the one we outlined for the original MMPI in Chapter 5 of this book (Seisdedos, Roig-Fusté, 1986; Roig-Fusté, 1993; 2020). In the following sections, we will discuss simulation processes, with a couple of examples, one of them involving the MMPI-2.

Simulation

To introduce simulation, we'll begin by discussing cellular automata, which have been used in physics, biology, and sociology to model phenomena such as population dynamics and disease transmission. In the social sciences, they have been used to explain events as diverse as the spread of gossip, the formation of gangs, ethnic segregation, and attitude change (Gilbert and Troitzsch, 2005).

As an example, we will look at the Game of Life by the British mathematician John Horton Conway (see Program 10-1).

The Game of Life consists of a grid, as large as you like, with elements or not, along with simple rules that define when one element causes another to appear or disappear over time; thus, elements can create other elements, under favorable conditions, or disappear due to overpopulation or isolation. The rules are as follows:

a) An element remains if it has two or three elements around it; if it does not have any, it disappears.

b) When there are three elements around a grid cell, a new element appears in it.

Program 10-1.

```
# Game of Life

import pygame
import numpy as np
import time
import sys

# Game window
pygame.init()
width = 600
height = 600
screen = pygame.display.set_mode ((height, width))
pygame.display.set_caption("Conway's Game of Life.")
bg = (0, 0, 255)
screen.fill ( bg )

# Number of cells on the x-axis and on the y-axis
ncX, ncY= 40, 40

# cell size
dimCW = width / ncX
dimCH = height / ncY

# we initialize all cells to 0
cells = np.zeros ((ncX , ncY))

# initial values for starting up the PLC
cells[11, 11] = 1
cells[12, 12] = 1
cells[12, 13] = 1
cells[11, 13] = 1
cells[10, 13] = 1
cells[12, 15] = 1
cells[11, 14] = 1
```

```
cells[10, 15] = 1
cells[13, 15] = 1
cells[13, 14] = 1
cells[13, 15] = 1
cells[9, 15] = 1
cells[9, 15] = 1
cells[9, 14] = 1
cells[9, 15] = 1

# Controlling game execution
pauseExect = False

# Execution loop
while True:
    ''' Create a copy of cells on which to make changes, to that
    are performed at the same time in each cycle of the loop'''

    newcells = np.copy (cells)

    # Color the screen on each cycle
    screen.fill ( bg )

    # introduces a time delay for smoother motion
    time.sleep (0.3)

    # Logs keyboard and mouse events
    ev = pygame.event.get ()

    for event in ev:
        if event.type == pygame.QUIT:
            pygame.quit ()
            sys.exit ()

        # Detects if pressed a key
        if event.type == pygame.KEYDOWN:
```

```
                if event.key == pygame.K_ESCAPE:
                    pygame.quit()
                    sys.exit()

            # pauseExect = not pauseExect

            # collects keyboard and mouse keystrokes
            mouseClick = pygame.mouse.get_pressed()

            if sum( mouseClick ) > 0:
                posX, posY = pygame.mouse.get_pos()
                celX, celY = int (np.floor (posX/dimCW)), int (np.floor
                (posY / dimCH))
                newcells[celX, celY] = 1

        for y in range(0, ncX ):
            for x in range(0, ncY ):

                # if not pauseExect:

                # We calculate the number of close neighbors
                n_neigh = (cells[(x-1) % ncX , (y-1) % ncY ] + cells[(x)
                % ncX , (y-1) % ncY ] +
                           cells[( x+1 ) % ncX , (y-1) % ncY ] +
                           cells[(x-1) %
                           ncX , (y) % ncY ] +
                           cells[( x+1 ) % ncX , (y) % ncY ] +
                           cells[(x-1)
% ncX , ( y+1 ) % ncY ] +
                           cells[(x) % ncX , ( y+1 ) % ncY ] +
                           cells[( x+1) % ncX ,
                           ( y+1 ) % ncY ])

                # Rule 1: An inactive cell is activated with 3 active
                neighbors
```

```
            if cells [x, y] == 0 and n_neigh == 3:
                newcells [x, y] = 1

            # Rule 2: An active cell with less than 2 or more than 3
active cells #around it becomes inactive.
            elif cells[x, y] == 1 and (n_neigh < 2 or n_neigh > 3):
                newcells[x, y] = 0
            # end pause pauseExect ------------------------------


            # We create the polygon of each cell to draw
            poly = [((x) * dimCW , y * dimCH),
                    ((x + 1) * dimCW , y * dimCH),
                    ((x + 1) * dimCW , (y + 1) * dimCH),
                    ((x) * dimCW , (y + 1) * dimCH)]

            # And we draw the cell for each pair of X and Y.
            if newcells [x, y] == 0:
                pygame.draw.polygon (screen, (0, 0, 0), poly, 1)
            else:
                pygame.draw.polygon (screen, (255, 255, 255),
                poly, 0)

    # update the game
    cells = np.copy (newcells)

    # Refresh the screen
    pygame.display.flip()
```

The program runs and displays its progress until the screen is closed or the Esc key is pressed. Figure 10-1 shows the game in progress.

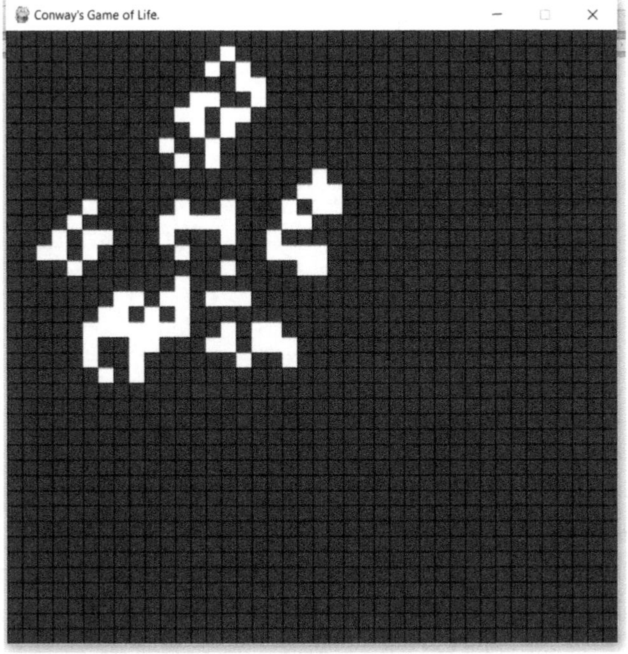

Figure 10-1. *Game in progress*

The following simulation program is a random response generation program for the MMPI-2, which can be useful for understanding how the results of this test appear when someone answers it randomly and for studying the test's ability to detect this problem.

The MMPI-2 is a 567-question personality trait questionnaire with two options: True or False' (Roig-Fusté, 1993; 2020). For our program, we will create a few response protocols, 500 and 1000. There could be many more, but they would surely not add anything to the results, to which a True or False response will be randomly assigned for each of the test items. We assume that the probability of assigning a True response is identical to that of assigning a 'False response; that is, it is 50%. This postulate could be discussed, and it would be interesting to see the test results with different response percentages, which we will not do for the sake of brevity.

Once the protocols have been generated, we will correct all the validity scales and those of the fundamental clinical profile, calculate the mean scores for each scale for the simulated cases, and transform these into typical scores to study the results and establish rules to detect protocols that respond randomly. These rules could be used in a new, subsequent procedure for generating random responses to determine how many cases can be detected by applying them. Here is the code:

```
1  # Simulation of MMPI-2 responses
2  # Dr. Roig / 09.12.24 /
3
4  from random import *
5  import numpy as np
6
7
8  nSubjects = 1000
9  nResponses = 567
10 rSubject = ''
11
12 replies = []
13 matriuPuntuacions = []
14 # Create answers ------------------------------------------------
15 for S in range(nSubjects):
16     for R in range(567):
17         aux = randint (0, 1)
18         if aux == 1:
19             rSubject = rSubject + 'T'
20         else :
21             rSubject = rSubject + 'F'
22
23 # responses.append (rSubject)
24     responses.append (rSubject)
25
26 # record a subject 's response   ......
27     with open('DatSimMMPI.dat', 'a') as f:
28         f.write (rSubject)
29         f.write ("\n")
30     rSubject = ''
```

Lines 4 and 5 import random libraries, generate random responses, and use NumPy to handle matrices.

Lines 8 to 13 define the variables number of subjects, the number of responses for each subject, and the set of responses for an individual subject, as well as an empty response matrix (`respostes`) and a score matrix (`matriuPuntuacions`).

From lines 15 to 22, there is the double loop that creates the set of responses for each simulated subject, with the inner loop generating 567 random numbers 0 or 1. If the number is 0, the response is assigned with a single character to V (true). Otherwise, it is assigned F (false). The string of 567 responses is added to the general response matrix that will contain 1,000 subjects, in line 25. This matrix is saved on the hard disk for later checks if desired in lines 27 to 31.

The next step is correction, which implies that the program knows the correction keys. The correction keys are in different Internet publications and in the original manual; they have also been published in various over-the-counter books such as the second edition of the book by Friedman, Lewak, Nichols, and Webb (2000). In the third edition (2015) they no longer appear. Since these keys are copyrighted, it is not possible to include them here. The program must contain them in the form of a matrix, with the scale number, the T or F key, and the specific items, to create a loop that checks item by item if the answer matches a point is added to the scale. If it does not, "match nothing" is added.

```
176   for S in range(nSubjects):
177       resp = replies [S]

260   # keys and correction loop...
261   ...
262   ...
263
264       matrixScores.append(pMMPI2)
265
266   # record scores of a subject ···········
267       with open('PEscalasSimMMPI.dat', 'a') as f:
              for jj in range(20):
268               f.write ( str ( pMMPI2 [ jj ]))
269               f.write(", ")
270           #Write the last value without including a comma
271           f.write(str(pMMPI2[17]))
272           f.write("\n")
273
274   pMMPI2 = [0, 0, 0, 0, 0, 0, 0, 0, 0, 0, 0, 0, 0, 0, 0, 0, 0, 0, 0, 0]
275
```

```
276   # print(matrixScores)
277
278
279   finalMatrix = np.array(matrixScores)
280
281   print( matriuFinal )
282   sum_columns = np.sum ( finalmatriu , axis = 0)
283   print( sum_columns )
284   print()
285
286   # Calculate means and deviations  ------------------------------
287   mean1 = np.mean (finalMatrix, axis = 0)
288   std1 = np.std(finalMatrix, axis=0)
      print ("Media: ")
      print (mean1)
      print (' Standard deviation')
      print (std1)
```

Lines 176 to 260 contain the correction loop; on line 260, the results for each subject are added to the overall results matrix. This matrix is saved, subject by subject, as the results are obtained on lines 262 to 268 in case any subsequent verification or analysis is required. Keep in mind that each time the program is run, it will produce slightly different results.

Line 270, still within the correction loop, resets each subject's score matrix to 0 before initiating a new correction. The remaining lines of the program print the screen shown in Figure 10-2, with the score matrix, the first three lines and the last three with the extreme values, the sum of the columns of said matrix, and the means and standard deviations of the corrected scales.

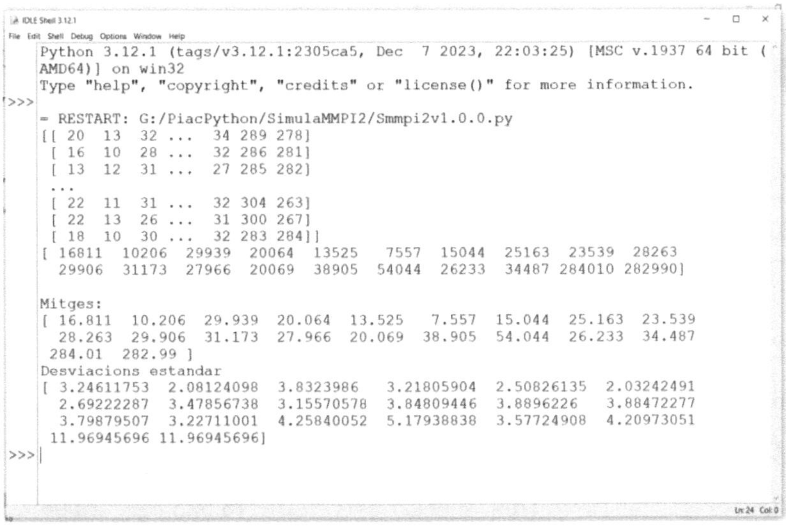

Figure 10-2. *Score matrix included*

These data was used to create the results graph in Figure 10-3, transforming the average obtained into a standard test score; that is, the graph would represent an average profile of all the subjects who responded randomly.

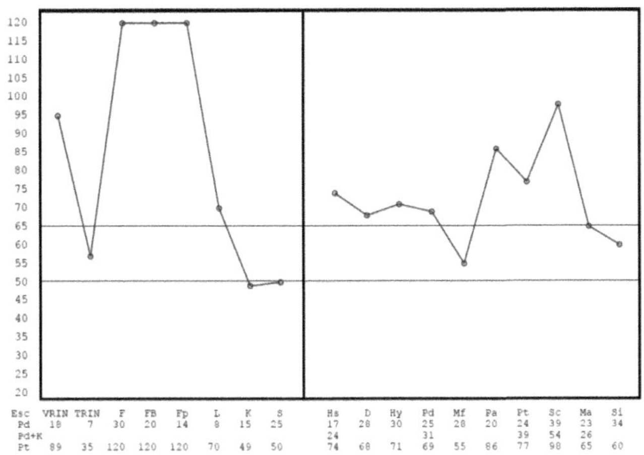

Figure 10-3. *Results graph*

Table 10-1 summarizes all the data needed to analyze the results: scale name (Esc), number of items it contains (N° items), number of true keys in the scale (V), number of false keys (F), mean of the scoring population rounded to the nearest integer in a sample of men (M), mean obtained by the simulation (Msim), standard deviation obtained by the simulation (SDsim), and typical score corresponding to the mean of the simulation (T).

Table 10-1. *Data Summary*

Esc	Number of items	V	F	M	Msim.	SDsim.	T
VRIN	67	-	-	5	16.811	3.246	95
TRIN	23	-	-	9	10.206	2.081	57
F	60	41	19	5	29.939	3.832	120
FB	40	37	3	2	20.064	3.218	120
F_p	27	18	9	1	13.525	2.508	120
L	15	-	15	4	7.757	2.032	70
K	30	1	29	15	15.044	2.692	49
S	50	6	44	25	25.163	3.478	50
Hs	32	11	21	13	23,539	3.155	74
D	57	20	37	18	28.263	3.848	68
Hy	60	13	47	21	29.906	3.889	71
P.S	50	24	26	23	31.173	3.884	69
MF-m	56	25	31	26	27,966	3.798	55
Pa	56	25	31	10	20.069	3.227	86
Pt	48	39	9	27	38,905	4.258	77
Sc	78	59	19	26	54,044	5.179	98
Ma	46	35	11	20	26.233	3.577	65
Si	69	36	33	25	34,487	4.209	60
No. V	567	-	-	-	284.01	11,969	-
No. F	567	-	-	-	282.99	11,969	-

As we can see, the graph obtained is characterized by very high scores in F, F_B, and F_p. The VRIN score is also high and, to a lesser extent, the corresponding L. The elevation of the scores of the scales is a function of the number of items in the scale and their content. The expected average score in the case of simulation is approximately a value close to half the number of items; if the content of the scale elements is avoided by many of the standardization subjects due to their extreme content, this will translate into a low average in the contrast group and therefore into a high typical score in the simulated subjects. Thus, for example, an F scale, with 60 items that are hardly accepted in the sense in which they score on the scale (note that the average in the normal population is close to 5), will tend to rise significantly if someone answers the test without taking into account the content of the items (the average of our simulated subjects is 30). That is, they respond at random. The same happens with F_B and F_p. Something similar happens with the clinical scales, Pa, Pt, and Sc. They are long scales with elements that are not easy for subjects of the general population to accept, although here we must take into account that Pt and Sc contain in their value the K correction, which is a scale that does not come out high in our simulation, contrary to what can happen in a contrast population. This would surely explain why the scores of these scales do not reach the level of F, F_B, and F_p. Naturally, the simulation can be repeated without K correction. Note also that the scores of the scale itself, K and Mf (males), are those that are closest to the mean. Theoretically, they are the most subtle and soft in their content, with 56 and 69 items, respectively. They reach an average in the general population close to 26 and 25, which minimizes their situation in the simulation graph. The same applies to the S scale, where an effort must be made to select the most favorable elements to obtain a high score; when this effort is not made, the score is average.

If we graphically analyze two extreme cases (Figure 10-4 and Figure 10-5), F and K, the difference becomes clear.

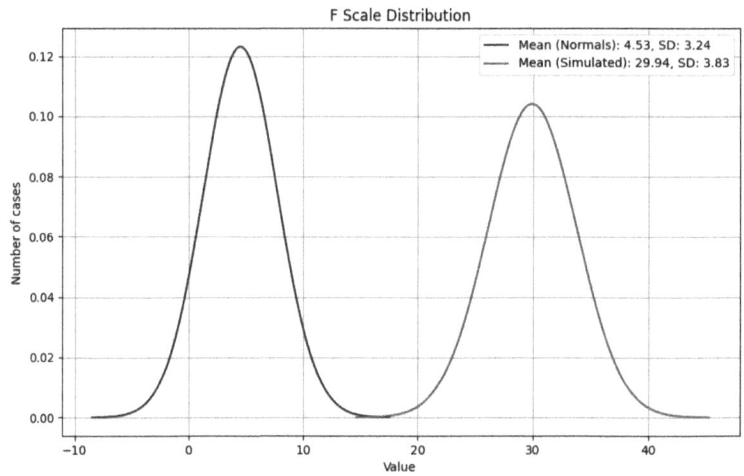

***Figure 10-4.** Two cases compared: case F*

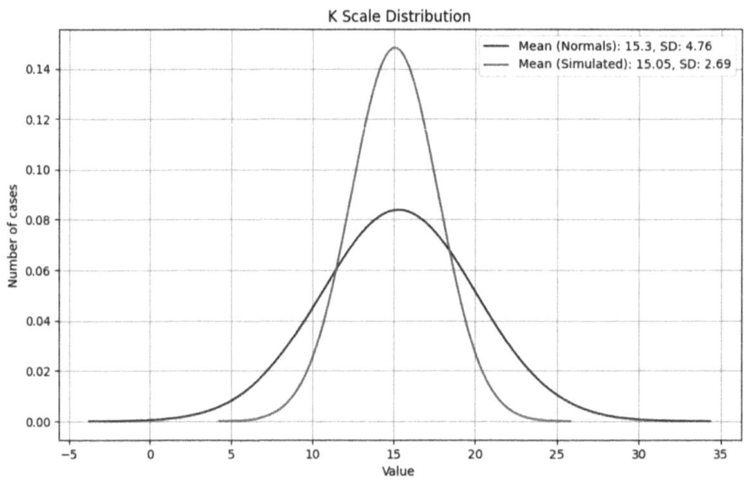

***Figure 10-5.** Two cases compared: case K*

These graphs have been drawn with a Python program, providing the means and deviations of each scale (the results of the contrast group are in blue, and those of the simulated group are in red):

```
import numpy as np
import matplotlib.pyplot as plt

# Parameters for the first Gauss curve
```

```
mean1 = 15.30
std_dev1 = 4.76

# Parameters for the second Gauss curve
mean2 = 15.05
std_dev2 = 2.69

# Generate 1000 values for each curve
data1 = np.random.normal (mean1, std_dev1, 1000)
data2 = np.random.normal (mean2, std_dev2, 1000)

# Create a range of values for the distributions
x1 = np.linspace ( mean1 - 4* std_dev1 , mean1 + 4* std_dev1 , 1000)
x2 = np.linspace ( mean2 - 4* std_dev2 , mean2 + 4* std_dev2 , 1000)

y1 = (1 / ( std_dev1 * np.sqrt (2 * np.pi ))) * np.exp (-0.5 * (( x1 -
 mean1 ) / std_dev1 )**2)
y2 = (1 / ( std_dev2 * np.sqrt (2 * np.pi ))) * np.exp (-0.5 * (( x2 -
mean2 ) / std_dev2 )**2)

# Graph the curves
plt.figure ( figsize =(10, 6))
plt.plot ( x1 , y1 , label = f"Mean (Normals): { mean1 }, SD: {
std_dev1
}", color="blue")
plt.plot ( x2 , y2 , label = f"Mean (Simulated): { mean2 }, SD: {
std_dev2
}", color="red")
plt.title ("K Scale Distribution")
plt.xlabel ("Value")
plt.ylabel ("Number of cases")
plt.legend ()
plt.grid ()
plt.show ()
```

Communication with the Machine

Another program that appears to behave intelligently is Eliza. This is a computer program designed by Joseph Weizenbaum (1966) at MIT. The purpose of the program was to study natural language by simulating a Rogerian psychotherapist, who was trying to maintain a coherent and meaningful conversation with the computer user. The author chose to represent (parody) the role of a Rogerian psychotherapist because "The Rogerian psychotherapist is relatively easy to imitate because much of his technique consists of obtaining information from the patient by feeding back his own testimony" (Weizenbaum, 1976). The author was surprised that some psychiatrists (Colby, Watt, & Gilbert, 1966) were enthusiastic about the Eliza program and its possibilities, since he was concerned about the gullibility of people using Eliza and the uses that could be put to it. In the prologue to his 1976 book, he makes clear two points that he believes are important: "...there is a difference between man and machine, and there are certain tasks that computers should not perform, regardless of whether they were built to do them."

The Eliza program works by searching for keywords in the sentence written by the user and responds with a programmed sentence that is coherent, if it exists, stored in its database. If it does not exist, it resumes the thread of the conversation reformulating what was expressed by the subject, as a Rogerian therapist would do, or it emits a more ambiguous or more general sentence that encourages the subject to continue with speaking without breaking the dialogue that is being maintained with him, such as "Tell me more..." and "How important could this be?" and "What does this mean to you?" with the hope that in what the subject continues saying they will find some pattern that has been programmed and will allow them to give a more specific response. See Program 10-2.

Program 10-2.

```
# A version of Eliza
# Dr. Roig Fusté / 20.07.22


import re
import random

```

```
person = {
"I am": "is",
"was": "was",
"I": "you",
"would": " would ",
"he": "has",
"hare": " you will hare ",
"my": "your",
"you are": "I am",
"you have": "I have",
"haras": "hare",
"you": "my",
"yours": "mine",
"yours",
"I": "you",
}

conversation = [
    [r'I need (.*)',
    ["Why do you need {0}?",
    "Would it really help him get {0}?",
    "Are you sure you need {0}?"]],

    [r'Why not\'? ([^\?]*)\??',
    ["Do you really think I don't {0}?",
    "Maybe I could {0}.",
    "Do you really want me to {0}?"]],

    [r'Why can't I ([^\?]*)\??',
    ["Do you think I should be able to {0}?",
    "If I could {0}, what would I do?",
    "I don't know -- why can't {0}?",
    "Have you really tried it?"

```

```
[ r'I can't (.*)',
["How do you know you can't {0}?",
"Maybe you could {0} if you try.",
"What would you require if {0} does it?"]],

[r'I am (.*)',
["Did you come to see me because you are {0}?",
"How long has it been {0}?",
"How does it feel to be {0}?"]],

[r'I am (.*)',
["What is it like to be {0}? How does it make you feel?",
"Do you like being {0}?",
"Why are you telling me it's {0}?",
"Why do you think it is {0}?"]],

[r'Is ([^\?]*)\??',
["Why does it matter if I'm {0}?",
"Would you rather it wasn't {0}?",
"Maybe you think I'm {0}.",
"I can be {0} -- who you think?"]],

[r'What (.*)',
["Why do you ask?",
"How would an answer to that help you?"
"What do you think?"]],

[r'How (.*)',
["How do you think?",
"Perhaps you can answer your own question."
"What are you really asking?"]],

[r'Because (.*)',
["Is this the real reason ? ",
"What other reasons can you think of?"
```

```
    "Does this reason apply to anything else?"
    "If {0}, what else must be true?"]],

    [r'(.*) sorry (.*)',
    ["There are many times when it is not necessary to apologize.",
    "What feelings do you have while apologizing?"]],

    [r'Hello (.*)',
    [" Hello... I'm glad you're here today.",
    "Hello..., how are you feeling today?"
    "Hi, how are you feeling today?"

    [r'I think (.*)',
    ["Do you have any questions {0}?",
    "Do you really think this?"
    "But aren't you sure {0}?"]],

    [r '(.*) friend (.*)',
    ["Tell me more about your friends.",
    "When you think of a friend, what comes to mind?"
    "Why don't you tell me something about a childhood friend?"

    [r'If ',
    ["Seems pretty safe",
    "Okay, but can you explain it a little more?"

    [r'(.*) computer(.*)',
    ["Are you really talking about me?",
    "Does it seem strange to you to talk to a computer?"
    "How do computers make you feel?"
    "Do you feel threatened by computers?"

    [r'Is (.*)',
    ["Do you think it's {0}?",
    "Maybe it's {0} -- What do you think?"
```

```
        "If I were {0}, what would I do ? ",
        "It may well be that {0}."]],

        [r'Is (.*)',
        ["He seems very safe.",
        "If I told you it's probably not {0}, how would you feel?"]],

        [r'Can ([^\?]*)\??',
        ["What makes you think I can't {0}?",
        "If I could {0}, what would happen",
        "Why are you asking if I can {0}?"]],

        [r 'Can I ([^\?]*)\??',
        ["Maybe I don't want {0}.",
        "Do you want to be able to {0}?",
        "If I could {0}, would I do it?"]],

        [r'You are (.*)',
        ["Why do you think I'm {0}?",
        "Do you like to think I'm {0}?"
        "Maybe you would like it to be {0}.",
        "Maybe he's really talking about you?"

    [ r'Is ? (.*)',
    ["Why do you say I'm {0}?",
    "Why do you think I'm {0}?",
    "Are we talking about you or me?"

        [r'I can't (.*)',
        ["Can't you really {0}?",
        "Why can't he? {0}?",
        "Do you want {0}?"]],

        [r'I'm sorry (.*)',
        ["Okay, tell me more about these feelings.",
```

```
        "Do you feel it often {0}?",
        "Usually, when do you feel it? {0}?",
        "When you feel it {0}, what do you do?"]],

        [r'I have (.*)',
        ["Why are you telling me you have {0}?",
        "Do you really have {0}?",
        "Now you have {0}, what will you do next?"]],

        [r'I would like (.*)',
        ["Could you explain why you would like {0}?",
        "Why would you like {0}?",
        "Who else do you know who would like {0}?"]],

        [r'There is (.*)',
        ["Do you think there are {0}?",
        "Is it likely that there is {0}.",
        "Would you like there to be {0}?"]],

        [r'My (.*)',
        ["I see your {0}.",
        "Why do you say that your {0}?",
        "When your {0}, how does it feel?"]],

    [ r'You (.*)',
    ["We should be talking about you, not me .",
    "Why do you say that about me ?"
    "Why do you care if I {0}?"]],

    [r'Why (.*)',
    ["Why don't you tell me the reason why {0}?",
    "Why does {0} think?"]],

        [r'I want (.*)',
        ["What does getting {0} mean to you?",
```

```
        "Why do you want {0}?",
        "What would you do if you got {0}?",
        "If you get {0}, what will you do? after ?"]],

        [r '(.*) mother(.*)',
        ["Tell me more about your mother.",
        "How was your relationship with your mother?"
        "How do you feel about your mother?"
        "How does this relate to your current feelings?"
        "It is important to have good family relationships."

        [r'(.*) parent(.*)',
        [" Tell me more about your father.",
        "How did your father make you feel?"
        "How did you feel about your father?"
        "Do you think the relationship you had with your father has
        anything to do with your current feelings?"
        "Do you have trouble showing affection to your family members?"

        [r (.*) child(.*)',
        ["Did you have any close friends as a child?",
        "What is your favorite childhood memory?"
        "Do you remember any dreams or nightmares from your childhood?"
        "Did the other children sometimes bother you?"
        "How do you think your childhood experiences relate to
your current
      feelings?"

        [r'(.*)\?',
    ["Why are you asking me this?",
    "Please consider whether you can answer your own question."
    "Perhaps the answer lies within?"
    "Why don't you tell me?"

    [ r'EXIT ',
```

```
["Thanks for talking to me.",
" Bye .",
"Thank you, I hope to see you again soon. Have a nice day !"

[ r '(.*)',
["Please tell me more.",
"Let's change the subject a bit... Tell me about your family."
"Can you elaborate on that?"
" Why does it say {0}?",
"I see.",
"Very interesting."
"{0}.",
"I see. What does this tell you?"
"How does this make you feel?"
"How do you feel when you say this?"
]


def reflect(fragment):
tokens = fragment.lower ().split()
for i , token in enumerate(tokens):
if token in persona:
tokens[ i ] = person[token]
return ' '.join(tokens)


def analyze(statement):
for pattern, responses in conversations:
        match = re.match (pattern, statement.rstrip (".!"))
if match:
response = random.choice (responses)
return response.format (*[reflect(g) for g in match.groups ()])


def main ():
```

```
248         print ("Enter 'EXIT' to exit")
249         print ("Hello. How are you feeling today?")
250
251         while True:
252         statement = input("> ")
253         print(analyze(statement))
254
255         if statement == "EXIT":
256             break
257
258
259     if __name__ == "__main__":
260         main ()
```

Lines 5 and 6 import the libraries necessary for the program to run: `re` and `random`. The former allows operations with regular expressions, while the latter generates random numbers.

Comprehensive information on the operation of the bookstore can be found on the Internet:

`https://docs.python.org/es/3/library/re.html`

Lines 8 to 229 contain the information the program will use for its operation. First, there is a dictionary (lines 8 to 23), whose purpose is to change a first-person pronoun to a second-person one; lines 25 to 229 contain a knowledge base. This is list of lists that is expandable if necessary containing patterns to recognize, which will determine the program's response.

Then two functions are defined: `reflect` (lines 232 to 237) and `analyze` (lines 240 to 245), which accept as a parameter the string entered by the subject.

Lines 248 to 257 contain the program itself, and lines 260 and 261 are the starting points for any Python program.

The program initially works by providing information, the way out, and issuing a greeting. From here, it waits for the user to enter some text. Then it analyzes the entered text and issues a response or comment that is minimally coherent with what the subject has said or attempts to encourage the user to continue interacting.

This program could be expanded or refined by using verbal rather than written language. We've already seen how it's possible to convert text to speech and speech to text in Python without facing major problems. This would undoubtedly add more realism and authenticity to the situation.

We have proposed and introduced into our Eliza program the recording of conversations. This can be used to refine the program by studying interactions between the subject and machine, identifying which ones are inappropriate, and finding a solution for them. We already know that our Eliza lacks consciousness, which drastically differentiates her from a human interlocutor, but incomprehensibly, she also lacks memory, which would surely be easier to achieve since we could save her conversation to use as a reference in future conversations. The real problem is not retaining the conversation but rather how to use previous data from the conversation in the current moment. Commercial bots do not usually have this feature, although with modern resources it should be easier to implement.

The Eliza program is the precursor to the bots that answer the phone in some companies or that call one phone after another to start commercial conversations aimed at getting new clients. However, these devices are currently programmed in another way using natural language processing (NLP). So, Eliza's next step was the ALICE program (Artificial Linguistic Internet Computer Entity) by Richard Wallace (2009). Information about this program can be found in Ciesla (2024) and in Python on the Internet:

`https://pypi.org/project/python-aiml/`

A simple way to test the new way of programming chatbots is shown in the following program:

```
1   from nltk.chat.util import Chat
2   from nltk.chat.eliza import eliza_chat
3
4   eliza_chat ()
```

There are other types of chats other than Eliza. Try replacing line 2 with one of the following lines to test them:

```
from nltk.chat.iesha import iesha_chat
from nltk.chat.rude import rude_chat
from nltk.chat.suntsu import suntsu_chat
from nltk.chat.zen import zen_chat
```

With these commands you will only be able to carry out conversations in English. Doing so in other languages is somewhat more complicated. In any case, you will have to install the nltk library with pip and to work, with other languages, you will have to execute the following commands from the Python interpreter prompt:

```
import nltk
nltk.download ()
```

The latter will bring up a window similar to Figure 10-6.

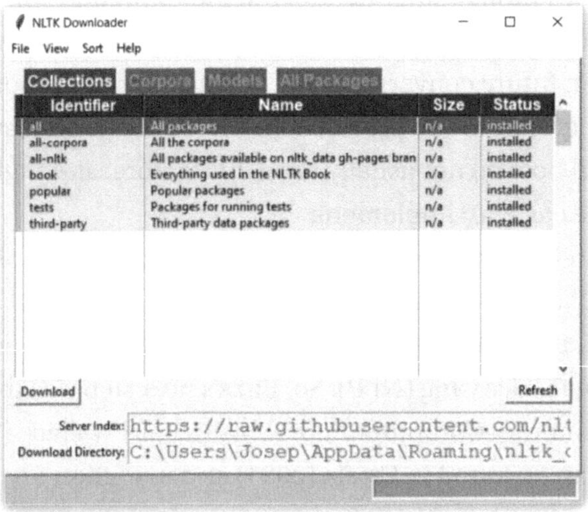

Figure 10-6. *English chat*

From here you can install all the documentation to work with other languages by selecting all-nltk and clicking the Download button.

To work with Spanish, it's better to use other, more adapted libraries, such as spacy. Let's look at an Eliza program using spacy; see Program 10-3.

Program 10-3.

```
import spacy

# Carry model spaCy
nlp = spacy.load (" es_core_news_sm ")

class ChatbotEliza:
```

```
    def __init__(self):
        self.responses =[
            ("I want", "Why do you want %s?"),
            ("need", "Why do you need %s?"),
            ("I feel", "Why do you feel %s?"),
            ("I am", "I understand you are %s. Why?")
        ]

    def analyze(self, text):
        doc = nlp (text)
        for token in doc:
            if token.lemma _ in [" want ", " need ", " feel ",
            " be "]:
return token.lemma _, doc
        return None, doc

    def respond(self, text):
        lemma, doc = self.analyze (text)
        if lemma:
            for pattern, response in self.responses:
                if lemma in pattern:
                # Extract the plugin straight from the phrase
                    plugin = " ".join([ token.text for token in doc if
                    token.dep _ == " obj "])
                    return response % complement
        return "Tell me more about that."

# Execute chatbot
if __name__ == "__main__":
    print ("Eliza: Hi, how can I help you? Type 'exit'
 to finish.")
    chatbot = ChatbotEliza()
    while True:
        user_input = input(" You : ")
```

```
        if user_input.lower () == " exit ":
            print ("Eliza: Goodbye!")
            break
        print ("Eliza:", chatbot.respond(user_input))
```

First you will need to install spacy or stanza with pip and the `es_core_news_sm` model:

```
pip install spacy
python -m spacy download es_core_news_sm
```

To check the installation, you must type this:

```
python -m spacy validate
```

This will return the name and version of the installed library.

Natural Language Processing with Python

Language is an essential tool in our lives and sets us apart from other animals in the world. It is primarily used to transmit information, ideas, and feelings; express emotions; give commands; or ask questions. Language is, without a doubt, a living thing that is constantly evolving; it can become ambiguous and changeable, which initially isn't an ideal situation for communication with a computer. However, for the user, the ability to communicate with the computer in their own language is a great advantage, which would explain the efforts that have been made to ensure that the computer "understands" and "can express itself" in human language.

What Is Natural Language Processing?

Natural language processing is a discipline that lies at the intersection of several sciences, such as computer science, artificial intelligence, and cognitive psychology. Its main objective is to empower machines to understand and use the languages we humans speak. NLP research aims to answer the question of how people are able to understand the meaning of a thought expressed in a sentence and how people understand what is said to them, using the context of the dialogue and the nuances of language, which involves differentiating between an assumption, a belief, or a fact.

Applications of Natural Language Processing

NLP algorithms are typically based on machine learning. Instead of manually coding large sets of rules, NLP can rely on machine learning to learn these rules, and it does so by analyzing a set of examples through statistical inference, which allows it to guess which word is most likely to follow a given word. In general, the more data analyzed, the more accurate the model can be. These algorithms can be used for applications such as the following:

- Summarize text to extract the most important ideas, ignoring irrelevant information.
- Create chatbots that can interact with people, like Eliza or ALICE, which we saw earlier.
- Generate keyword tags for content analysis, leveraging the LDA algorithm used in natural language processing to assign keywords to paragraphs of text to search for similar texts.
- Conduct sentiment analysis to identify the tone of a text string, from very negative to very positive, including a neutral position.

Python Libraries for Natural Language Processing

Currently, Python is one of the most popular languages for working in this field. To address problems related to NLP, Python provides several libraries:

- **NLTK**: This is most used in NLP and has many lexical resources, in addition to a set of text processing libraries for classification, labeling, analysis, and semantic reasoning (Perkins, 2014; Raj, 2019).
- **Spacy**: This is a relatively new library that stands out for its ease of use and speed in word processing.
- **Stanza**: This is a Python natural language parsing package based on neural networks, developed by researchers at Stanford University that supports many languages.
- **Textacy**: This is designed from Spacy to make related tasks easier.
- **TextBlob**: TextBlob simplifies text processing by providing an intuitive interface to NLTK and is packed with features.

There are many other libraries for natural language processing, both paid and free and open-source.

Linguistic Corpus

A linguistic corpus is a large and structured set of real-life examples of the language we are considering. These examples can be either written text (the most common) or oral samples. It must be relatively large, must be created independently of its possible forms or uses, and must reflect a language as accurately as possible. Its usage and representation must be realistic, allowing NLP models to learn the patterns necessary to understand it.

Machine Learning

Machine learning is the science of teaching computers to make predictions based on data. The goal is for a computer to learn from experience. This type of performance was impossible a few years ago, given that computers couldn't store enough data or process it quickly and complexly enough to learn effectively. Spectacular advances in computer hardware have solved this problem.

Machine learning (deep learning) is a method that allows a computer to learn how to perform a complex task so that it can then perform it independently. This involves developing programs capable of generalizing knowledge from a wide range of information supplied in the form of examples. Machine learning can be applied to many fields of knowledge such as statistical research, DNA sequence classification, natural language recognition, image recognition, search engine development, credit card fraud detection, computer programming, game development or robot construction, spam identification, among many others.

The development of machine learning began in 1959 when Arthur Samuel (IBM Software Engineer), from his desire to teach his computer how to play checkers, thought he could achieve this by playing many games against his computer so that it could learn and improve its performance. So, in 1962 the machine could already win state competitions of the game on its own.

For machine learning in Python, you can use the Scikit-Learn module, which contains the algorithms needed for this type of task.

Scikit-Learn interacts with other libraries such as NumPy and Scipy. It contains simple and efficient tools for data mining and advanced data analysis. Information about this library can be found at `https://scikit-learn.org/`.

Machine learning algorithms are radically different from traditional computer programs. The latter involves coding a series of rules that anticipate all the circumstances the program will encounter and therefore cannot be better than the programmer who designed them. Machine learning programs are based on neural networks that can learn from experience.

Neural Networks and Simulation of Mathematical Models

A neural network is a structure made up of units called neurons that connect to each other to transmit information. This information passes through the network, from the input to be modified, and provides output values. Networks must have at least two neurons, one input and one output (Figure 10-7), but can have millions of them, in which case they are distributed in layers. The intermediate layers are called hidden layers. Neurons have connections that are assigned a value, and each neuron has a bias, another numerical value, which influences the result.

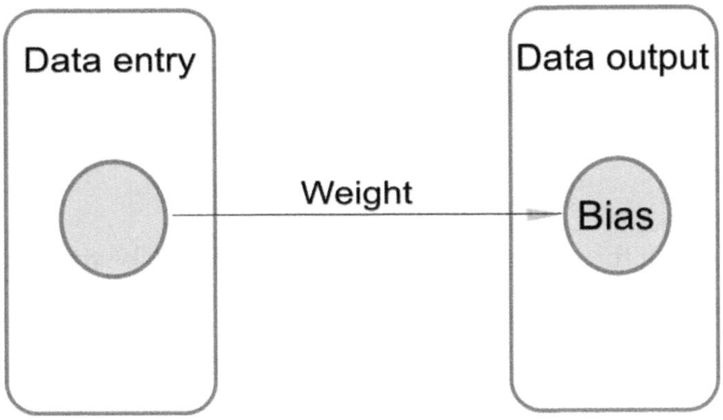

Figure 10-7. *Example of a network*

To understand how neural networks work, we will choose a simple example: creating a network that learns to transform degrees Celsius into Fahrenheit.

We already know the exact formula to make this conversion:

$$F = 1.80\ C + 32$$

But that's not the point here; it's about seeing how the network learns to convert from practical data. For that, we'll need some Celsius data with their Fahrenheit equivalents. The more data, the better, but since this is a very specific and simple problem, 10 or 20 will probably be enough. To create the data, we'll write a program that generates 100 random numbers, between -50 and 150, placing them in a list that will be the Celsius values. From this, we'll create a list of equivalent Fahrenheit values, applying the formula we already know:

```
import random

c = []

for i in range(100):
    c.append ( random.randrange (-50, 150))

print(c)

f = c

for i in range( len (c)):
    f[ i ] = round(c[ i ] * 1.8 + 32, 1)

print(f)
```

These two lists that the program writes to the screen will be the basis for learning the program shown in Program 10-4.

Program 10-4.

```
import tensorflow as tf
import numpy as np

```

```
c = np.array ([-17, 27, 54, 79, 131, 138, 53, 46, 106, 128, 147, 117,
58, 123, 147, 85, 55, -28, 36, -5, 119, 16, 116, 14, -19, 107, 69, 3,
6, -35, 68, 1, -47, 2, 96, 149, -33, 18, -23, 133, -15, 80, 28, 52,
64, 75, 57, 20, 81, -29, 52, 63, 3, 27, 45, 126, 111, -34, -43, 9, 57,
87, 40, 15, 109, -43, 79, 126, 22, 148, 85, 22, 15, 15, -35, 70, 64,
84, 94, 79, 123, 13, -10, 137, 51, -46, 138, 95, -41, 125, 27, -23,
112, 131, 119, 61, 44, 55, 29, 113], dtype =float)

f = np.array ([1.4, 80.6, 129.2, 174.2, 267.8, 280.4, 127.4, 114.8,
222.8, 262.4, 296.6, 242.6, 136.4, 253.4, 296.6, 185.0, 131.0, -18.4,
96.8, 23.0, 246.2, 60.8, 240.8, 57.2, -2.2, 224.6, 156.2, 37.4, 42.8,
-31.0, 154.4, 33.8, -52.6, 35.6, 204.8, 300.2, -27.4, 64.4, -9.4,
271.4, 5.0, 176.0, 82.4, 125.6, 147.2, 167.0, 134.6, 68.0, 177.8,
-20.2, 125.6, 145.4, 37.4, 80.6, 113.0, 258.8, 231.8, -29.2, -45.4,
48.2, 134.6, 188.6, 104.0, 59.0, 228.2, -45.4, 174.2, 258.8, 71.6,
298.4, 185.0, 71.6, 59.0, 59.0, -31.0, 158.0, 147.2, 183.2, 201.2,
174.2, 253.4, 55.4, 14.0, 278.6, 123.8, -50.8, 280.4, 203.0, -41.8,
257.0, 80.6, -9.4, 233.6, 267.8, 246.2, 141.8, 111.2, 131.0, 84.2,
235.4], dtype =float)

layer = tf.keras.layers.Dense (units=1, input_shape =[1])
model = tf.keras.Sequential ([layer])

model.compile(
              optimizer= tf.keras.optimizers.Adam (0.1),
              loss='mean_squared_error'
)

print ("Start training...")
history = model.fit (c, f, epochs =500, verbose =False)
print ("End of training")
```

Here is the screen output:

```
Start training...
End of training
```

tensorflow and numpy libraries. Lines 4 and 6 contain the training examples material we created with the previous program. Lines 9 and 10 define the neural network and its model based on a framework called keras that allows you to specify the layers of the neural network and the chosen network model. This model must be compiled to prepare for the training phase, which is done in lines 12 to 15. The model needs to be specified with certain properties; here we specify the optimizer call and the loss function; the learning rate (0.1) indicates the adjustment of weights and biases. If the value is large, it makes it less accurate; if it is small, the program increases accuracy but slows down.

In lines 17 to 19, the program is trained by looping through the data several times and adjusting the results. Here, it has been instructed to loop through the data 500 times, which will likely be sufficient for the proposed objective. The `verbose = False` command indicates that it should not provide information about what it is doing to prevent the program from providing an endless stream of information printed on the screen.

After completing the training, we will request a result of how the model was adjusted in its operation:

```
import matplotlib.pyplot as plt
plt.xlabel ("# Cycles ")
plt.ylabel ("Loss Magnitude")
plt.plot ( history.history ["loss"])
```

Figure 10-8 shows the results in a graph.

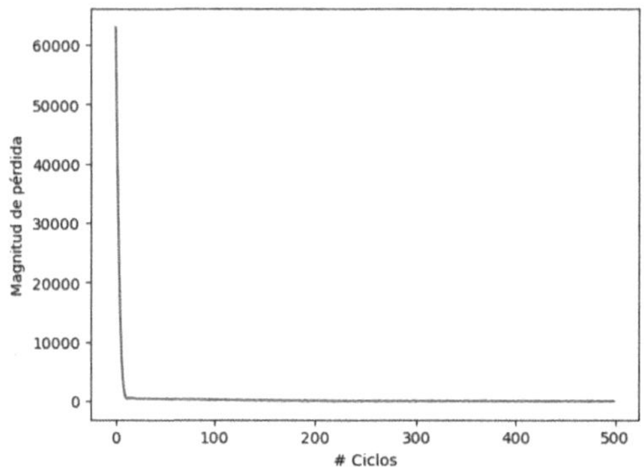

Figure 10-8. *Graph*

In the graph, we can see how it adjusted with the first few runs but then didn't improve at all in the following runs. This shows that 25 runs would have been more than enough to achieve the same result. You can run the program again with an epoch value of 25 on line 18 to see that it works just as well.

Let's finish with an example of a prediction:

```
print ("Prediction Example")
result = model.predict ([100.0])
print ("Result: " + str (result) + " fahrenheit .")
```

Screen output:

```
Example of prediction
1/1 [=============================] - 0s 115ms / step
Result: [[211.99219]] Fahrenheit.
```

As we can see, the result was very good.

It would be possible to write the program specifying several layers of neurons, for which lines 9 and 10 would have to be replaced by the following lines:

```
hiddencap1 = tf.keras.layers.Dense (units=3, input_shape = [1])
hiddencap2 = tf.keras.layers.Dense (units=3)
output = tf.keras.layers.Dense (units =1)
model = tf.keras.Sequential ([hiddenCap1, hiddenCap2, output])
```

These lines specify two intermediate, hidden layers, each with three neurons. This allows for better fitness and predictions, as shown in the graph in Figure 10-9 and the screen output.

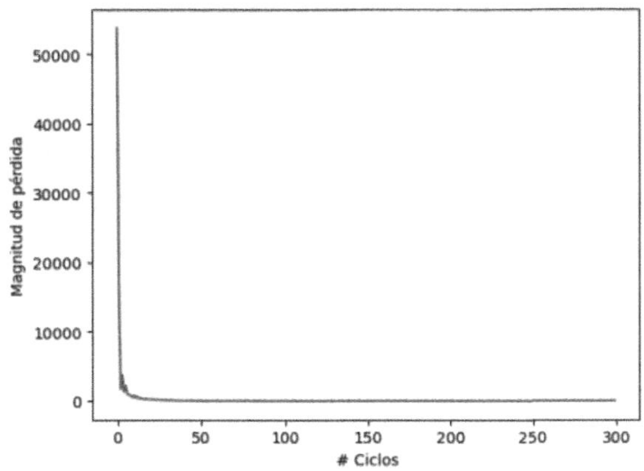

Figure 10-9. *Graph*

Here is the screen output:

```
Example of prediction
1/1 [==============================] - 0s 141ms / step
Result: [[211.99998]] Fahrenheit.
```

A multilayer neural network would respond to the scheme shown in Figure 10-10.

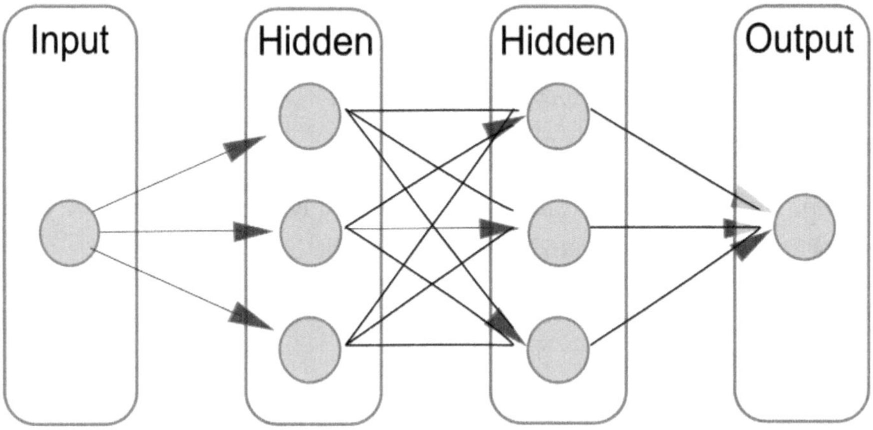

Figure 10-10. *Multilayer network*

Neural networks have been used in facial recognition and character recognition, both print and handwritten, and it would be interesting to see how they can be used in psychology, social sciences, and education. I hope you will become interested in these topics and will be able to develop valuable applications in the future. I said at the beginning of the book that having a goal to apply programming helps you learn. My goal was to get the computer to produce textual reports based on psychological test scores, and that was achieved some time ago (Seisdedos, Roig-Fusté, 1986). This goal also helped me learn to program.

Recognizing someone by their face could improve a chatbot that would greet someone it has previously interacted with by name without first mentioning their name; this is one of many improvements that can be made to a chatbot beyond the already difficult task of providing a minimally coherent response to any interaction from a subject.

Summary

In this chapter, you saw examples of artificial intelligence that can be useful in human sciences, developed with the help of Python. In the next chapter, we will talk about virtual reality.

CHAPTER 11

Virtual Reality

In this chapter, we will make a small foray into some aspects of virtual reality that can be programmed with Python.

Creating a virtual reality application is a complex task since you must consider both the programming and the content to be included. This requires carefully designing everything to be included and how it will be included, before starting to write the application code. To get an overview of virtual reality, prior to the programming work, the following books may be useful: *Understanding virtual reality: interface, application and design* (Sherman and Craig, 2018) and *Complete virtual reality and augmented reality* (Glover and Linowes, 2019). Here we will focus on presenting some aspects and possibilities of virtual reality programming in Python and leave the question of content to your creativity.

The rapid technological advances of recent years have allowed virtual reality to reach many fields and can be developed with the means most people have available. Today's personal computers are very powerful, capable of hosting high-quality 3D graphics, and the availability of specialized software predicts exponential growth in the field in the coming years.

3D development platforms were developed long ago for game programming and are now often applied to the programming of virtual reality elements that provide tools and interactions for the development of a virtual reality environment.

Virtual reality can be used with standard displays, mice, and keyboards, but it incorporates more typical elements such as motion trackers, sensors that track the subject's movements in real time, which replace the devices. The standard display is also replaced by virtual reality headsets, in other words, a head-mounted device (HMD) display, that projects stereoscopic images directly into each eye of a subject from a close distance, using special devices suitable for such close-range images. It is equipped with motion trackers that provide positional information so that the display can adapt to the subject's head and eye movements and display consistent visual content.

J. M. Roig-Fusté, *Python for Psychology, Social Sciences, and Education*,
https://doi.org/10.1007/979-8-8688-2355-8_11

A Three-Dimensional Presentation

For virtual reality development, you need to design three-dimensional spaces. This can be done with Pygame and OpenGL or with other libraries specialized in virtual reality, which we'll look at later.

A three-dimensional visualization with Pygame looks like Program 11-1.

Program 11-1.

```
import pygame
import numpy as np
from OpenGL.GL import *
from OpenGL.GLU import *

# We define the faces of the die
vertices = [
            (1, -1, -1),
            (1, 1, -1),
            (-1, 1, -1),
            (-1, -1, -1),
            (1, -1, 1),
            (1, 1, 1),
            (-1, -1, 1),
            (-1, 1, 1),
]

edges = [
          (0, 1),
          (1, 2),
          (23),
          (3, 0),
          (4, 5),
          (5, 6),
          (6, 7),
          (7, 4),
          (0, 4),
```

```
        (1, 5),
        (2, 6),
        (3, 7),
]

colors = [
        (1, 0, 0),
        (0, 1, 0),
        (0, 0, 1),
        (1, 1, 0),
        (1, 0, 1),
        (0, 1, 1),
]

def draw_dice ():
    glBegin (GL_QUADS)
    for i , color in enumerate(colors):
        glColor3fv (color)
        for vertex in edges[ i ]:
            glVertex3fv (vertices[vertex])
    glEnd()

    glBegin(GL_LINES)
    for edge in edges:
        for vertex in edge:
            glVertex3fv (vertices[vertex])
    glEnd ()

def main():
    pygame.init ()
    display = (800, 600)
    pygame.display.set_mode (display, pygame.DOUBLEBUF | pygame.
    OPENGL )
    gluPerspective (45, (display[0] / display[1]), 0.1, 50.0)
    glTranslatef (0.0, 0.0, -5)

```

```
clock = pygame.time.Clock ()
angle = 0

while True:
for event in pygame.event.get():
if event.type == pygame.QUIT:
    pygame.quit()
    return

        glRotatef (1, 0, 1, 0) # Rotate the die
        glClear (GL_COLOR_BUFFER_BIT | GL_DEPTH_BUFFER_BIT)
        draw_dice ()
        pygame.display.flip ()
        clock.tick (60)

if __name__ == "__main__":
    main ()
```

At the beginning of the program, we imported the necessary libraries: Pygame, NumPy, and OpenGL.

We define the vertices, faces, and edges of the die.

The `draw_dice` function draws the die using OpenGL.

The main function sets up Pygame, initializes OpenGL, and enters a loop where the die rotation is updated and redrawn every frame.

With Python we can also use platforms or libraries specifically designed for 3D design such as env and Vizard.

The first one can be obtained at `https://virtualenv.pypa.io/en/latest/`.

The second one from WorldViz.com is located at `https://pypi.org/project/vizard/`.

The scenarios and the desired world map for a virtual reality are created with specialized programs such as Autodesk's 3D Studio Max and Blender's Blender (Ezra, 2020). These will allow us to create the prefabricated 3D objects (prefabs) that we will use in the application. These objects are stored, for Vizard, in files with the extension `.osgb` for their use and are imported for the application with the `viz.add()` and `viz.addChild()` methods.

Objects are positioned on the stage along three axes (x, y, z) and are also oriented with reference to the same axes, using the so-called Euler angles.

The created world must be as realistic as possible. This means that if we try to go over a wall, we will crash or collide, and it must also have gravity, which will influence the behavior of the various objects in the scene. Enabling collision also activates gravity under Earth-like conditions (9.8 m/s^2). This value must be adjusted if the scene is supposed to be on another planet or in outer space.

Virtual reality has already been used in psychological and neuropsychological treatments (Rizzo and Bouchard, 2019), mainly in phobias to face feared scenarios, which usually gives good results.

Summary

In this chapter, you were introduced into some aspects of virtual reality that can be programmed with Python. In the next chapter, we conclude our discussion.

CHAPTER 12

Conclusion

If you have come this far, you have an idea of the possibilities of computer science in psychology, but there is still a long way to go. Experienced programmers say that you can only learn to program by programming, but you can hardly program if you don't know how to do it.

If you feel that you need further basic knowledge on the subject, you can refer to a general Python programming book. If the chosen book is too difficult for you, then choose an easier one. Keep in mind that there are also Python books for children and teens, and perhaps one of them could be useful for you as a starting point. In addition, many universities teach Python courses online (many of them are free).

Working alone is generally ineffective, more boring, and less motivating. You can create your own group of people who encourage and support each other, or you can sign up to join an existing community of Python users. You can also sign up for a newsletter such as Python Weekly or PyCoders Weekly to receive news, articles, tutorials, or even job offers related to Python. Private programming classes (in person or online) can be found on the Internet at reasonable prices. Find a teacher you trust who can also help you at specific moments when you are stuck.

You also can connect to AI teachers (Porter and Zingaro, 2023). There are free AI options that are skilled in teaching Python programming. AI teachers are often found to be kind, polite, and helpful, and they can answer almost everything that is asked of them. But they can also make mistakes. Their proposals must be reviewed and tested to ensure their correctness.

You can use AI to present problems that you have not been able to solve on your own. When AI offers you a solution, you can continue to ask questions or ask AI to explain how the proposed solution works or if there is a simpler solution. You must analyze the task or project that is proposed and evaluate the steps you would need to follow.

J. M. Roig-Fusté, *Python for Psychology, Social Sciences, and Education*,
https://doi.org/10.1007/979-8-8688-2355-8_12

Where to Find Resources?

Learning to program and use programming to carry out projects or activities is complex, so it requires a lot of dedication at the beginning. Everything you can read about computer science or Python programming will help you, give you ideas, and expand your experience and knowledge. There are many books on Python (especially in English). Many books can be found on the Internet, including tutorials, libraries, and documentation.

A description of the Python standard libraries and Python documentation in its different versions and in various languages can be found at `https://docs.python.org/`.

There are many useful packages for science and psychology (some mentioned throughout this book), and Table 12-1 includes books that cover the basics.

Table 12-1. *Recommended Python Books Covering the Basics*

Name	web	Description
Expiration	`https://expyriment.org/`	Library for cognitive and neuroscience experiments
Keras	`https://keras.io/`	Is an open-source deep learning framework
Neuropsychia	`https://neuropsydia.readthedocs.io/en/latest/#`	Python module for creating experiments, assignments, and quizzes
NumPy	`https://numpy.org/`	High-level math functions and array support
OpenSesame	`https://osdoc.cogsci.nl/`	
Pandas	`https://pandas.pydata.org/`	Tools for data analysis
Psychophysics	`https://github.com/wisions/mPsy3`	Creation of psychophysical experiments
PsychoPy	`https://www.psychopy.org/`	Library for the design, execution, and analysis of psychological experiments
Pygame	`https://www.pygame.org/`	Library for creating games
PyGaze	`http://www.pygaze.org/`	Eye movement tracking

(*continued*)

Table 12-1. *(continued)*

Name	web	Description
Pyglet	`https://pyglet.org/`	Development of games and other visual applications
Scikit-learn	`https://scikit-learn.org/stable/`	Library for machine learning applications
SciPy	`https://scipy.org/`	Library for scientific calculations
TensorFlow	`https://www.tensorflow.org/learn`	Machine learning
Tkinter		Graphical interfaces

The description of the standard libraries can be found at `https://docs.python.org/` and on the pages of each library.

APPENDIX A

References

The bibliographic references cited parenthetically in short form in each chapter are listed fully in this appendix, alphabetically, by the last name of the first author. They are not listed by the chapter number in which they appear.

ABELSON, R. P., CARROLL, J. D. (1965). Computer simulation of individual belief systems. American Behavioral Science. 9. 24-30.

ADCOCK, C. J. (1954). Factorial analysis for non-mathematicians. Carlton: Melbourne University Press.

ADLER, J. (2010). R in a nutshell. A desktop quick reference. Cambridge: O'Reilly.

AGER, A. (1991). Microcomputers and clinical psychology: issues, applications and future developments. New York: Wiley.

AHONNISKA, J., AHONEN, T., ARO, T., LYYTINEN, H. (2000). Suggestions for revised scoring of the Tower of Hanoi test. Assessment. 7. 3. 311–319.

ALDRICH, C. (2005). Learning by doing. A comprehensive guide to simulations, computer games, and pedagogy in e-learning and other educational experiences. San Francisco: Pfeiffer.

APTER, M. J. (1970). The computer simulation of behaviour. London: Hutchinson and Co. Ltd.

APTER, M. J., WESTBY, G. (1973). The computer in psychology. New York: John Wiley and Sons.

AXELROD, B. N., GREVE, K, W., GOLDMAN, R. S. (1994). Comparison of four Wisconsin Card Sorting Test scoring guides with novice taters. Assessment. 1. 2. 115-121.

BEAUMONT, J. (1981a). A PASCAL program to administer a digit span test. Current Psychological Reviews. 1. 1. 115–117.

BEAUMONT, J. (1981b). A PASCAL program to administer the wisconsin card sorting test. Current Psychological Reviews, 1(1), 113–115.

BERMAN, J. J. (2011). Methods in medical informatics. Fundamentals of Healthcare Programming in Perl, Python, and Ruby. London: CRC Press.

J. M. Roig-Fusté, *Python for Psychology, Social Sciences, and Education*,
https://doi.org/10.1007/979-8-8688-2355-8

BERRY, S. (1996). Diagrammatic procedure for scoring the Wisconsin card sorting test. The Clinical Neuropsychologist, 10. 1. 117–121.

BERTAMINI, M. (2018). Vision, illusion and perception; Vol. 2. Programming visual illusions for everyone. Heidelberg: Springer International Publishing.

BEXTER, A., KAMPA, B. M. (2020). Mazemaster: an open-source python-based softwarepackage for controlling virtual reality experiments. bioRxiv.

BIRD, R. J. (1981). The computer in experimental psychology. London: Academic Press.

BLEIDORN, W., HOPWOOD, C. J. (2018). Using machine learning to advance personality assessment and theory. Personality and Social Psychology Review. 1-14.

BORGO, M., SORANZO, A., GRASSI, A. (2012). MATLAB for Psychologists: New York: Springer.

BRADLEY, V. A., WELCH, J. L., SKILBECK, C. E. (1993). Cognitive retraining using microcomputers. Hove: Lawrence Erlbaum Associates.

BROOKER, P. D. (2020). Programming with Python for social scientists. Los Angeles: Sage.

BROOKS, A. L., BRAHNAM, S., JAIN, L. C. (2014). Technologies of inclusive well-being. Serious games, alternative realities, and play therapy. London: Springer.

BRENT, E. E., ANDERSON, R. E. (1990). Computer applications in the social sciences. New York: McGraw-Hill.

BRIGGS, J. R. (2012). Python for kids: A playful Introduction to Programming. San Francisco: No Starch Press.

BUTCHER, J. N. (1987). Computerized psychological assessment. A practitioner's guide. New York: Basic Books.

CAI, Y., VAN JOOLINGEN, W., VEERMANS, K. (2021). Virtual and augmented reality, simulation and serious games for education. Singapore: Springer.

CHEN, D. Y. (2017). Pandas for everyone. Python data analysis. Boston: Addison-Wesley.

CHILD, D. (1990). The essentials of factor analysis. 2a. ed. London: Cassell.

CIESLA, R. (2024). The book of chatbots. From ELIZA to ChatGPT 2024. Cham: Springer.

COLBY, K. M., WATT, J. B., GILBERT, J.P. (1966). A computer method of psychotherapy: preliminary communication. The Journal of Nervous and Mental Disease. 142. 2. 148-152.

CONNOLLY, I., PALMER, M., BARTON, H., KIRWAN, G. (2016). An introduction to cyberpsychology. London: Routledge.

COPERLAND, B. J. (1993). Artificial Inteligence. A Philosophical Introduction. Malden: Blackwell.

DALMAIJER, E. S. (2017). Python for experimental psychologists. London: Routledge.

DALMAIJER, E. S. (2024). Python for experimental psychologists. A fun way of learning how to code your experiments and analyses. 2. Ed. Abingdon: Routledge.

DALMAIJER, E. S., MATHÔT, S., van der STIGCHEL, S. (2013). PyGaze: an open-source, cross-platform toolbox for minimal-effort programming of eyetracking experiments. Behavior Research Methods. 46. 4. 913–921.

DAMIAN, M. F. (2010). Does variability in human performance outweigh imprecision in response devices such as computer keyboards? Behavior Research Methods. 42. 1. 205–211.

DANN, P. L., IRVINE, S. H., COLLINS, J. M. (1991). Advances in computer-based human assessment. New York: Kluwer Academic Publishers.

DEL GROSSO, N. A., SIROTA, A. (2019). Ratcave: A 3D graphics python package for cognitive psychology experiments. Behavior Research Methods.

DENI, R. L. (1986). Programming microcomputers for psychology experiments. Balmont: Wadsworth.

DICKTER, C. L., KIEFFABER, P. D. (2014). EEG methods for the psychological sciences. Los Angeles: Sage.

DOWNEY, A. (2012). Think Python: An introduction to software design. Needham, MA: Green Tea Press. Disponible en: `http://greenteapress.com/thinkpython/thinkpython.htm`

DUCHOWSKI, A. T. (2017). Eye tracking methodology. Theory and practice. 3 ed. Cham: Springer.

EICHENBERG, C. (2012). Virtual reality in psychological, medical and pedagogical applications. Rijeka: InTech.

ELOSUA, P. (2011). Psicometría. Conceptos básicos y aplicaciones prácticas con Rcommander. Bilbo: Euskal Herriko Unibertsitatea.

EZRA, T. M. G. (2020). Creating game environments in Blender 3D. Learn to create low poly game environments. New York: Apress.

FARRELL, J. (2013). Introducción a la programación. Lógica y diseño. 7 ed. México: Cengage.

FARRELL, P. (2019). Math adventures with Python. An illustrated guide to exploring math with code. San Francisco: No Starch Press.

FITZPATRICK, M. (2019). Create simple GUI applications, with Python & Qt5. The hands-on guide to building desktop apps with Python. Leanpub.

FLASHMAN, L.A., MANDIR, AS., HORNER, M.D., FREIDES, D. (1991). Increasing interscorer reliability on the Wisconsin Card Sorting Test (WCST) using clarified scoring rules. Journal of Clinical and Experimental Neuropsychology. 13. 431-431.

FRIEDMAN, A. F., LEWAK, R., NICHOLS, D. S., WEBB, J. T. (2000). Psychological assessment with the MMPI-2. Hove: Lawrence Erlbaum Associates.

FRUCHTER, B. (1954). Introduction to factor analysis. New York: Van Nostrand.

GEBEN, B. F., NULL, C. H., FURNAS, G., HAGEN, M., RUMELHART, D. (1985). Advanced computing in psychology. Behavior Research Methods, Instruments, & Computers. 17. 2. 331–338.

GHOSH, C. (2022). Data analysis with machine learning for psychologists. Crash course to learn Python 3 and machine learning in 10 hours. Cham: Springer Nature Switzerland AG.

GILBERT, N., TROITZSCH, K. G. (2005). Simulation for the social scientist. 2 ed. Open University Press.

GOLDEN, C. J. (1978). Stroop color and word test: a manual for clinical and experimental uses. Chicago: Skoelting.

GORSUCH, R. L. (2015). Factor analysis. New York: Routledge.

GOSLING, S. D., RENTFROW, P. J., SWANN, W. B. (2003). A very brief measure of the Big-Five personality domains. Journal of Research in Personality, 37. 6. 504–528.

GROTH-MARNAT, G., WRIGHT, A. J. (2016). Handbook of psychological assessment. 6ª edición. Hoboken: John Wiley & Sons.

GUTTAG, J. V. (2016). Introduction to computation and programming using Python. With application to understanding data. 2 ed. Cambridge: The MIT Press.

HALSTEAD, W. C. (1947) Brain and intelligence. Chicago: University of Chicago Press.

HARWANI, B. M. (2018). Qt5 Python GUI programming cookbook. Building responsive and powerful cross-platform applications with PyQt. Birmingham: Packt Publishing.

HASLWANTER, T. (2016). An introduction to statistics with Python. With applications in the life sciences. New York: Springer.

HATHAWAY, S. R., MCKINLEY, J. C. (1940). A Multiphasic Personality Schedule: I. construction of the schedule. Journal of Psychology. 10. 249-254.

HELLMANN, D. (2017). The Python 3 standard library by example. Boston: Addison-Wesley.

HINZ, A. M. (1989). An iterative algorithm for the Tower of Hanoi with four pegs. Computing. 42. 133-140.

HINZ, A. M., KLAVZAR, S., MILUTINOVIC, U., PETR, C. (2013). The tower of Hanoi – Myths and maths. Heidelberg: Springer Basel.

HOWELL, S. L., HRICKO, N. (2006). Online assessment and measurement: case studies from higer education, K-12 and corporate. Hershey: Information Science Publishing.

HOWELL, S. R., MULLER, R. (2000). Computers in psychotherapy: a new prescription.

HOWLETT, C. A., MOSELEY, G. L. (2024). An improved diagrammatic procedure for interpreting and scoring the Wisconsin Card Sorting Test: an update to Steve Berry's 1996 edition. Behavior Research Methods. 56. 8715–8719.

IDRIS, I. (2015). NumPy beginner's guide. Third edition. Birmingham: Packt.

JOHNSON, M. J. (2012). A concise introduction to programming in Python. Boca Taton: CRC Press.

JOHNSON, M. J. (2018). A concise introduction to programming in Python. 2 ed. Boca Taton: CRC Press.

JONES, M. N. (2017), Big data in cognitive science. New York: Routledge.

KALB, I. (2018). Learn to program with Python 3. A step-by-step guide to programming. 2nd Ed. Berkeley: Apress Media.

KEMENY, J. G. (1972). Man and the computer. New York: Charles Scribner's Sons.

KETKAR, N. (2017). Deep learning with Python. A hands-on introduction. New York: Apress.

KINSLEY, H., McGUGAN, W. (2015). Beginning Python games development with Pygame. 2 ed. New York: Apress.

KLEINMUNTZ, B. (1969). Clinical information processing by computer. An essay and selected readings. New York: Holt, Rinehart and Winston.

KLINE, P. (1994). An easy guide to factor analysis. London: Routledge.

KOSINSKI, M., WANG, Y., LAKKARAJU, H., LESKOVEC, J. (2016). Mining big data to extract patterns and predict real-life outcomes. Psychological Methods. 21. 4. 493–506.

KRAUSE, F., LINDEMANN, O. (2013). Expyriment: a python library for cognitive and neuroscientific experiments. Behavior Research Methods. 46. 2. 416–428.

KRAUSE, F., LINDEMANN, O. (2014). Erratum to: Expyriment: A Python library for cognitive and neuroscientific experiments. Behavior Research.

KRONTHALER, F., ZÖLLER, S. (2021). Data analysis with RStudio. An easygoing introduction. Berlin: Springer.

LACHAR, D. (1973). The MMPI: Clinical assessment and automated interpretation. Los Angeles: W.P.S.

LANE, D. (2021). Machine learning for kids. A project-based introduction to artificial intelligence. San Francisco: No Starch Press.

LEWIS, N. D. (2015). Build your own nural network today. AusCov.

LEZAK, M. D., HOWIESON, D. B., BIGLER, E. D., TRANEL, D. (2012). Neuropsychological assessment. 5 ed. Oxford: Oxford University Press.

LYNCH, B. (2002). Historical review of computer-assisted cognitive retraining. J. Head Trauma Rehabil. 17. 5. 446-457.

LÓPEZ, J. (2012). Introducción al análisis de datos con R y R Commander en psicología y educación. Almería: Editorial de la Universidad de Almería. Disponible en: `http://hdl.handle.net/10835/1658`.

LU, C. H., PROCTOR, R. W. (1995). The influence of irrelevant location information on performance—A review of the Simon and spatial Stroop effects. Psychonomic Bulletin & Review. 2. 2. 174–207.

LUBANOVIC, B. (2015). Introducing Python. Modern computing in simple packages. Sebastopol, CA: O'Reilly.

LUCAS, E. (1893). Récréations mathématiques III. Paris: Gauthier-Villars et Fils.

LUCE, R. D. (1986). Response times: their role in inferring elementary mental organization. Oxford: Oxford University Press.

LUISELLI, J. K., FISCHER, A. J. (2016). Computer-assisted and web-based innovations in psychology, special education and health. London: Academic Press.

LYNCH, B. (2002). Historical review of computer-assisted cognitive retraining. Journal of Head Trauma Rehabilitation. 17. 5. 446-457.

MA, M., JAIN, L. C., ANDERSON, P. (2014). Virtual, augmented reality and serious games for healthcare 1. Berlin: Springer Verlag.

MA, M., OIKONOMOU, A., JAIN, L. C. (2011). Serious games and edutainment applications. London: Springer.

MAIR, P. (2018). Modern psychometrics with R. New York: Springer.

MAKOWSKI, D., PHAM, T., LAU, Z. J., BRAMMER, J. C., LESPINASSE, F., PHAM, H., SCHÖLZEL, C., CHEN, S. H. A. (2021). NeuroKit2: A Python toolbox for neurophysiological signal processing. Behavior Research Methods. 53. 1689–1696.

MANOLAS, C., XANTHIDOU, O. K., XANTHIDIS, D. (2022). Virtual reality application development with Python. En: Dimitrios Xanthidis, Christos Manolas, Ourania K. Xanthidou, Han-I Wang, Handbook of computer programming with Python. Boca Raton: CRC Press.

MARJI, M. (2014). Learn to program with scratch. A visual introduction to programming with games, art, science and math. San Francisco: No Starch Press.

MARKS, P. A., SEEMAN, W. (1963). Actuarial description of abnormal personality; an atlas for use with the MMPI. Baltimore: Williams & Wilkins.

MARTIN, D. W. (2008) Doing Psychology Experiments. Belmont: Thomson.

MATHÔT, S., MARCH, J. (2022). Conducting linguistic experiments online with OpenSesame and OSWeb. Language Learning.

MATHÔT, S., SCHREIJ, D., THEEUWES, J. (2012). OpenSesame: An open-source, graphical experiment builder for the social sciences. Behavior Research Methods. 44 .2. 314–324.

MATTHES, E. (2022). Python crash course. A hands-on, project-based introduction to programming. Third edition. San Francisco: No Starch Press.

MATTHEWS, M. COYLE, D. (2010) Therapeutic Computer Games. En The use of technology in mental health: applications, ethics and practice. Anthony, K., Nagel, D.M. y Goss, S. Charles C. Thomas Pub. Ltd.

McMANUS, S. (2018). Mission Python: code a space adventure game! San Francisco: No Starch Press.

MEIER, B. (2019). Python GUI programming Cookbook. Develop functional and responsive user interfaces with tkinter and PyQt5. 3 ed. Birmingham: Packt Publishing Ltd.

MICHAEL, D., CHEN, S. (2006). Serious games: games that educate, train and inform. Boston: Thomson.

Misirlisoy, E. (2017). Programming behavioral experiments with MATLAB and Psychtoolbox. 9 simple steps for students and researchers. Abingdon: Routledge.

MOORE, A. D. (2019). Mastering GUI programming with Python. Develop impressive cross-platform GUI applications with PyQt. Birmingham: Packt Publishing Ltd.

MORALES, A. (2019). Desarrollo de serious games para rehabilitación de función motora. Madrid: Autor.

MUELLER, S. T., PIPER, B. J. (2014). The psychology experiment building language (PEBL) and PEBL Test Battery. Journal of Neuroscience Methods. 222. 250-259.

MULLER, E., BEDNAR, J. A., DIESMANN, M., GEWALTIG, M., HINES, M., DAVISON, A. P. (2015). Python in Neuroscience. Lausanne: Frontiers Media.

NANDY, A., BISWAS, M. (2018). Reinforcement learning. With Open AI, TensorFlow and Keras using Python. New York: Apress.

NAVARRO, D. (2013). Learning statistics with R: A tutorial for psychology students and other beginners. Adelaide: University of Adelaide.

NAWAZ, M. W. (2020). Statistics crash course for beginners. Theory and applications of frequentist and bayesian statistics using python 2020. AI Publishing.

NEUMAN, Y. (2016). Computational personality analysis. Introduction, practical applications and novel directions. Cham: Springer.

NOKERI, T. C. (2022). Artificial intelligence in medical sciences and psychology: with application of machine language, computer vision, and NLP techniques. New York: Apress.

NORTON, P. (2006). Introducción a la computación. 6ª ed. México: McGraw- Hill Interamericana.

NORVIG, P. (1998) Paradigms of artificial intelligence programing: case studies in common lisp. 4 ed. San Francisco: Morgan Kaufmann.

O'NEIL, C. (2016). Weapons of math destruction, how big data increases inequality and threatens democracy. New York: Crown.

PAPERT, S. (1980). Minndtorms. Children, computers and poweful ideas. New York. Basic Books.

PASTUKHOV, A. (2021). Python for social and experimental psychology. Disponible en Internet: `https://alexander-pastukhov.github.io/python-for-experimental-psychology/`

PAYNE, J. R. (2019). Python for teenagers. Learn to program like a superhero! New York: Apress.

PAYNE, B. (2015). Teach your kids to code: a parent-friendly guide to python programming. San Francisco: No Starch Press.

PEIRCE, J. W. (2007). PsychoPy-Psychophysics software in Python. Journal of Neuroscience Methods, 162. 1-2. 8–13.

PEIRCE, J. W. (2009). Generating stimuli for neuroscience using PsychoPy. Frontiers in Neuroinformatics. 2. 1-8.

PEIRCE, J. W. (2019). PsychoPy - Psychology software for Python. Release 3.2.4.

PEIRCE, J., GRAY, J. R., SIMPSON, S., MACASKILL, M., HÖCHENBERGER, R., SOGO, H., KASTMAN E., LINDELØV, J. K. (2019). PsychoPy2: Experiments in behavior made easy. Behavior Research Methods. 51. 195–203.

PEIRCE, J., HIRST, R., MACASKILL, M. (2022). Building experiments in PsychoPy. 2 ed. Los Angeles: Sage.

PEIRCE, J., MacASKILl, M. (2018). Building Experiments in PsychoPy. Los Angeles: Sage.

PERKINS, J. (2014). Python 3 text processing with NLTK 3 cookbook. 2 ed. Birmingham: PACKT.

PLANT, R. R., HAMMOND, N., TURNER, G. (2004). Self-validating presentation and response timing in cognitive paradigms: how and why? Behavior Research Methods, Instruments, & Computers. 36. 2. 291-303.

PLANT, R. R., TURNER, G. (2009). Millisecond precision psychological research in a world of commodity computers: new hardware, new problems? Behavior Research Methods. 41. 3. 598-614.

PORTER, L. ZINGARO, D (2023). Learn AI-assisted Python programming, With Copilot and ChatGPT. San Francisco: Manning Publications.

QUIRK, T. J. (2016). Excel 2016 for social science statistics. A guide to solving practical problems. Cham: Springer.

RAJ, S. (2019). Building chatbots with Python. Using natural language processing and machine learning. New York: Apress.

RASHID, T. (2016). Make your own neural network. Createspace Independent Publishing Platform.

REYNOLDS, J. H. (1987). Computing in psychology. An introduction to programing methods and concepts. Englewood Cliffs: Prentice-Hall.

REITAN, R.M. (1969). Manual for administration of neuropsychological test batteries for adults and children. Indianapolis.

RICHARDSON, C. (2015). Learn to Program with Minecraft: Transform Your World with the Power of Python 2015. San Francisco: No Starch Press.

ROIG-FUSTÉ, J. M. (1993). MMPI y MMPI-2 en la exploración de la personalidad. Barcelona; MTRpsicologia.

ROIG-FUSTÉ, J. M. (2007). Prueba de aptitudes intelectuales SIEP. Barcelona; MTRpsicologia.

ROIG-FUSTÉ, J. M. (2017). Historia de los tests psicológicos. Barcelona. MTRPsicología.

ROIG FUSTÉ, J. M. (2018). La informática aplicada a la psicología. Barcelona: Bosch Editor.

ROIG FUSTÉ, J. M. (2020). La interpretación del MMPI-2. Barcelona: MTRpsicologia.

ROME, H. P., SWENSON, W. M., MATAYA, P., MCCARTHY, C. E., PEARSON, J. S., KEATING, F. R., HATHAWAY, S. R. (1962). Symposium on automation technics in personality assessment. Proceedings of the staff on the Mayo Clinic. 37. 61-82.

ROSEMAN, M. (2021). Modern Tkinter for busy Python developers. Late Afternoon Press.

ROSENBAUM, D. A., VAUGHAN, J., WYBLE, B. (2015). MATLAB for Behavioral Scientists. Second Edition. New York: Routledge.

ROTHMAN, D., LAMONS, M. KUMAR, R., NAGARAJA, A., ZIAI, A., DIXIT, A. (2018). Python: Beginner's guide to artificial intelligence. Build applications to intelligently interact with the world around you using Python. Birmingham: Packt.

RUSHKOFF, D. (2010). Program or be programmed. Ten commands for a digital age. New York: OR Books. (Hay edición castellana: Programa o serás programado, Madrid: Debate, 2020)

SACH, L., O'HANLON, M. (2020). Create graphical user interfaces with Python. How to build windows, buttons, and widgets for your Python projects. Cambridge: Raspberry Pi Trading.

SAHA, A. (2015). Doing math with Python. Use programming to explore algebra, statistics, calculus, and more! San Francisco: No Starch Press.

SAUNDERS, J. (2018). Veusz documentation. Autor.

SEISDEDOS, N., ROIG-FUSTÉ, J. M. (1986). MMPI. Suplemento técnico e interpretación clínica. Madrid: TEA.

SHAPIRO, A. G., TODOROVIC, D. (2017). The Oxford compendium of visual illusions. Oxford: Oxford University Press.

SHIMIZU, H. (2002). Measuring keyboard response delays by comparing keyboard and joystick inputs.Behavior Research Methods, Instruments, & Computers. 34. 2. 250-256.

SOMMA, R. (2020). Coding in the classroom. Why you should care about teaching computer science. San Francisco: No Starch Press.

STEIN, D. J., LUDIK, J. (1998). Natural networks and psychopathology. Connectionist models in practice and research. Cambridge: Cambridge University Press.

STOET, G. (2010). PsyToolkit: A software package for programming psychological experiments using Linux. Behavioral Research Methods, 42 (4), 1096-1104.

STOET, G. (2011). PsyToolkit manual. Leeds University. Leeds, United Kingdom.

STRAUSS, E. SHERMAN, E. S., SPREEN, O. (2006). A compendium of neuropsychological tests: administration, norms, and commentary. 3ª ed. Oxford: Oxford University Press.

STROOP, J. R. (1935). Studies of interference in serial verbal reactions. Journal of Experimental Psychology. 18.6. 643–662.

STRUB, R. L., BLACK, F. W. (1983). The mental status examination in neurology. Philadelphia: F. A. Davis.

SUMMERFIELD, M. (2008). Rapid GUI programming with Python and Qt. The definitive guide to PyQt programming. Upper Saddle River: Prentice Hall.

SWAN, M. (2013). The quantified self: fundamental disruption in Big Data science and biological discovery. Big Data. 1. 2. 85–99.

SWEIGART, A. (2017). Invent your own computer games with python 4 ed. San Francisco: No Starch Press.

TEUBER, H. L., BATTERSBY, W. S., BENDER, M.B. (1951). Performance of complex visual tasks after cerebral lesions. Journal of Nervous and Mental Disease. 114. 5. 413-429.

TIWARI, S. (2021). Build your own neural network in Python. Leanpub.

TOLLERVEY, N. H. (2018). Python in education. Teach, learn, program. Sebastopol, CA: O'Reilly Media, Inc.

TOMKINS, S. S., MESSICK, S. (1963). Computer simulation of personality. Frontier of pdychological theory. New York: John Wiley and Sons.

van ROSSUM, G. (2012). The Python Library Reference. Release 3.2.3. Python Software Foundation.

van ROSSUM, G. (2020). Tutorial Python Documentation Release 3.6.3 Python Software Foundation.

WALLACE R., S. (2009). The anatomy of A.L.I.C.E. En: Epstein R, Roberts G, Beber G, editors. Parsing the Turing Test: Philosophical and Methodological Issues in the Quest for the Thinking Computer. Cham: Springer. pp. 181–210.

WANG, Z. (2021). Eye-Tracking with Python and Pylink. Cham: Springer Nature.

WECHSLER, D. (1939). The measurement of adult intelligence. Baltimore: Williams and Wilkins.

WECHSLER, D. (1958). The measurement and appraisalof adult intelligence. Baltimore: Williams and Wilkins.

WEINACHTER; D. (2016). Cahier d'activités python pour les kids. Paris: Eyrolles.

WEIZENBAUM, J. (1966). ELIZA - A computer program for the study of natural language communication between man and machine. Computational linguistics. 9. 1. 36-45.

WEIZENBAUM, J. (1976). Computer power and human reason. San Francisco: W. H. Freeman.

WELSH, M. C., HUIZINGA, M. (2001). The development and preliminary validation of the Tower of Hanoi-revised. Assessment. 8. 2. 167–176.

WESTRA, E. (2016). Modular programming with Python. Birmingham: Packt.

WILLIAMSON, B. (2017). Big Data in Education. The digital future of learning, policy and practice. London: Sage

WOO, S. E., TAY, L., PROCTOR, R. W. (2020). Big data in psychological research. Washington DC: American Psychological Association.

Index

J. M. Roig-Fusté, *Python for Psychology, Social Sciences, and Education*,
https://doi.org/10.1007/979-8-8688-2355-8

Q

R

S

GPSR Compliance

The European Union's (EU) General Product Safety Regulation (GPSR) is a set of rules that requires consumer products to be safe and our obligations to ensure this.

If you have any concerns about our products, you can contact us on ProductSafety@springernature.com

In case Publisher is established outside the EU, the EU authorized representative is:

Springer Nature Customer Service Center GmbH
Europaplatz 3
69115 Heidelberg, Germany

Batch number: 10054597

Printed by Printforce, the Netherlands